SNAP
strategies
for couples

40 fast fixes for everyday
relationship pitfalls

Dr. Pepper Schwartz
& Dr. Lana Staheli

SEAL PRESS

Snap Strategies for Couples
40 Fast Fixes for Everyday Relationship Pitfalls
Dr. Pepper Schwartz
Dr. Lana Staheli
Seal Press

ISBN 978-1-58005-562-8

Library of Congress Cataloging-in-Publication Data

Staheli, Lana.

Snap strategies for couples : 40 fast fixes for everyday relationship pitfalls / by Lana Staheli and Pepper Schwartz.

    pages   cm

ISBN 978-1-58005-562-8

1. Couples--Psychology. 2. Interpersonal relations. 3. Interpersonal conflict.
    4. Man-woman relationships. I. Schwartz, Pepper. II. Title.

HQ801.S756 2015

306.7—dc23

2014035558

Published by
Seal Press
A Member of the Perseus Books Group
1700 Fourth Street
Berkeley, California
sealpress.com

Cover design by Erin Seaward-Hiatt
Interior design by Kate Basart/Union Pageworks
Printed in the United States of America
Distributed by Publishers Group West

With love and gratitude to my man, Fred Kaseburg, and my children, Cooper and Ryder.

—Pepper Schwartz

To my husband, Lynn Staheli, M.D., for a lifetime of love, guidance and support.

—Lana Staheli

CONTENTS

Introduction

Snap Strategies is our plan for quick and enduring answers to most common relationship issues. We help you modify your reactions to relationship aggravations so that you can stop repetitive arguments and move out of the past and into the present and future. If you take our advice, we believe you can reduce bickering, drama, and disappointment and make your relationship fun again. Conversation becomes a mutual skill, not the beginning of a clash. You build intimacy and work through problems while building love and passion for one another.

Why do we feel so sure about our advice? Well, for one thing, Lana is an accomplished coach who works wonders, quickly. With hundreds of couples over forty years of counseling and coaching on the radio, on TV, or in person, her quick assessment of the situation has changed people's lives in minutes. She doesn't believe that you need lengthy sessions of therapy or long hours of agonizing emotional discussions. Her sharp insights and practical, effective relationship revisions have immediately changed the emotional climate of many troubled relationships. Pepper is a nationally respected relationship expert herself, but Lana is the coach that various kinds of therapists go to when they need a consult on a sticky issue. Lana is the author of *Affair-Proof Your Marriage*, and her book, *Bounce: Be Transformed*, was written to offer people a step-by-step guide to seeking joy, not just survival. Pepper has written several books (including The *New York Times* bestseller, *The Normal Bar*) and created workshops based on her research into what makes relationships happy, durable, and loving.

As friends, we have consulted with one another over the years, and Pepper became an admirer of the unorthodox and amazing methods that Lana used to save couples who were just about to kick each other out of their marriage. We decided to join forces and gather up our collective knowledge to bring you this book. From our combined years of successfully solving marital problems quickly and effectively, we have developed *Snap Strategies*.

Our strategies have an unusual approach that underlies everything we recommend. We are not in favor of letting it "all hang out." Yes, we want honesty, but no, we don't believe honesty that is cruel does anybody any good. Things said in therapy linger long after therapy is over. We get to the heart of the matter without insults or revelations that can poison the couple's future. We avoid emotional payback for historical events that are deadly if they are brought up again and again. Instead we give you practical skills to bring out the best in you and your partner. We respect emotions, but they are fluid, exciting, and unstable: They can bring a relationship down when they turn into nasty venting and accusations. We teach you to make your relationship fun again, to reignite love and passion for one another.

Our new way of transforming your relationship without lengthy sessions of therapy or agonizing discussions will steer you away from the emotional roller coaster that damages many relationships. Going against some of the prevailing therapeutic approaches to couples, *Snap Strategies* does *not* hinge on sharing all of your feelings and working through problems no matter how long it takes. We believe that approach kills more couples than it saves. There's a common but destructive vision of intimacy that says because we are close, we can, and should, say everything we feel or believe. This is not true. In fact, intimate relationships take tender loving care, which sometimes requires a badly bitten tongue. Love and goodwill flourish when people feel safe, accepted, admired, adored, and complimented. Feedback has to be done carefully, lovingly, and—most importantly—briefly. Talking to your partner has to be choreographed if it's about something important. Brutal honesty has no place in a marriage or any other kind of committed relationship.

Our rules of the road have scooped couples out of the doorway of divorce court hundreds of times. And they have made happy relationships even better, halting escalation of a problem before the issue gets so big that damage is inevitable. At its core, this approach is about living in the present and finding ways to create lifelong love, at least in part by leaving the treacheries or tragedies of the past far behind.

Snap Strategies is a compendium of rules to live by, mistakes to avoid, and ordinary and understandable reactions that need to change. We know this sounds as if it's too good to be true, but it is. You will see that many of the couples in this book who look like they have an insoluble problem actually only need to reframe the problem and their approach to it to get what they need. We are practical, but we are also romantics: We are all about supporting love and saving relationships. We won't let you down.

—*Dr. Lana Staheli & Dr. Pepper Schwartz*

Chapter 1

Redundant Conversations

THE SNAP

If there is no new news, why are we talking about this, again?

A Closer Look

Stop repeating old conversations. Rehashing old wounds and wars will only create more conflict. Refuse to engage in reruns, whether it's over that critical comment he made about your hair or the time she forgot your birthday. Repetitive conversations, in which each person already knows the other's point of view and exactly what the other is going to say, are just plain destructive to relationships. Going over and over the same territory casts a negative pall on conversations and makes both of you feel pessimistic about the relationship's future happiness or durability.

The more often you recall bad experiences, the worse you both feel. It is normal and even necessary to disagree, but once you know your partner's thoughts or feelings, you know, right? So going back over the same discussion is either refusing to accept that the two of you don't agree or, as the saying goes, "beating a dead horse."

If you think you are going to change your partner's mind by repeating old conversations, think again. That is a very remote possibility, and in fact, this kind of regurgitation is more likely to cement their position. It may even feel incredibly insulting. Your partner may be thinking: "Does she think I'm dumb? I get what she's saying; I don't need it said forty-two different ways!" Believe us: All repetition does is train the other person to stop listening.

Does it seem as if your partner tunes you out on difficult issues that involve recurring themes in the relationship? Well, you are right; your partner is trying to be somewhere else. Even if she is standing right next to you, she is in psychological retreat. Pounding away at your point serves to build and perpetuate bad feelings and inhibit any kind of communication on difficult issues. Ultimately, this form of argument builds a wedge between two people.

Some relationship therapists allow their clients to keep venting about misdeeds and trying to correct misunderstandings. But often, this keeps rubbing a sore spot and prevents the couple from moving forward. We believe that once each person's point of view has been expressed and the situation has been stated, further arguments over "the truth" just mire the couple deeper in their own past mud.

The Situation
Ripples

Mateo and Lucia have been married twenty-two years. They have two children who left for college and now live on the opposite coast. Lucia has found the "empty nest" difficult. She works and has friends, a full life, but still she is often sad, telling Mateo, "My life feels sort of empty. I'm busy and happy overall, but kinda down. I miss the kids; I miss being a family."

Mateo is an emotional kind of guy. And he is a "pleaser," the kind of person who feels responsible for other people's emotions and who wants to be liked and admired all the time. He feels bad that Lucia is down so much of the time, and he wants to make her happy. So, he comes up with what he thinks is a brilliant idea. Mateo, who owns a convenience store, has been putting aside money for a year, planning to give Lucia a fantastic gift for their anniversary. On multiple weekends he has secretly gone out shopping for a good deal on a slightly used SUV. After many dead ends he found one, two months before their anniversary celebration.

Mateo enlisted their friends to garage the car for him to help make this a total surprise for her.

When Mateo and Lucia arrived at their friend's home for what she thought was dinner with another couple, she was happily shocked to find ten of their friends inside and waiting. She was genuinely surprised and grateful to Mateo and her hosts for taking the time and doing the planning on her behalf. The evening was wrapping up when Mateo excitedly put the last part of his plan into action. He said, "Oh, I almost forgot—there is one more little thing from me. Come outside." Mateo, Lucia, and their friends went outside and there at the curb, smack in front of the house, was a forest green SUV, with a bow on the front door handle. Lucia was stunned; it took her a minute to realize this was her present. Because she was unsure of what was happening, she did not hide her feelings, the first of which was complete confusion. Mateo saw her reaction and took it for a good kind of disorientation. He smiled broadly and announced to his wife, "This is yours. I love you." The party crowd clapped and yelled. Lucia, however, was still experiencing disbelief—and something more. Looking more shocked than happy or grateful, she searched for clarity.

Why hadn't Mateo conferred with her first? They usually talked about any purchase over $1,000, and this was a lot more than that. She just stared at the SUV, not knowing what to say. Mateo finally said proudly, "This wonderful car is for you!" Then the shock really set in. Did he not remember that she hates SUVs? He knows that she almost exclusively drives in the city. Parking one of those monsters? It would give anyone a migraine. What in the world possessed him to buy this expensive, huge, unwanted car? Lucia didn't want to cause a scene, so she gave him a weak "thank you" and a hug. Mateo was impervious to her feelings. He was jumping up and down with excitement at the extravagance of his gift and her genuine surprise. Because Lucia was still in front of all the party guests, she redoubled her efforts to try and act pleased. But she had to work at not crying. All through the rest of the goodbyes and thank-yous to her hosts, she hoped no one noticed the sweat on her brow and the forced smile she was wearing to hide her real feelings.

But the masquerade ended as soon as she and Mateo had some privacy. Lucia let Mateo have it: "What were you thinking? Why would you buy some enormous car, and not talk to me? This is the dumbest stunt you have ever pulled!"

Mateo was stunned. His happy face disappeared, and now it was his time to feel confused. He tried to explain his reasoning to his beloved wife: "I know you missed the kids, and I wanted to get you something special." Lucia wasn't placated in the slightest. His explanation only made her angrier: How could he think an SUV would affect her feelings about her life or children? In anger and despair, she said, "Don't you know me at all? I can't tell you anything without you messing up. Didn't I talk about gas and how a Mini Cooper would be a nice idea? Don't you have any common sense at all? Where do I drive, Mateo? Huh? Where? I drive downtown. They do not have parking places for tanks. I would have loved a new car like a Mini Cooper, but this thing is as big as a tank. Can't it go back?" Mateo told her it could not, and so from then on she called her SUV "Mateo's Tank."

Lucia suffered with the SUV for a year. She didn't know how to drive a big car and she wasn't interested in learning. Everything irritated her: She couldn't park in the building she used to because the Tank was too tall. Within four months she had two fender benders, both while backing up, because she could not see the car behind her. The second accident did it for her: She went to the Mini Cooper dealer and traded the Tank in for a used Mini Cooper. But that didn't put an end to the Tank episode. From then on Lucia carried around her anger, nursing it whenever anything would displease her about Mateo (which was often). Incredibly, two years of their twenty-two-year marriage have gone by since that incident and Lucia's anger has not softened or disappeared. She is convinced that Mateo really doesn't know who she is, what she needs, and what she would want.

So, a full two years later, she still blows up from time to time about that "stupid Tank." On the morning of her fifty-fifth birthday, after Mateo gave Lucia a beautiful pair of diamond earrings, she thanked him but couldn't resist saying, "At least it's not an SUV."

Mateo, of course, has gotten the message loud and clear. He is hurt and angry with her continued verbal attacks and he has stopped buying her things. Lucia resents that too; in addition to Mateo's other flaws, he has no generosity anymore. She does not think the SUV debacle should affect his gift giving, even though they argue about the incident on almost every birthday or holiday.

Blasts

Bernard and Angie have an ongoing battle because Angie feels that Bernard has switched his allegiance from her to his mother. They have been married only three years, which basically makes them newlyweds. Originally, they were both enthusiastic about having children and wanted to wait only a short time after marriage because they felt that their biological clocks were ticking.

But this all went sideways when Bernard seemed to listen to his mother more than Angie and even allowed his mother to trash their relationship. Angie feels that their situation is unbearable because no matter what they do—sit down for dinner, go on a walk, or even when they have sex—everything stops when Bernard's mother calls. Even if they are in a particularly delicate part of lovemaking, he will take his mom's call. When Angie goes ballistic about this, he defends his actions as being those of a dutiful son. He believes that his mom is very lonely, especially since his father's death two years ago, and that he, Bernard, an only child, must make his mother's life happier.

In Angie's opinion, Bernard has turned into an over-obsessive slavishly responsive son, who encourages all his mother's worst behavior. Angie feels his mother is extremely manipulative and that Bernard is her puppet. When his mom calls, she is usually weepy and complains that no one cares about her. Bernard immediately feels guilty and inadequately filial, and says yes to whatever she asks for. He promises to see her more often. He even promises that Angie will visit her, too. These calls can last an hour and sometimes there are several a day.

All of this is even worse because Angie feels that Bernard's mother holds her personally responsible for her lack of grandchildren. In fact, his mother said as much to Bernard, which Bernard reported back to Angie. He never indicated that he found his mother's comment to be out of line. Angie feels so distraught that she doesn't want Bernard to even touch her, and has continued to use birth control. She doesn't feel their relationship is in good enough shape to have a baby right now, and it is upsetting to her that Bernard doesn't even comment on the fact that she is still on the pill.

Angie is looking for an answer. She wants Bernard to place restrictions on the calls and stop his mother from, as she states it, "taking over their life." When she is totally frustrated, she loses her ability to edit her feelings. So she recently started a real fissure between them when she yelled, "I want you to man-up and act like my husband instead of acting like your mother's husband." After that, Bernard shut down and refused to talk about anything for a week. These hostile exchanges now happen several times a week, and both spouses are exhausted and depressed. They are at a stand-off and Angie has been thinking about leaving.

The Doctors' Advice

Neither of these couples has "news." There is no new information and nothing has been added for them to be discussing. When one, or both, of you can't seem to put a painful topic to rest, it's going to put your relationship in jeopardy. Going over the same topic without progress, new information, or change leads to hopelessness, and the longer it goes on, the more intense its consequences. Ultimately, the couple create a gulf between themselves and communication itself seems useless.

Of course, if you are the one who is bringing up these issues time and time again, you have a right to your feelings. It's o.k., even appropriate, to feel angry when an important issue remains unresolved. But let's be practical: It's not productive to keep voicing your frustration or anger or, for that matter, to keep holding onto these feelings without figuring out a new way to deal with the problem.

This *is not* impossible. Progress can happen either by getting more information, eliciting professional help, or learning a better way to talk to each other. That means finding a conversational style that does not include personal attacks or take place in the same emotional climate. We're not underestimating or unappreciative of how much pain the issue has caused, but stirring it up again and again simply won't solve anything.

Mateo and Lucia know that they are in a bad cycle. The SUV is the go-to insult that Lucia uses whenever she feels upset with him, and she can't resist a potshot every so often, even when it's totally uncalled for. But the reason these digressions exist is because the car fiasco has never really been put to rest. It's necessary for Lucia to forgive Mateo for doing something that did not take her tastes and desires into account, and for Mateo to know what he did wrong so that he and Lucia can know each other better, more intimately, with more trust between them.

Some of the warmth that they could have together has disappeared because gift giving has become an unsafe area for both the giver and the receiver. They need to talk about how to safely give gifts and how to celebrate important events in a loving, caring way. If the real problem is that Lucia doesn't feel that her husband "knows" her, then it's her responsibility to show him what she likes.

One way to do that is to go shopping for things together, but it can't be a setup. Lucia has to curb her sharp tongue and not chide Mateo if he asks her if she likes something that she feels he should know she hates. It's her job to educate Mateo, since no spouse is a mind reader and not every person has a good intuitive knowledge of his or her partner's tastes or style. Mateo, for his part, has to take the risk of winning or losing his wife's approval, and understand that she will ultimately love his efforts to know and please her.

Here is a checkpoint for everyone to think about: Happy couples take risks with each other, so spouses must make it safe for each other to do so. The key point is that instead of moving away from each other by bringing up old failures, you need to pull closer together. Relationships require long-term partner education and if that sounds like work, it shouldn't. As Lillian Hellman said in a different context, "People change and forget to tell each other." The past doesn't predict the future, and you should not use the past to predetermine what your partner is thinking or feeling.

If Lucia will admit that Mateo can grow and learn and "know her," she will be more able to let go of the past and concentrate on how she and Mateo can know each other better. If Mateo can trust that Lucia will not go after him all the time, he will be able to communicate with her more and take risks in gift giving. This is a marriage that could easily go from combative to collaborative and more loving.

The case of Bernard and Angie is much more serious. But sadly, their problem is not rare. Bernard and Angie feel isolated and dispirited because both of them feel disrespected, wounded, cornered, and stuck. We don't think this is an intractable problem, but we do think it has gotten so ugly and repetitive that they probably need a cognitive therapist or a relationship coach to help them work through their feelings and come up with some practical solutions.

Angie can take a step back and remember what she really does want: She wants her husband to love her, support her, and be the father of her children. It seems that Bernard may have retreated from her partially because he feels so guilty about his mother's circumstances and partly because he feels attacked without a way to resolve the competition between his responsibilities as a son and as a husband.

Often one person has to take the lead to solve a problem. It may seem best that both people change together, and that is ideal, but it just doesn't always happen that way. One way to find a road back to spousal collaboration is for Angie to let Bernard know that she is committed to him and their home; then he can feel encouraged and feel that he has a chance to reconnect to her. Bernard currently believes that everything he is doing is wrong, with his mother and his wife. Angie can tell Bernard that she can see him struggling to take care of her and his mother and that she knows he is in a lose-lose situation.

She can reassure him that their relationship is the center of her life and that she wants it to be the center of his, and for that they need time together with no intrusions from anyone. It's not all about his mother; it's about the kind of focus that any two spouses need to give each other.

She can start by telling Bernard that she needs to talk to him and she would like to do that after dinner, before they clean up the dishes. We would like Angie to give him a safe place to open up to her by letting him know she is committed to him and that they can solve their problems together. She can start the conversation on an upbeat note with her reassurances. Then Angie can tell Bernard that more conversation, more planning for the future, and more companionship in their relationship will allow her to be more generous about everything. If she assures him that she is not trying to cut his mother out but rather is trying to make sure that their marriage is prioritized and protected, she can feel more secure, and more sexually open as well. Bernard, for his part, needs to focus on the needs of his wife and their future family and to get some help figuring out how to be a good husband as well as a good son.

Next, they need to make a plan to get together with his mother on a regular basis. Here's how it could go:

ANGIE: *Bernard, for us to be a strong couple, I need a beginning and an end to our day together. I want us to have half*

an hour when we wake up and before we go to bed when
nothing interrupts us, especially the phone.

BERNARD: *But you know Mother calls in the morning and at*
night because she is scared and lonely.

ANGIE: *O.K., do you want to have intimate couple time set*
aside for us?

BERNARD: *Yes, of course. I do, Angie, I really do. I love you,*
and I want us to be a family.

ANGIE: *Do you want to suggest other times we could have that*
are reserved for just the two of us?

BERNARD: *Maybe I could tell mother that I will call her on*
the way to work, and I'll call her in the evening to say
goodnight, and tell her not to call again unless there is a real
emergency.

ANGIE: *Great, let's try it. If that doesn't work, we will try some-*
thing else until we figure it out.

The marriage has to come first. Angie and Bernard can find other
ways to support his mother. He could do some practical things to
help by agreeing to meet his mom one night a week for dinner, and
maybe for lunch as well. Angie can show goodwill and support by
agreeing to invite his mother for dinner on Sundays.

Sometimes these practical, structured actions seem too light for
the deep crevasses that emerge when two people have not found an
answer to a serious, recurring problem. But simply not allowing
calls after a certain time at night unless there is an utter emergency
could start a whole new era of peace and understanding between
the spouses.

If you are going around and around on a painful topic and no
new elements have been brought in to carve away at the problem,
then that is a signal that you need intervention to put new ideas
and solutions into the mix. And, if there is no news, stop and think
about what you are feeling and what you want before you start talking, and leave out the past.

Chapter 2

Refusal to Change

THE SNAP

"That's just the way I am" is a relationship destroyer.

A Closer Look

When you or your partner says, "That's just the way I am," it's not only a refusal to change. It is a commitment to the past rather than the present or the future. It forsakes the possibility of growth, compromise, or new insight. It is a refusal to even engage in an important conversation that might allow for change. These words cut off innovation, the ability to reexamine oneself, and the ability to listen attentively, or indeed, at all.

The stubborn negation of even the consideration of change isolates partners from each other because no further discussion is possible. These few words, "I am what I am," deliver a death sentence to a living relationship and turn it into an inert shadow of its hopeful beginning. The person who hears these words almost always feels hopelessness about the future of their relationship.

Couples therapy often encourages people to analyze why they act or feel the way they do, and trace that back to early family patterns. The bad news here is that this process sometimes makes people feel that they are wired or destined to be "the way I am," and that all change has to flow from this insight. We find this regrettable. Individuals, like relationships, have to grow and change and anything that gets in the way is dangerous. Although there may be some fixed personality characteristics (for example, research has indicated that shyness has a genetic origin), they can usually be

11

tinkered with and, by effort or experience, modified, grown, or truly changed.

Think of the long arc of life. Think of changes from childhood fears, angers, self-doubts, or ambitions. Even if there are behaviors that have not changed, do we really want to be uninfluenced by our lives or our partners? Do you really want to be exactly the same twenty years from now, with the same issues, blocked by a belief that you are destined to stay the way you are? We know that people are capable of new insights and new ways of behaving.

Modern brain research has shown that the brain keeps developing even into old age, if you choose to think and behave in new, different ways. Your brain will rewire to make that possible. So not only is it untrue to say, "That's just the way I am," but it's more willful than real, and more than that, it's dysfunctional and unhealthy for both individuals and relationships.

The Situation
Ripples

Barb and Ross met when they were in their late twenties and have been together ten years. Barb's marriage to Ross was her second marriage and she has complex feelings about marriage. Her first marriage ended because her high school sweetheart husband became physically abusive. She was desperate but felt ashamed that she had picked a man who would beat her and she didn't want anyone to know what was happening.

Nonetheless, it became apparent to others who knew her well that something was terribly wrong because of the contempt Barb's husband would show to her in public. Evidence of abuse ultimately surfaced, and her parents finally intervened when she had no believable excuse for a third black eye. Barb's dad came over to her house, loaded up her stuff, and took her away. He reported her husband to the police, resulting in humiliating court action for Barb, who dreaded her demeaning situation becoming public. She was so traumatized and bewildered after the divorce that she withdrew from everyone and everything. She had been trained as a nurse but she couldn't focus on work, and depression set in. Fortunately, her parents got her help and medication, her sisters supported her, and she got back on her feet. But the fear from the emotional trauma never left her. She did not want to ever go through that kind of terror or loss of self-respect again, so she decided to give up on marriage and children.

True to her avoidance of dishonor and pain, Barb never actually dated Ross. They were casually acquainted through their favorite coffee shop and became friends. Ross was a kind and gentle man who was very active with homeless kids and the more she knew of his big heart and compassionate nature, the more she felt safe with him.

They became particularly tight when Ross opened up to Barb about his own story of abuse. His outward self-composure was developed after a lot of therapy because he, like Barb, had an abusive background. His father believed the saying, "Spare the rod, spoil the child." Ross knew what it was like to fear someone bigger and stronger than he was. He felt terrible about what Barb had suffered and wanted to give her a better, protected life. Their friendship grew into a loving relationship and they married three years later. Ross felt they understood the world in a way that only people who had suffered in the same way could feel. He had never felt so connected to anyone before.

Unfortunately, their work schedules, and their different responses to exhaustion, have started to affect their feelings of comfort and mutual understanding. Ross's work as a construction manager for large city projects means that he works long hours making sure jobs are done correctly. He loves his work and gets great satisfaction in preserving old buildings and seeing them become valuable again, but it's physically difficult. Because Ross often comes home exhausted by the end of the week, his ideal weekend involves kicking back and watching TV.

Barb eventually went back to nursing and her long hours sometimes absorb whole weekends. Their schedules make it hard to plan time together. They are still very much in love, but Barb wants more time when they can be alone and talk or do something fun, just the two of them.

But it is hard for Barb to ask for more time. She learned how to be timid when she was in an abusive relationship, but she is trying to listen to her own heart and feelings to get more time with the man she loves. She feels guilty because she knows Ross works so hard, but she is upset that his work gets his good energy and, increasingly, she does not.

Ross loves Barb, but he is frustrated that she says she needs more from him. Barb suggests they go out on Friday even though he has always reserved Friday nights to recover from the week. The idea of going out somewhere on Friday nights just makes him feel angry. He finally lost his usual low-key manner and barked at her, "Stop asking me out. You can go out if you want, but let me stay home. Friday nights are the only time I can truly relax. I need to unwind; that's just the way I am."

His outburst made Barb cry, which was the last thing Ross wanted to do. He apologized and tried to find a better compromise. He said, "Sorry, Hon" (he knew she loved being called her pet name), "I just need to rest up on weekends. You can go out. How about Sunday? We can spend all day together on Sundays. I'll do anything you want. I love you and want you to be happy, but Friday night is sacred."

Barb appreciated his effort. He had a point; she loved spending Sundays with him. But Barb's complaint is about never going out on Friday nights. Several of the couples they are closest to meet after work on Fridays for happy hour and she would like to join them once in a while. But Ross would not even discuss it. He used the fateful words, "Friday night is my TV night, always has been, always will be. That's just the way it is."

Barb feels shut out, even though he has tried to compromise. At this point she has resigned herself to going out alone on Fridays since her way of relaxing after a hard week is to go out with friends or do something. Watching TV with Ross just doesn't do it for her—in fact, it makes her feel more alone. Barb has had things so much worse that she feels bad about pushing this issue, but still, she can't understand why Ross is so absolutely stubborn about even considering a change in his routine.

Blasts

Jackson, forty-two, a big guy with a big personality, works as a salesman for a sporting goods company. His charm and charisma make him a great salesman. Everyone loves Jackson. He is the guy with a great story, a new joke, and a hug for every kid or close friend. His clients feel well treated and admire his knowledge, so he has a huge bank of repeat customers. His wife, Audrey, thirty-five, is a homemaker, and even as a little girl she dreamed of having three kids and the time to be an active advocate for her kids at school and in the community. She loves taking her children to lessons, tutoring, and sports events while creating a welcoming environment for their friends and having a well-run household. She likes to cook healthy meals, keep the house clean and organized, and manage their budget. She also likes to work out and walk every day and is proud of her ability to take good care of herself. She is the kind of person every community admires: a dependable neighbor and a good friend. She loves her life with Jackson.

Jackson is a traditional guy. When he got serious about finding a wife, a woman like Audrey was exactly what he was looking for. He admires Audrey's success as a homemaker and believes that they share the same central value that home and family need a woman there full time to make everything run right. He feels good about his role in the equation: He makes the money, and that's his job; he doesn't feel he should do more. As a result, he does very little around the house, but he plays with the kids every night and reads to them in bed. He always takes them to the park or somewhere on the weekend so Audrey can get a break. As the boys have gotten older and require more of her time, Audrey has found that it's harder to keep the house and their schedules up to her standards.

Jackson thinks of himself as a loving, caring father and husband, but he is not particularly aware of how much he ups the ante by creating more work for his conscientious wife. Being a true extrovert, Jackson often invites people to come over for a bite or to watch a football or basketball game. He doesn't think this is a big deal and he knows Audrey likes having people in the house. She is able to entertain on the spot, provide a good meal if need be, and maintain a clean house. He loves showing off his family, and he is proud of Audrey for being the "perfect wife."

Audrey generally likes these challenges; overall it's the life she wanted and got. But sometimes too many things happen at once and she just needs a break, and an extra pair of hands to make sure that their home is in order and the kids taken care of.

So from time to time, she asks Jackson to pitch in, always noting that it is an exceptional time and she is overwhelmed. But when she asks for a little help, Jackson always says the same thing: "I'm the breadwinner; you're the homemaker." This rebuke is getting to Audrey. She feels that although he appreciates her, he does not understand how overwhelmed she is.

The breaking point came when Jackson started having a Friday night poker party without talking to her about it. Six of Jackson's buddies would show up and settle down at the dining room table for a late night of beer, poker, and laughter. They were so noisy that Audrey could not get the kids to sleep and she couldn't sleep herself. Recently Jackson came up to bed after his buddies left and wanted to have sex. Audrey was so tired and angry she pushed him away. He was outraged and told her to sleep somewhere else, and she did.

It took a few days for them to settle down before they could even talk to each other. Jackson was fuming. He said, "My home is my castle, and I am king of the castle. That's the way it was with my folks, and that's the way it is here." Audrey finally said, "I am not going to live like this. I am going to go stay with my sister. I need time to think." Jackson was stunned. He could not understand how this was happening. His words were, "How could you do this to me?" Her retort was, "How could *you* do this to *me?*"

They are both surprised by the intensity of their emotions and how far apart they suddenly find themselves. Neither of them really saw this crisis coming until they were in the midst of it. But relationships require growth, change, and a willingness to adapt to each other if couples want to have a long, fulfilling life together.

The Doctors' Advice

We understand Ross's need to unwind after a tough workweek. But we don't think that making blanket pronouncements is an acceptable marital tactic. Although patterns can seem natural and normal, there should be almost nothing in a relationship that is not discussable and modifiable.

Barb has to tell Ross that eliminating Friday nights from their time together is a serious problem in their marriage for her. She needs him to consider what is important to their relationship, and "That's the way I am" is not o.k. with her. Because of the scars from her first marriage, it is hard for Barb to ask for what she wants. But she musters the courage and lets him know that she wants to go out on Fridays when something special is happening. She tells him it is painful for her to believe that her desire to have more fun together is not important to him.

Ross responds, "What you want is very important to me. I love you and want you to be happy. I thought Saturdays and Sundays were enough." Ross even suggests he could record his Friday night program and watch it later. He says he prefers to do something that isn't stressful on Fridays, and she agrees. This is a good start, but we also suggest they reserve a different time for him to watch his recorded games, like Saturday mornings, when Barb goes to the gym and runs errands.

If Barb wants to throw in a bribe, such as agreeing to eat at his favorite restaurant, she can do that. Doing a little extra to say thank you for being flexible is always a nice touch. At some point, when the new system is working, she will want to talk about how great it is that he changed his pattern for her and how much she appreciates that.

For Jackson and Audrey, however, there's a level of urgency. They both believed they had a deal: He had his job and she had hers. That attitude is hurting their marriage. Audrey has changed, their circumstances have changed, and although Jackson may not recognize it, he has changed too. We think there are several ways to approach this, without threats, but also without accepting their separate fixed roles.

We recommend that they go someplace they can talk privately for an hour to an hour and a half. It is better to have more short talks than long ones. Couples often talk in circles and become defensive if they talk too long at any one time.

Audrey can tell Jackson she loves him and wants to be married to him. It is important to start with reassurance; otherwise, Jackson may dig in his heels because he thinks he is being threatened. Audrey can tell him how her life has changed and that she didn't realize she could not do it all, and simply ask Jackson to think about it. Jackson loves Audrey, and if he has a chance to think he will see that their life has changed. They will both need some time and an ongoing conversation about the changes in their life and how they can make life smoother for each other.

By talking about the changes in their circumstances, neither one has to be wrong, and they don't have to rehash the past. They can look at life in the present and find solutions that are practical and enhance their life as a couple and as a family.

In loving relationships, there must be a sense that the two of you can keep growing, learning, and changing. Changing together betters and enriches your daily lives. People leave relationships that are stagnant and boring. We want to save you from that.

Chapter 3

Snarky Comments

Making snarky comments poisons your relationship.

A Closer Look

A snarky comment is something nasty that is said about someone else. It is a hit-and-run criticism. The snark can be veiled or straightforward, but it's negative and unprompted. If it's about your partner, he or she will feel cut and insulted without a fair chance to respond. When the snark is about others, it only breeds negativity and causes your partner to see you as petty.

Sometimes it can seem like you are only passing on interesting information or a funny story, but it comes across as mean-spirited gossip and criticism. As a habit, making these comments diminishes others' respect for you. Whoever the victim is, you will be seen as untrustworthy because there is nothing useful or constructive in what you are saying; it is only hurtful and harmful. Sooner or later, the potshots you throw at your partner will be seen as vicious, cowardly, and unloving. People naturally move away from someone who says ugly things about them, and that will happen in a marriage just as much as it happens in a friendship. No one really wants to be around someone who frequently lashes out.

The comments can seem benign, such as, "Well, honey, I married you for your beauty, not your brains," or "Grocery store flowers again, wow, that really makes my day." Or something that is superficially funny but stings, such as, "You can't find your keys again? Maybe you should look where you lost mine the last time you borrowed them."

19

We wonder if you might be masking some real problems in your relationship. Instead of communicating directly, are you making snarky comments and bitter remarks because it's hard to express your feelings? It's important to trace where such negative feelings come from so you can figure out how to stop making these nasty quips.

The Situation
Ripples

Emma and David are in their sixties, and they've been married for forty-two years. They met while working at a department store and both of them have been in retail in one form or another all of their working lives. Emma worked in fine women's clothing and when management decided to eliminate her department, she thought it was time for her to retire. Suddenly, she has a lot of spare time to spend on herself and her husband, which isn't entirely easy for her. She had spent a lifetime working and raising her daughter and now, retired and an empty nester, she feels out of sync with the life she is living. The house seems too quiet and lonely.

Emma hadn't anticipated how terrible she would feel once her daughter Joyce left home. Raising Joyce was a pure pleasure for both David and Emma, and the years of her childhood were some of the happiest in their lives. When Joyce did get married and move away, Emma felt intensely alone and very sad. She had trouble facing each day, and after confiding to friends that she might be depressed, she took a friend's advice and went back to work. Her best friend owned a small boutique that specialized in women's clothing and was delighted to have Emma's help a few days a week. The store profited from her presence and pretty soon she was working 10:00 A.M. to 7:00 P.M. five days a week and a half day on Saturday. Emma's mood cleared up considerably and she looked forward to being at the shop each day.

David, who has been a manager in the appliance section of a large department store for thirty-five years, is still gung ho about his job. He has no intention of retiring. In fact, he has a small side business as an appliance repairman that he enjoys. He has made peace with the fact that Joyce and her husband, and their two children, live more than three hours away. He likes driving there every three weeks or so, but he doesn't want to go any more than that. Emma would like to go there more often, but the drive is difficult, so the distance is just a little too far for Emma to see Joyce's family as often as she would like.

Emma has put some of her unused energy into becoming the unofficial neighborhood watch captain, and it's her pastime to be "in the know." She comes home daily with news about other people, and she generally can't wait to tell David about other people. He usually responds with "Uh huh." He hopes that is enough to truncate what he finds a tiresome new habit of hers: gossiping. But she rejects his disinterest and tries hard to make him her confidant. David finds her behavior so unflattering that it is affecting his perception of her character. Here is what they told us was a typical discussion:

EMMA: *Poor Lila. She came in the shop today. Her husband took away all her credit cards and took her name off the bank account because she keeps giving their son and daughter-in-law money.*

DAVID: *Uh huh.*

EMMA: *I told her, "Don't spend what you don't have," but you know Lila.*

DAVID: *Uh huh.*

EMMA: *David, I am talking to you. Say something. She picked out an awful dress. I could have found her something that didn't make her look so fat, but she wouldn't listen.*

DAVID: *Well, I don't care what she wears or what she spends or who has what. You should hear yourself talking this way about your friend.*

EMMA: *You don't care about anything I say. I'm just trying to have a little conversation about something that's important to me. Lila is my friend.*

Blasts

Natalie and Juan are in their mid-fifties. They met on a cruise where it was easy for single people to meet each other casually. They both said it was love at first sight and have now been married for seven years. Falling in love and getting serious so quickly was surprising to both of them. Each had been married before, but both had unpleasant divorces. In fact, both of them had told all their friends that they were never going to get married again. They laugh now about failing to follow through on their vows to stay single!

Juan was on the boat as a perk because the hotel chain he works for was having its anniversary celebration and all the employees were given the chance to go on the cruise for a very minimal fee. He has had many jobs at the hotel but now works in reception. He has an eye for detail and a warm personality; both coworkers and guests adore him. Natalie started out as a manicurist and now has a storefront manicure- pedicure business of her own. She has a grown daughter, Ana, who is a very successful radio host.

Unfortunately, Juan has started to make some drive-by nasty comments about Ana, either out of the blue or as a "joke." Natalie feels seriously annoyed at Juan and has complained about it, but Juan seems unaffected by her distress or comments. Here's the way it goes:

JUAN: *Hey, last night when we stopped by Ana's house, I was amazed. I've never seen her house so clean.*
NATALIE: *Why don't you leave my daughter alone? It's not your house.*

JUAN: *I didn't say anything. I said the house looked nice. I was complimenting on how nice the house looked. Why are you so grouchy?*

NATALIE: *I am not going to be a part of this. It's late. I am going to bed.*

The Doctors' Advice

Snarky comments reflect badly on everyone; they do not make anyone feel better. Both of these couples are hurting their relationships because of unfortunate conversational patterns that judge people so harshly as to offend their partners.

In the case of Juan and Natalie, Juan is not taking responsibility for his comments (which is part of the problem). But the immediate issue is that he is making an indirect judgment about his wife's daughter's habits; that kind of comment hits a nerve because just about all parents feel protective of their children. When you repeatedly make negative comments about another person's child (true or not), you are going after the parent because at some level, conscious or not, you know it will upset them. Juan is critiquing his stepdaughter by complimenting her "unexpectedly" good housekeeping, a so-called left-handed compliment. You say something that sounds nice but is really a slam. We've all heard these kinds of "compliments." For example, someone tells you, "You look thinner in that dress," or "I'm so glad you changed your hair style," or "You finally got a report done on time." Juan gets some pleasure, it seems, by doing this kind of under-the-radar shot at Natalie, and these comments hurt her. She knows that something is making him feel like going after her through her daughter, and she calls him on it. When he refuses to deal with his comment and his intent, or why he cares at all about her daughter's housekeeping, Natalie abruptly ends the conversation and withdraws. It is understandable, but it's not going to end Juan's potshots.

Emma has gotten into a bad habit of telling stories about people that include snarky comments about them. We can see that Emma is lonely and bored, but that is not an excuse for derogatory commentary about others. The more negative or snide comments a person says (and thinks) about others, the worse it actually makes that person feel, even if they don't recognize it at the time. Negative comments create negative feelings. Although Emma's snarky comments are not directed at David, they do not make him feel closer to her; in fact, it is quite the opposite. He distances himself from her because he doesn't like gossip. Emma is showing a nasty, petty part of her personality, and her husband doesn't want to participate in what he thinks is an unattractive and unnecessary review of how people dress or behave.

If your partner is making snarky comments, there are three steps you have to take:

1. You have to recognize that a snarky comment has been made. How do you recognize it? By being aware of your own discomfort, irritation, or anger. Sometimes, it may take a while to figure out what it was that upset you. It's amazing how sometimes we protect ourselves by choosing not to recognize when we've been emotionally assaulted.

2. You need to decide that you are going to take this on because it's damaging your relationship. It lessens your respect for your partner, even if you are not aware of it at the time. You will begin to distance yourself from him or her because the safety of the relationship has been breached. Although it's easier just to "not notice" unwanted behaviors and it avoids a bigger blowup to let a snarky remark go by, you are losing an opportunity to change things for the better by withdrawing. For example, David's behavior is merely prolonging his wife's new habit, which hurts both of them. He needs to talk about why he doesn't want to participate in these

kinds of conversations, and he needs to look deeper: His wife needs more contact, and more fun and affection from him.

3. Partners who are upset about their spouse's proclivity to diss them or others need to *clearly identify the behavior at that time* and say, "STOP, I don't want to hear bad things about other people, ever. There is no good that comes from snarky, critical, or gossipy talk. So, please, just don't do it." You have to immediately identify the kind of conversation or comment you hate because your partner may truly be unaware of how you perceive these comments. Your partner may think these remarks are clever or witty, so you really have to tell them exactly when it bothers you.

Your partner might not fully understand the damage he or she is doing and may not want to take responsibility for being snarky. Many people will turn this back on their spouses and call them "thin-skinned." Perhaps that is true; perhaps they are sensitive and pick up on a possible insult too readily. But it is still the responsibility of the snarky person to stop the negative quips and comments. When you ask your partner to stop, you need to handle the accusations about your "oversensitivity" or "inability to take a joke" by saying something like "They aren't jokes. Notice, I am not laughing. A comedian isn't funny if no one laughs."

Because we feel this behavior is really damaging to your goodwill and good opinion of your partner, we suggest a strategy that can be effective without having to do a major overhaul of your partner's personality. Here is the model to follow:

JUAN: *I've never seen her house so clean.*
NATALIE: *Juan, when you say you've never seen the house so clean, you're implying that it's always dirty. That's criticizing my daughter and I don't like it. If you can't say something*

nice about her—or for that matter, other people we know—I
don't want you to say anything.

JUAN: *Hey, I am just telling you. I didn't mean anything bad*
by it.

NATALIE: *O.K., but either way, it upsets me. I want you to stop.*
And I don't want to talk about it anymore. I just want you
to stop.

JUAN: *But I don't understand why you are so touchy about this.*

NATALIE: *I know you don't. But I don't want to argue about*
this. I just want you to stop talking about other people to me.
It makes me really unhappy and angry, and it's best for our
relationship to just stop it.

JUAN: *O.K., geez, you're really sensitive.*

NATALIE: *Yes, I am.*

If you are the one who's making the snarky comments, and you
get called on it, or you recognize yourself in this chapter, it would
be wonderful if you would talk to your partner about whether or
not you've bothered them or offended them. You could talk about
what changes need to be made with them and, even more important, review in your own mind why you are making these negative,
needling remarks.

Of course, many of us don't always recognize or accept the harm
and ugliness of snarky comments. We may truly have no insight
into why we make them, but here are some of the reasons: You
might feel jealous or competitive or have a need to feel superior. Or
you may be expressing anger and getting back at someone over past
insults or other infractions. These are very human and understandable feelings, but they need to be understood and dealt with rather
than manifesting themselves in snarkiness.

That solution—understanding what's bothering you—gets rid of
not only the ugly comments but also the ugly feelings that prompt
them. The only exception is someone who genuinely gets pleasure
from other people's misfortunes and likes wounding people—but
we are not dealing with that extreme personality flaw here.

If you are the perpetrator of snarky comments, you might want to consider cognitive therapy. The therapist or coach can explain why what you are saying is snarky, sarcastic, or critical and can teach you alternative ways to express your thoughts that are not offensive to others. If you don't want therapy or counseling, then monitor yourself. Try some self-talk such as, "If you can't say something good, don't say anything at all."

But without therapy and without a divorce, you can do the next best thing, and that is to stop the behavior that's harming the relationship. So for Natalie and David, the recipients of these snarky comments, the best *Snap Strategy* is to simply say "STOP"—and say it unequivocally so there's no lack of clarity.

Chapter 4

Insensitive Remarks

THE SNAP

When your partner makes an insensitive remark, just say "Ouch" and let it go.

A Closer Look

It's normal to feel hurt in an intimate relationship. Hurt feelings are part of life and happen from time to time in every relationship. Most of the time, they are simply a matter of different expectations or different perceptions of what is important. Men and women often see things differently, perhaps because of biology, different treatment by mothers and fathers, or just a variety of life experiences. For example, a woman may feel threatened by a male stranger who stands very close to her in a chance meeting, while a man might experience the same kind of close encounter with a woman as a flattering flirtation. Differences in male and female expectations can also occur in a relationship and be influenced by cultural values and traditions and what we observed as children in our families or from prior relationships.

We have rarely seen partners set out to hurt one another. But careless comments or forgotten manners can lead to more distress than is warranted. We've seen one person's unintentional, hurtful remark to his or her partner turn into a dramatic dialogue or spark a torrent of anger and defensiveness. Frequently, insensitive remarks are meant as jokes or "just kidding," but when they are hurtful they need to be called out and addressed. Often a light reminder is all it takes. It can be as simple as saying "Ouch" to remind your partner that he or she is treading in a sensitive area.

The Situation
Ripples

Chloe and Mason have been together for twenty years, and early on they decided not to have children. They enjoy their freedom, their friends, and their hobbies. Chloe loves antiques and enjoys browsing through markets and street fairs. She finds treasures that she can restore and sell on eBay. Mason loves tennis; he plays as often as possible. They both work in health care management and love their work.

Chloe is fashionable. She cares about what she wears and has a sizable shoe collection. She likes to be a little edgy; she has great legs and shows them off with short skirts and high heels. She also likes makeup, often wearing jewel tone lipstick and purple eye shadow with dark mascara. Mason frequently makes remarks about her clothes, and especially about her shoes, such as, "You look like you are going someplace fancy tonight, not to a movie," or, "How can you walk in those shoes? I'd fall on my face."

Understandably, Chloe is hurt. Her appearance is very important to her, and she wants Mason to appreciate her good looks. She reacts by telling him that he doesn't know what he's talking about or calls him a "nerd."

She shrugs it off, but she's hurt. Often it damages what should have been a really nice evening together. Mason has not noticed how deflating his comments are to her.

Blasts

Eli and Camilla have been together for more than a decade and over that time Eli has put on twenty-five pounds, so weight has changed his appearance. Eli owns a deli and loves food; he cannot seem to stop himself from sampling the goods.

A big part of Camilla's attraction to Eli when they first met was his physique. She actually gasped the first time she saw him while she was waiting in line at this very popular deli. She was so stunned she could not take her eyes off him. When it was her time to order, Eli came from behind the counter, took her hand, looked into her eyes and said, "I would like to help you." Camilla said, "Yes," but couldn't utter another word. That was the beginning of their intensely sensual and sexual love affair.

Now Camilla cannot seem to admit to her feelings about the change in his appearance and instead just drops zingers. She once even said, "Is there a balloon under your shirt or is all that you?" It was an insult buried in a giggle. Sometimes when Eli wants to have sex, she will pinch his fat. He gets upset and goes cold. He understandably turns away and that is the end of lovemaking. Once after a string of hurtful comments, he cancelled their plans for the evening and told her to just go by herself. Camilla thinks he's over-reacting and that most of the time she is just trying to make him aware and perhaps go on a diet.

The Doctors' Advice

We believe that not every comment, remark, or oversight needs to be taken seriously. You can let your partner know that he or she has struck a nerve that hurts without delving into explanations or dis-section. Just say "Ouch." We have rarely seen a partner consciously and deliberately set out to do damage to a loved one. If one of you is deliberately hurting the other, that is a different problem, and one that requires a serious solution.

We would like Chloe to tell Mason that his comments about her clothes and shoes leave her feeling hurt and disappointed. Like it or not, we do care about our partner's approval or at least acceptance of whatever passions or quirks we have. She may simply need to tell

Mason that she wants him to comment on things about her appearance that he finds attractive, rather than commenting on what he doesn't like or maybe just doesn't understand. He used to comment on her legs a lot, and she would like him to do that again. And in turn, Mason can try to see her point after she creates a new frame for him to use to understand her fashion style. She can point out Katherine Hepburn, who wore pants before it was "acceptable," and Diane Keaton, who has a unique way of putting herself together. That might help Mason to see there isn't just one way to look good. Whether or not he "gets it," however, he has to learn to keep his negative judgments to himself.

Camilla's actions hit deeper and darker because she is ridiculing Eli, and not taking ownership of her disapproval of his appearance, so it's time for her to cease making mean remarks altogether. His weight is now a health issue, and she has to figure out a way to respond to how he looks without creating more anxiety and tension, which makes him edge closer and closer to heart-attack territory. Not only might he eat more out of self-loathing if she makes him feel unworthy, but nasty comments will so damage the solidarity of the relationship that he might refuse any help or advice from her.

We want Eli to have a serious talk with Camilla before she makes her next remark. He can tell her that he is carrying more weight than either one of them would like and that her approach of kidding and joking about his weight is not helping him and in fact is hurting him. He can tell her that when she makes these comments, they leave him feeling unwanted, defeated, and unloved. He can ask her to stop kidding about something that hurts both of them. Then they can put together a plan that makes him feel loved and gives him a sense that they are tackling this issue together. It could entail cooking healthy food together, going to the gym together, or seeing a doctor together.

We believe it is important to have an air of lightness and forgiveness in your relationship. We all make mistakes. It is part of being human to say the wrong thing at the wrong time, and when this happens it is often best just to let it go. Trust that you are loved and respected and that sideswipes are minor mistakes. You and your partner are not wired exactly the same and expectations can run the gamut, but that does not mean there is something wrong between you. You simply have differences. A smile, a chuckle, or a simple "Ouch" is all you need to signal that you feel hurt. Dwelling on these feelings makes them bigger than they need to be.

Chapter 5

Lack of Play

THE SNAP

Couples who play together stay together.

A Closer Look

Couples who play together stay together. Every relationship needs play that is fresh and fun, activities that arouse friendly, frivolous feelings. Couples who play together, sharing laughter and spontaneity, are happier individually and as a couple than those who don't. Fun together doesn't happen just by chance often enough to keep you connected. Play dates or fun at home produce badly needed endorphins that keep us connected to one another. Be original and keep playing and laughing. Be intentional about creating time and energy to be playful with your partner.

Mammals play for solidarity, for joy, to show affection and trust. Play is hardwired in our DNA and we really can't afford to ignore it. We were not meant to be serious all the time, and we need occasions to be silly, lively, athletic, creative, and funny. Trust is built through risk and so some of our play involves a certain amount of risk. For example, hiking or climbing together, taking a trip together (even if it's just to a different neighborhood), playing bingo, jointly doing a video game, going to a nightclub—or even gambling—raises the excitement level in a relationship and often requires interdependence and communication. But above all, play gives you those great endorphins that provide pleasure. It casts a good mood over the two of you.

The Situation
Ripples

Mia and Matthew are stuck in a rut. Mia is a manager in a software company, and Matthew is a software engineer. They are in their early fifties, and their kids are grown and live out of state. Every Saturday night, they have dinner and a movie. They take turns walking their dog, Jimmy. Neither of them is athletic, and in their spare time they work or read books. It's not a bad life, but Mia complains that it seems too routine, and she is envious of her girlfriends who travel with their partners, go to book salons, and have season tickets to the theater. She has mentioned this to Matthew, but Matthew is really content with things exactly the way they are. Mia isn't angry, but she wonders, "Is this all there is?"

Blasts

Carlos and Eva, a couple in their mid-thirties, got married two years ago. They are both devoted to their religion and waited to have a sexual relationship until they were married. Carlos loves sports. He golfs, he is in a bowling league, and he rarely misses watching his hometown teams play, either at the field or on television. At least a couple of times a week, he stops after work at a local bar to discuss the week's games with his buddies.

Eva likes sports, but she is upset about how much time they take up in their life together. She feels that there's very little time that she has to share alone with Carlos. She is especially annoyed when he turns the TV on to ESPN as soon as he walks into the house. Unless she turns it down, he turns the TV on so loud that she can hear it in every room. She feels shut out of his life and sometimes driven out of her own home. She has coped by creating a lot of activities with her friends and logging onto various computer games for three or four hours a night. But she has realized lately that she and Carlos are living parallel lives and that the fun has gone out of their relationship. She doesn't desire him the way she used to and she worries that they are so distant from one another that they will never find a way back.

The Doctors' Advice

Play dates, having adventures, romping in the park, or rollerblading on the sidewalk develop a type of intimate connection that is essential to maintaining a happy, loving, long-term relationship. Fun at home produces badly needed endorphins that keep us connected to one another. Interestingly, most play is free. It is the interaction between the two of you that is free, fun, and maybe even a little wild. It can be child's play like board games, tossing a ball back and forth, or chasing each other, the kinds of play we did as kids. Like other mammals, humans build confidence in each other through laughter, friskiness, even being mischievous.

There is also adult play: flirting, strip poker, dressing up or role-playing, as well as undressing each other. Try feeding each other grapes, candies, or chocolates as foreplay. Or even consider taking sexuality education classes for grownups sponsored by local sex shops. If that's way out of your comfort zone, you can find serious sex play tips on Babeland.com, Libida.com, Trojan.com, AARP.org/relationships/love-sex or on Menshealth.com and Womenshealth.com.

These couples are experiencing a common cultural habit that is turning into a common cultural problem. A 2008 study by sociologist Paul Amato, entitled "Alone Together: How Marriage in America Is Changing," found that spouses are interacting less than in previous periods of history. The good news is that when partners generate activities together, they are much more likely to be happy and stable.

Mia and Matthew are on the right track. They have "dates," but that's not the same as fun. Mia has become dispirited and envious, which is a good indication that things have to change. You can take a perfectly good relationship and bore each other so much that it starts to undermine what was a pretty decent foundation. So Mia, who has noticed the problem while Matthew is unfazed by their lifestyle, has to be the one to get the energy and interest back into their lives.

Mia can take the situation into her own hands by thinking of new things to do that are simple and convenient and offering Matthew choices. Matthew needs to pick one. Since Matthew basically just wants to please her, he will probably be on board for at least some of the things she suggests. Easy new activities for couples include having a game night or an indoor picnic; taking a tour of a factory (chocolate factories are particularly fun); getting season tickets to sporting events or plays; roller-skating; or going to a casino, an amusement park (catering to that inner child), or a shooting range—in other words, opening up the world of possibilities and having fun exploring them. There will be more laughs, perhaps a new real interest, and ultimately a feeling of being closer.

Carlos has filled up his life with sports. It is an addiction because more never seems to be enough. Eva can see that, but unfortunately, she has adapted to it by creating her own life apart from his. In the end, she's lonely. What she doesn't realize is that her tack is enabling him to continue his separate life. We think at this point she should confront the issue directly by telling him, "I am starting to feel like I am not married. But I want to be. And I want to be married to *you*. And for me that means we do things together, like we did when we were dating." She should then take it to action mode: "Are there things you would like to do with me that would be fun for you?" After he says, "Sex," she can say, "Sure, what else?"

Perhaps he will say, "Well, I used to like going to games together," and even though she doesn't want a life wrapped around sports, she can say, "Yes, let's do that. Could you get the tickets?" It's still sports, but it's also a re-connection. Then she can suggest something she would like to do, by asking him if he would be willing to do something they used to like, such as playing cards with another couple or going out to listen to music. The more fun they start to have together, the more they will feel like doing other things. It's that first step back together that may be the hardest, but once the pattern has been modified, more change is not so unthinkable.

Being silly, fumbling around, doing things you are not good at—just for the fun of it—builds intimacy and trust. And don't forget to frolic between the sheets. Relationships in which perfection is required for entertainment are missing one of the best parts of love, which is joy. Put some energy and focus into creating experiences that bring out the child in you and share that part of you with one another. Couples who play together stay together.

Chapter 6

Damaging Arguments

Going to bed mad might be your smartest move.

A Closer Look

Your mother may have told you never to go to bed mad. Many people believe this to be true. We don't. The problem is that when you are mad, you are often in no shape to deal with anything well, least of all a difficult problem or hurt feelings.

When we are really, really mad, the human brain reverts to survival mode. The only options are fight, flight, freeze, or surrender. Although the human brain has evolved to do more thinking, problem solving, and creativity under duress, those basic survival instincts still set in even if we consciously know our survival is not at stake. Doctors John and Julie Gottman have done research indicating that people, especially men, can get angry fast, and it takes longer to cool down than you might think. While you are still angry, you are much more likely to be irrational or to say things that are mean and make it harder to reach a good solution. It is better to sleep on it, even though you may really want to keep at it because you feel like you need to resolve the problem immediately. That feeling is understandable, but it is likely to be counterproductive. Not only that, if you push too hard, you might end up saying things that are more damaging than good.

The Situation
Ripples

Isaac and Zoe have been a couple for six years, and they decided not to marry or have children. They love their jobs: Isaac is an actuarial agent for an insurance company, and Zoe is a tour guide. They are each other's best friend and play pals. They have a lot of fun together. But when they do have disagreements, they find themselves harshly divided.

Isaac has trouble leaving unfinished business on the table. When he and Zoe have a disagreement, he wants to clear it up as soon as possible. He wants issues resolved. Zoe prefers to think about things and doesn't want to be pushed to a conclusion before she feels ready. Sometimes she is much more upset than Isaac realizes because she keeps it in. She does a slow burn, whereas when he's upset it is readily observable. They have a pattern in which he can see she's upset or distant about something and he wants to know what's bothering her. He doesn't stop pressing her, even when she says, "I don't want to talk about it now." He will respond, "We don't need to talk about it, but I just need to know what it is." He will say the same thing ten different ways and protest, "I can't sleep unless you tell me what it is." And he worries, "Is it something I did?" Or, "Is it important?" Or, "Is it about last night's conversation about your sister?" Zoe puts her hands on her head and says, "I can't think. Leave me alone." He presses until she yells at him, "God damn it. Leave me alone," goes into the bedroom, and slams the door behind her.

Blasts

Ethan and Madeline, in their late twenties, just bought their first home. They previously lived in a tiny apartment furnished with hand-me-downs. They saved for years to buy their new house and a few pieces of nice furniture. Ethan thought Madeline would be happy and grateful, but she isn't. Madeline is unhappy and Ethan is frustrated.

They are currently at verbal fisticuffs over Ethan's sloppiness and his lack of regard for Madeline's desire for a neat, clean house.

Ethan throws his stuff on whatever table or chair is nearby, leaving a trail behind him wherever he goes. He opens the mail and scatters everything on the kitchen table. He leaves every sink wet and dirty. There's half-eaten food at his desk, or unwrapped in the refrigerator. It's driving Madeline crazy. She takes pride in having a house that is tidy and organized. She feels like it's a personal attack when he shows no respect for all the work she does to make a nice home. They don't see each other until dinnertime, although he leaves the house later in the morning than she does and often creates a new mess. So when she gets home from work, the place is in shambles again. She is so angry that the first thing she says to him when he gets home is usually critical. Madeline starts with, "You did it again; you left a huge mess. You are a disgusting pig! Didn't your mother teach you anything? I am not your mother, housekeeper, or maid."

Ethan gives it back. The other night, he screamed, "I worked my ass off to buy this house and all you do is bitch, bitch, bitch. You are selfish. You are a spoiled brat. This is it. I am fed up with you and I am tired of all the criticism and carping that goes on the moment I get back home."

Things are pretty raw between them, and there is a lot of door slamming and yelling. The level of conflict is so harsh and degrading on both their parts that we consider it verbal abuse. It will permanently damage the relationship if it does not come to a complete and clear end very soon.

The Doctors' Advice

You may be surprised to know that the absence of conflict in an intimate relationship is a predictor of divorce. Conflict, disagreement, struggle, and clashes are essentials in a healthy relationship. There are two people in the relationship and each should have differences, and those differences need to be expressed. Intimacy is knowing the other's deepest nature. The only way to peel away the layers and see your partner's core is through communicating both your similarities and differences. The state we want you to reach is one of mutual acceptance. And that does entail conflict, but there is a big difference between conflict and cruelty. Cruelty is intentionally using your partner's vulnerabilities against him.

Isaac gets obsessive when fear rears its head, but he really needs to figure out another way to soothe himself and calm down. Zoe is sending him every signal in the book that she can't operate on his time schedule. But her approach winds him up even more and gives them both heartburn. When Zoe walks away and closes the door, she is shutting him out without giving him any sense of her emotional state and how they as a couple are in danger. He doesn't know if she is going to pack her bags or read a book.

We would like Zoe to reassure him that she loves him and that everything is o.k., and that they can talk tomorrow. She can give him a light kiss and say goodnight. Most of the pressure he puts on Zoe comes from insecurity and fear, and if he knows that things will be o.k., he will be able to wait until a better time to talk. So we believe that sleeping on it and letting your emotions settle down is the best medicine in this type of conflict. Neither Isaac's nor Zoe's survival is at stake, so a good night's sleep can do wonders, helping them to come up with reasonable solutions and allowing them the opportunity to understand their needs are simply different.

Ethan and Madeline are a different story, although there is some similarity: Both couples are caught in a conflict over opposing styles. The partners in this Blasts couple, however, have very dissimilar needs for order in their environment. But they need to understand how important this issue is to each of them and that they literally do not see their environment in the same way. This issue will never be solved through explosions, contempt, or personal attacks. They truly need to stop this type of conflict.

The relationship threat comes from the contempt they now feel for each other. Contempt is different from anger because when you show contempt for your partner, it's like aiming arrows at his or her heart. When Madeline calls him a "disgusting pig" or Ethan calls her "a spoiled brat," that's contempt. It is malicious and it has to stop, but it needs to be discussed under less fraught conditions.

Name-calling has no place in an intimate relationship. This couple has to find a time to apologize for the ugly words exchanged. They also need to explore their motivations regarding this issue. Some understanding of the importance of cleanliness is necessary— for each of them. Ethan is treating Madeline's need to have a neat and tidy house as trivial, until he feels attacked. We want Ethan to accept that Madeline needs him not only to stop attacking her but to appreciate the fact that her efforts benefit him.

Ethan would also benefit from reconnecting to Madeline. We want him to focus on how she improves his life. He does not have the same need for order that she does. He doesn't even see what she sees, and that is not going to change either.

We want them to step back from this level of verbal abuse and remember that they are on the same team. We would like them to remember that they are partners, not enemies, and they live in a home, not a war zone. It may help for Madeline to add a bit of self-deprecating humor about her over-the-top cleanliness, just to remind both of them not to take it so seriously.

Taking a break to remember all the good that you have done as a team will remind you of your bond, which is more important than what you don't agree on. Going to bed mad might be your smartest move if cooling off can lead to finding reasonable solutions and remembering what does work for the two of you.

Chapter 7

Doubting Your Partner's Intentions

THE SNAP

Assume goodwill from your partner and show goodwill to your partner.

A Closer Look

Assuming goodwill is an easier way to go through life, and adds lightness to your relationship. When you believe your partner wants the best for you, it is easier to stay calm, centered, and open. Use self-talk to remember that your partner loves you and wants you to be happy. Use a mantra such as "I love her and she loves me," "Every day isn't a ten," or "This too will pass."

Love and respect are not constant emotions that permeate every minute of every day, and despite our best intent all of us have bad days or grumpy moods. Couples make mistakes in reading each other. One of you may be grumpy because your sports team lost or your pants don't fit the same as they did last year. His or her mood may have absolutely nothing to do with you. Generally, if a bad mood or grouchy tone is about you, you will know soon enough.

In the course of daily life it may seem that your partner doesn't think about you. It is easy to assume that your partner is ignoring your needs or waving them off as relatively unimportant. Unfortunately, many of us make unjustified assumptions that take us down a path of unwarranted resentment. Assuming "goodwill" and "good intent" can help bring you closer and feel less resentment.

It is easy to think the worst. It is easy to feel that your partner just does what he or she wants to do, without concern for you. You may whip up a whole scenario about how selfish your partner is, about how he or she doesn't take your feelings into account. But we notice that many of us make assumptions that are terribly wrong. So we suggest a mantra that reminds you that you are loved, that you are needed, that you are appreciated and cared for. Unless you have major evidence to the contrary, this mantra will put things in perspective.

The Situation
Ripples

Nicholas and Grace are in their late thirties and the parents of two kids under the age of ten. They both work at banks and are very frugal. They would like to buy a house and it's going to take saving as much as possible to eventually be able to buy the kind of home they want. So they are living a no-frills life, but there are certain luxuries they can afford because their family helps them out with the kids. Both sets of grandparents babysit occasionally on weekends and Nicholas's parents help on a regular basis during the week. Once a year, Nicholas's parents take the kids and Nicholas and Grace go away on vacation, just the two of them. They have a limited budget, so Nicholas looks for the cheapest place he can find in a good location. Grace agrees on the price, but when she gets to the hotel she feels depressed and disappointed because she and Nicholas don't agree on a "good location." For Nicholas, a good location is in the center of the city, near all the attractions like museums. He doesn't seem to notice when he has found a motel that is in a truly sketchy neighborhood. This has happened more than a few times, and Grace now feels that Nicholas doesn't care if she is safe. Her reasoning goes something like this: "He knows I won't be able to sleep in a place like this. He should know that this place spoils the trip for me." By now, she thinks, Nicholas should know where she feels comfortable staying. She is convinced that if he were thinking about her, he would have picked a different place. So when he continues to book "finds" in neighborhoods where she is nervous walking around after dark, she gets more than a little upset. When this happens, as it does most years, she tends to sulk and doesn't want to do anything. She thinks she has given him more than enough feedback, but in fact, Nicholas has no idea why she gets "snitty" and thinks she is unreasonably moody on their rare vacations. That upsets him.

Blasts

Tyler and Olivia have been married for twenty years. They married when she was thirty-five and he was thirty. When they met, she had two very young children from a short-lived marriage. Tyler has been a champ about the kids. He adopted them when he and Olivia got married and they raised the children together. Once the kids left home, they sold their large family home and now they are living out by the lake in their dream house. Olivia does some freelance editing from home and Tyler is general manager of a popular restaurant.

Olivia's early life was marked by the unfortunate and painful circumstances of her accidental pregnancy at age nineteen and her short, unfulfilling marriage to the feckless father of the kids. She and the baby's father married as soon as they found out they were having a baby. Within six months of the baby's birth the relationship became contentious, and they separated for a month. But this made things very difficult for Olivia with her family and his family, and after a lot of family pressure and some counseling sessions with their priest, they both felt it was important to try again. Getting together again was soon followed by another pregnancy, which they thought would solidify the marriage and their feelings for one another. It didn't. Money became even tighter and her husband needed to pitch in more. He resented being tied down, and he started disappearing without telling her where he was going. Olivia challenged him and soon he stopped making excuses and just left when he felt like it, returning home less and less often. Finally he disappeared for good and never again made contact with either her or the kids. Olivia filed for divorce when she was twenty-nine. She took a number of jobs, working at a day care center part-time to get her kids covered and starting a freelance editing service, which eventually took off and provided her with quite a bit of work. Her life was difficult but happier than when she was married.

Olivia's first marriage left wounds that never really healed, and sometimes she fears that something will happen to Tyler and cause him to disappear. She feels that life could take him away from her, and she can only calm herself by being in almost constant contact with him.

When Olivia gets really upset she starts to believe that Tyler, like her first husband, does things to purposely make her mad. She is good about reminding herself that Tyler is such a different man than her first husband, because Tyler is loving, generous, and responsible. But when Tyler is out of touch, she gets anxious. Very anxious. She starts to pace the floor and she looks at the clock every few minutes. When she sees him, she is a mess. She can be in tears. She reminds him that when she doesn't hear from him, it frightens her. She has tried to tell him that when he is out of touch, she imagines the worst, but he still forgets to call or text.

Some of her fears are legitimate. She worries about Tyler's long commute on a difficult highway, especially because he is often tired when he leaves work. He has told her that sometimes he has trouble staying awake, and that has added fuel to her fears. She has asked him to call her when he's leaving so she knows what time to expect him and she doesn't have to worry. But half of the time, he doesn't call, and she starts worrying that something may have happened to him. She will call him to check and when he says, often with some irritation in his voice, "Everything is fine—I'm just on my way home," she gets angry and starts telling herself, "He knows this makes me anxious and he doesn't care. He does it anyway." Or "He's paying me back for wanting to move to the lake and now he has a half-hour drive." As the minutes tick by, she looks at the clock and gets more and more anxious, thinking, "This is some kind of rebellion against doing what I asked. I don't ask for much. He should do this for me." By the time he gets home, she has worked herself up. When Tyler walks through the door, she's standoffish and very cool or in tears. She is upset because she believes he doesn't love her enough to take just a minute to tell her what he's doing so she could worry less. She's upset that she has to call him to calm her fears. After she knows he is safe, she gets mad, feeling that he puts her through this unnecessarily and way too often.

The Doctors' Advice

Assume goodwill with your partner. Believe he or she wants the best for you, even if it's difficult. These two couples need to take a step back and remember this: You are with someone who loves you, cares for you, and wants the best for you. Your partner may not always get it right or act according to your needs and expectations, but he or she is not intentionally trying to disappoint you or make you mad. Very few people get off on making their partner mad.

Nicholas and Grace are in different worlds about acceptable places to stay. We have observed that perceptions of safety are often a gender issue. Men feel safe in more places than women do, and women's fears are based on reality in that they are not usually as physically able to defend themselves as men are. Grace has an issue that we understand—her deeper fears stem from a concern for personal safety. But Grace has jumped to an interpretation that is neither necessary nor true: that Nicholas doesn't care about her fear. The truth is he actually doesn't know about her fear, at least in the way she feels it. When Grace tells him she's afraid, he underestimates the true degree of her panic, and even when he does try to take her fears into account, he simply doesn't perceive places the way she does. For example, he sees a good hotel in the business district, but she sees streets that are deserted at night without any witnesses around if someone should accost them. Furthermore, when Nicholas does think about her discomfort, he tends to think he can handle what she's afraid of and reassures her that he can take care of things. But this doesn't do it for her and she remains afraid regardless of his confidence about handling the neighborhood. She seethes privately, and he actually doesn't realize how much the locations he picks affect her enjoyment of the trip.

On one level, this is such an easy fix. If they talked about this issue and decided to pick a place only if both of them agreed on it, they could end the problem easily by going online and picking a place that suits both their budget and her need to feel safe. But to get to the heart of the issue, Grace must realize that this is a problem of location, or of a lack of sensitivity, or perhaps even of Nicholas's inflated self-confidence about handling trouble should it arise—but it is not evidence of a lack of love or care for her safety. There is no reason—and at some level Grace knows it—that Nicholas would want to put Grace in harm's way. They have differences about where she will be safe, but there is no lack of love in this couple. Grace could adopt mantras like these: "Nicholas loves me and sometimes he simply misses the mark"; "Nicholas wants me to be happy; this is a small mistake"; "Nicholas loves me in his way." Nicholas is simply not a good psychologist. He doesn't understand primal fears and he may never truly understand how quickly and deeply Grace experiences fear. When she uses her mantra, Grace can reassure herself that she is loved as well as soothe her panic.

Doing these things can help her look more clearly at the place he has chosen and decide if she really has reason to be afraid. Using her mantra will help her de-escalate the rising fears that can turn into a fear frenzy. She can take a few deep breaths before deciding if this neighborhood is really scary, and if it is she can tell him that she is scared and they need to move elsewhere, or take cabs to and from the hotel, or together find a way to reduce her very real feelings of vulnerability. Nicholas has to agree that they will move if they get there and Grace is uncomfortable.

Olivia and Tyler have a bigger and more worrisome misunderstanding. Olivia mistakenly believes that Tyler doesn't care enough about her to do something simple to alleviate her anxiety. She needs a mantra like this: "Tyler loves me deeply. We moved out to the lake to make each other happy" or "Tyler says I am the center of his world and I believe him." In fact, Tyler is in a hurry to get home to see her. Yes, he has a problem remembering to call, but no, that doesn't mean he is consciously trying to torture her. When she told Tyler that she felt responsible and guilty for his longer commute and that is part of her worrying, he told her that he loves living at the lake and the extra time driving is no big deal. In fact, he likes the commute most of the time because it gives him time to change from his "work self" to his "lake self."

The impact on Olivia is so severe that it's clear that they need a new system of keeping her in the loop so she doesn't worry. Tyler is forgetful, and that probably isn't going to change, so they can set a reminder on his smart phone so that he calls her at the same time every night to give her an update. We all come with some baggage from the past and we need our partners to go the extra mile, even when they don't fully understand the problem.

Olivia can forgive herself for old wounds that still hurt even though they have nothing to do with Tyler. She has to use her own tools to help herself feel better, because only she can know the precise moment when her tension starts to rise out of control. She can use her mantra to remind herself that she is the center of his world, and she will be truly glad to see him walk through the door, embrace him, and tell him she's glad he's home.

Assume goodwill from your partner. Most of the time, that is a good bet.

Chapter 8

Unavoidable Issues

If you can't work through it, go around it.

A Closer Look

If you cannot work through an issue, go around it. Not everything in a relationship is fixable, changeable, or movable. Sometimes you honestly disagree and no amount of conversation or evidence is going to change your mind or your partner's. There are ways to move past a blocked subject rather than be stuck in a torturously repetitive revolving door.

It is a myth that problems, issues, and disagreements have to be resolved. They don't. You and your partner will get exhausted if you try to bring everything in your relationship to consensus. Even if you are "soul mates" and the best of friends, the fact is that two different people will have some conflicting perceptions, needs, and beliefs that never fit together, no matter how hard you try. These conflicts may range from the trivial to the critical and it is not dishonest to work around some of them rather than take them on headlong.

It might seem that you can agree to disagree: That is great if it works, but often it isn't a solution either. It can be hard to let go of something your partner wants or does when you simply believe it is wrong and every time the subject comes up the hair on the back of your neck stands straight up.

The Situation
Ripples

Brianna and Daniel have both been married before. They met at Brianna's office, when Daniel came in for a doctor's appointment. For him it was love at first sight. They dated three years before moving in together. They are both nervous about "failing again," so they are sometimes tentative about disagreements and hesitate to admit something is bothering one of them.

Their latest challenge is about dog hair. Daniel loves dogs, he always had dogs as a child, and dogs are an important part of life to him, which is why a year ago they adopted the retriever puppy they named Brandy. Brianna did this more for Daniel than for herself because she had not been around dogs much. She grew up in the city and didn't have pets.

Brianna was happy for Daniel and at first enthusiastic about the puppy adoption. She loved making Daniel happy and she knew that having a dog was important to him. She thought the puppy was adorable, and since they have a large fenced yard, she didn't think the dog's welfare or care would create any problems. Daniel assured Brianna he would be responsible for Brandy, walking her every day, taking her to the vet, whatever she needed. Brianna appreciated Daniel's willingness to handle everything, but she wanted it to be "their" puppy and she wanted a role in Brandy's care. The puppy was so much fun that she became a positive addition to the household and to the relationship; Brianna and Daniel were overjoyed with Brandy. What Brianna did not anticipate was that when Brandy grew larger she would shed so much.

Brianna loves Brandy, and is glad they have her, but the mess has become overwhelming to her. Brianna is particularly aggravated because she vacuums the carpet, the couch, the corners of their apartment, the drapes, everything. But the next day the house is again covered with long blond retriever hair. She has to roller off all of her clothes just before she walks out the door because they are always covered with hair. But it's not just on her clothes. No matter how much she works at it, there is continually hair all over the carpet, the couch, and even the towels in the bathroom. She has tried to encourage Daniel to brush the dog every day, as he agreed to do when they bought the dog as a puppy. He does it periodically, but not enough to make a difference. Brianna feels that he broke their deal and it causes her a lot of extra day-to-day frustration with the way the house looks. Daniel says he doesn't see the hair and what he does see, he doesn't mind. He says, "Dogs have hair. It's not a problem, really, is it? You love Brandy, don't you?"

Blasts

Adrian, a forty-two-year-old architect, and Kylie, a forty-year-old who works from home as a salesperson for a cosmetic company, have been together eight years. They were originally attracted to each other because they found it so easy to be together. It seemed they were always on the "same page." Other couples admire their marriage because it seems so peaceful. It is true that they have never raised their voices with one another, nor do they disagree at all about basic values, politics, or goals. However, they do in fact have two different personalities. He is an extrovert, and she is a homebody and introvert. This would be no big deal, but it does present some problems because they share a marital philosophy that dictates that couples should spend most of their lives together. Adrian is very social, but Kylie is not. Adrian can make new friends at the grocery store standing in line. Kylie is cautious and private.

Adrian likes to go out with friends almost every day of the week, and he wants Kylie with him. She wants to be with him but not with all these people. They are in a struggle about what their nights and weekends should look like. They feel very differently about it, but neither wants the other to be on his or her own. Adrian wants to go out and get together with friends on the weekends, while Kylie's perfect weekend is hanging out together at home. If it were up to Adrian, they would be out with friends every Friday and Saturday night. If it were up to Kylie, they would be home alone watching a good movie after collaborating on an interesting new recipe. They would go out with friends once every two or three weeks.

The Doctors' Advice

Life and love would be easier if we could get others to do what we want, when and how we want, but neither of us has found that to be realistic. Reminding our partners to do what they have agreed to or what we believe they should be doing sounds reasonable, but over time it comes across as nagging or criticism. That is not only ineffective but also damaging.

Brianna realizes that Daniel is never going to take care of that dog the way she wants him to. Daniel has good intentions and he thinks he takes good care of Brandy, including brushing her. Neither Daniel nor Brianna likes conflict, so they are both hesitant to disagree, but in this case they can work around the problem rather than through it. Brianna can find solutions that work for her and that she can control. They started by sitting down and agreeing on "dog zones." After discussing Brianna's frustration with walking out of the house covered with dog hair, Daniel has agreed that the places she gets dressed (the bedroom and the bathroom) can be off limits to Brandy. This solution wasn't possible until Brianna reframed the issue and thought of a way to work around it. Together, Daniel and Brianna installed dog gates that confined Brandy to the kitchen when they were not home, and they also agreed that Brandy would stay off the furniture. They went out and got a nice, comfy dog bed and spent some time teaching Brandy that the dog bed was her go-to place for the night.

It is important to figure out how to get at least some, or maybe most, of what you really need, and not stick to the notion that your partner do what you want because you are right. The new arrangement—dog on dog bed, dog in kitchen— worked out well for all three of them, and it happened without Brianna having to bang away at Daniel's inability to be as fastidious about the dog as she would have liked him to be.

The biggest threshold that Adrian and Kylie have to cross is to agree that they don't have to do everything together. They have to believe that they can still be a couple and not have to experience the world the same way at the same time. Unfortunately, this is hard for Adrian because his parents got divorced when he was fourteen, and his dad said it was because his mother never wanted to do anything. They've been struggling over this, so they recently went to their pastor, who is also a couple's counselor. Here is the dialogue that helped them feel secure about having some separate time and interests.

> **PASTOR:** *What are you afraid might happen if Adrian goes out without you?*
>
> **KYLIE:** *Well, to be honest with you, I would be afraid that he would meet someone else. He goes to a lot of social events and women come on to him.*
>
> **ADRIAN:** *I don't like going out alone. I think marriage is spending time together. I have always wondered about men or women who show up alone. I don't think it's a good thing.*
>
> **PASTOR:** *Well it's important for you to go out together and have experiences together, but I think you have a strong marriage and you will not make your relationship vulnerable with an occasional outing alone. You could have some ground rules that protect you from awkward situations. For example, what if Adrian goes to a cocktail party to see someone but is always home by 8 and never has more than one drink? Would that reassure you, Kylie?*
>
> **KYLIE:** *Yes, as long as I felt I could call him and he would take my call.*
>
> **PASTOR:** *Well, that seems doable. What about you, Adrian? What would make you feel comfortable about going to some event by yourself when Kylie wasn't interested in going?"*
>
> **ADRIAN:** *Well, I want to be able to check in with her and make sure everything is O.K. And I don't want her to feel*

left out. And honestly, I worry that my friends might think we are not doing well, not getting along and that I have some other agenda like pretending I'm available—when I'm absolutely not.

PASTOR: *Why don't you go to these events with a guy friend or with a couple? That ought to do it. And you can talk about your wife a lot. Would that feel comfortable?*

ADRIAN: *What do I say when they ask, "Where is your wife? They might think she doesn't want to know them."*

KYLIE: *Tell them the truth—I like more alone time than you do—tell them I'm a true introvert. But if you think we are in danger of insulting them, then we can plan on having them over to dinner sometime. I would rather have people come here than go out.*

ADRIAN: *Ok. I think we have a deal. I just like seeing people, and if we can have some over more that will do it for me.*

PASTOR: *Problem solved!*

Remember that you are two individuals, with different perspectives and personalities, as well as a couple. Problems are not always solved through agreement; many times going around the issue is much better.

Chapter 9

Criticism

THE SNAP

Constructive criticism is still criticism and it will
destroy your relationship.

A Closer Look

There's no such thing as constructive criticism. Don't think your
partner will appreciate it or learn from it. Negative commentary
about your partner is going to sting and separate both of you. There
are other ways of influencing one another. We show how to influence your partner in ways that help the relationship grow in a positive, happy climate. We suggest the motto "The person is not the
problem; the problem is the problem."

Criticism is a complaint with an edge, a sharp edge, meaning
that it usually cuts a piece off the other person. Criticism that is
masked with humor or "just trying to help" generally fools no one.
It almost always ends up wounding your partner, the relationship,
or both. There is plenty of research that shows negative judgments,
even when nicely phrased—"Honey, you just don't get it. I love you,
but you are no math whiz"—generate defensiveness and resistance.

It's hard not to complain about things your partner does or says
that offend or irritate you, but listing or highlighting their deficits
not only drives you apart it is useless at effecting change. However,
you don't have to live with the problem behavior. There are some
very effective ways of motivating your partner to please you.

The Situation
Ripples

Marianna is a professional nanny who cares for three children under the age of ten. Jazmin is a loan officer for the bank. They were friends for five years before they became lovers and moved in together. Typically, Marianna walks in the door, glad to be home and eager to see Jazmin. She drops her heavy bag on the kitchen table and can't wait to wrap her arms around her wife.

But the first thing Jazmin says is this: "Why didn't you take the chicken out of the freezer this morning? I could have started dinner."

Marianna stops in her tracks. She doesn't know what to say but stammers, "I guess I forgot."

Jazmin, who is stirring tomato sauce in a pot, responds, "Honey, you are always forgetting something. Why don't you write stuff down, like I've told you? Make a list or put it on your calendar. It is just not that difficult, sweetie."

Marianna is apologetic at first. "I know, I just wasn't thinking about dinner this morning. I had to get to work earlier than usual because Mrs. Kellogg was leaving early. I can fix something else."

Jazmin chuckles, and tells her that won't be necessary. She says, "I already took care of it. We are having spaghetti. It is a good thing your pretty head is attached or you would forget that too."

That does it for Marianna; she is crestfallen and offended. "I don't think I'm that forgetful." She turns and walks away, muttering, "You know, you forget things too."

Blasts

Emily and Sam have been married forever, it seems. This year, they celebrated their twenty-fifth wedding anniversary. They have just come back from dinner with friends. Emily had a lot of fun and is in a great mood. But Sam felt embarrassed by Emily's behavior at the party. After a couple glasses of wine, she turned into such a chatterbox. As they are getting ready for bed, Emily asks him if something is bothering him. He turns to her and says, "You talked a lot tonight. In fact, no one else got a chance to say much of anything. When I was asked about our vacation, you told the entire story."

Without stopping to let her respond, he continues, "It wasn't just me you cut off. Every time someone at the table brought up a topic, you jumped in and pretty much did a monologue."

Emily's face drops—she's clearly hurt—but Sam keeps digging in: "I can't imagine you learned anything about anyone else at that table. I think you really have to watch how much you talk and I am telling you this because I think your constant talking is the reason we are not invited more often."

Emily is stunned. And hurt. She blurts out, "What are you talking about? There was lots of interest in what I was saying, and everyone was talking. I think you just have problems getting your own two cents in and you're projecting your discomfort on me. If you're uncomfortable and you can't think fast enough to keep up with the conversation, that's your problem."

Emily folds her arms across her chest and ends with, "o.k., I'll just keep quiet, if that's what you really want."

The Doctors' Advice

We are entirely sure there is no such thing as constructive criticism. It sounds like you're passing judgment, which usually makes your partner feel bad, angry, or defensive—or all three. Presumably, you are not your partner's teacher or mother, so trying to teach them a lesson or educate them by explaining what they don't know or don't do right is a dead end with little chance of success and a high probability of resentment. Instead, think about what you *want* your partner to do, rather than what you don't want them to do. The best way to get them to do the desirable behavior is to come at it from a positive direction.

Remember the old saying, "You catch more flies with honey than with vinegar"? That may sound dated, but it's true. Think about it. What motivates you—compliments, praise, and appreciation or insults, demands, and complaints? It is in our nature to go in the direction of positive reward, so we have to find a way to change behavior by rewarding what we want. Think about how to bring out the best in your partner with rewards and bribes. Rewards are compliments, reminders of past successes and pats on the back, or hugs. Bribes are exchanges or barters. For example, "I'll give you something you like if you give me something I like." This can sound a bit cold, but it doesn't have to be: Keep your bribes upbeat and playful. For example, "I'll give you a neck rub if you'll walk the dog."

Jazmin has to find a way to remind Marianna about things that are important, since she sometimes forgets. In therapy, Marianna said that having her partner comment on her forgetfulness as she came in made her feel "like an animal balloon being shot with a pellet gun." Instead of confronting her when she walks through the door, Jazmin needs to find the right moment to remind Marianna in advance so that Jazmin doesn't just approach her partner when she has already "failed." For example, Jazmin can send Marianna a text asking her to defrost the chicken if she has time. She can add an emoticon (like a heart with wings) so Marianna knows she is being reminded in a loving way, not a critical one. Most importantly, she is being prompted so that she can do a task that is important to Jazmin, do something that she meant to do, and not have to apologize or cope with any problems. And Jazmin needs to hold her tongue if Marianna forgets, and make dinner from whatever is available or go out. No more comments or reminders, which are in fact criticisms.

Emily and Sam have a tougher problem. A lot of nasty words have been exchanged. This kind of exchange leaves partners feeling demoralized, stung, and angry. What could they do differently? As a start, they could separate fact from fiction. If Sam has been reacting to what he perceives as Emily's takeover of dinner conversation, he needs to do a reality check to see if his perception is correct. He could talk to a close friend who was at the dinner and see if he or she actually felt that Emily was hogging all the conversation.

This is risky because the friend might go back to Emily, but it's necessary because this criticism is damaging enough to seriously hurt the relationship. So, the first step is to find out if it's valid. Let's say his opinion is confirmed (if not, he has to apologize and find out why he misjudged the situation). In this case, how does he modify her behavior without this kind of destructive exchange?

Sam needs to think about *what he does want—rather than what he doesn't want.* Knowing what we don't like is often easier than knowing what we do want. He doesn't want her to talk so much, and he doesn't want her to "shut up" either. Thinking about what he wants allows him to approach her in a way that elicits her help, not her anger. He realizes he wants to participate more in conversations with their friends and he wants to have the opportunity to hear what other people have to say.

He can tell her this in a nice way, saying, "I probably talk a little slower than you do, so if you could invite me into the conversation, I would like that. I would like you to let me finish my stories even if they are a little slower and more sluggish than yours."

Or, he could approach it this way: "You are so lively and interesting that everyone wants to listen to you, but I think it might intimidate people who aren't such easy storytellers. I think there are some other people at the table who might need a little more time to tell their stories, so maybe we need to give them time and space to get in the mix."

If Emily says, as she well might, "Well, how do I know when you, or they, want to talk more? I'd be happy to hand over the air time, but do you think I am a mind reader and can tell when someone else wants to say something?" Fair enough, so Sam might volunteer, "Well, I'm not an expert, but if I need more time, or if I think one of our friends does, I could just tug my ear or hold your hand or something like that." She says, "O.K., let's try it." Voila—crisis and criticism averted.

Your guide to figuring out how to handle your partner's undesirable quirks and habits is to always remember to focus on the positive, rather than go negative and rail at the behavior. Take some time to think about the behavior *you do want to see* and prepare a well-thought-out request before you start talking. Check your tone and body language and keep it short and sweet. Criticism is criticism; do not let it destroy your relationship.

Chapter 10

Missing Manners

A Closer Look

Manners matter, especially with the people you love. So, please mind your manners. If your partner needs a hand, lend it. When he or she walks into the room, flash a little smile. If you're saying goodbye, do it with a kiss and a hug. Manners show your partner that you honor him or her and hold him or her in the highest personal regard.

At the beginning of most relationships people are on their best behavior, and that means being courteous, polite, and thoughtful. As times goes by, we relax; we do not monitor ourselves so closely. But an unfortunate outcome of what we think is just a process of becoming more casual and comfortable is often a loss of common but important forms of etiquette. Partners stop treating each other with the care and thoughtfulness that they tried so hard to practice in the beginning. We can tell you for sure that that is a terrible mistake. When you start coasting in your relationship, there is only one way it can go—downhill. You cannot coast uphill.

Many traditional manners are based on kindness and respect, two elements of relationships that always need upkeep. We are not going to turn into Miss Manners here, but we think all couples need to keep saying these things to stay happy: please, thank you, excuse me, and may I help you.

Other manners are less obvious but still important. Here are some of the most despised bad manners: not covering your face when you sneeze or cough, not holding the door, chewing with your mouth open, cussing, or borrowing money and not paying it back promptly. Some interesting surveys have indicated that the breaches in men's manners that women hate most are bad table manners and body noises. The surveys also suggest that women's bad habits that annoy men the most are interruptions and assumptions.

These lapses in manners are important because happy relationships require care and thoughtfulness every day. Granted, it may be harder to do than one thinks. Good manners require focus and attention and even some discipline, but if you want a happy relationship, that's what it takes to let your partner know that you love, honor, and respect him or her.

The Situation
Ripples

Robert, forty-two, and Fabien, thirty-six, both work at large corporations. Robert markets a luxury car line and Fabien teaches new employees about legal standards and practices in the television industry. They met at a party at a mutual friend's house, were immediately attracted to one another, and ended up spending the night together. Although popping into bed right after meeting someone was not unusual for Fabien, it was quite unusual for Robert, who has strict standards about whom he has sex with. But there was some deeper connection from the beginning and the two of them have been together ever since. They just had their seven-year anniversary and had a big celebration with a very large guest list at a fashionable bar in D.C. Robert is a very accepting, calm kind of guy, and very much in love with Fabien, but he is getting really tired of Fabien's habit of starting an important conversation without taking into account what else is going on.

Specifically, in the morning, when he's just about to go to work and he's usually a bit late and in a hurry, Fabien will introduce a topic that requires discussion—and Robert has no time for it at that moment. When Robert reminds Fabien that they can talk about it at dinnertime, Fabien gets upset. He retorts, "You forget to talk about it later." If Robert doesn't fold immediately and deal with the issue, Fabien gets offended and says somewhat petulantly, "O.K., I'll just take care of it myself." Sometimes Robert stays because he really needs to be involved with that particular subject before the day is over, but then he's late for work.

Even though his office is pretty casual about arrival time, Robert personally is a very punctual kind of person, and it annoys him when he gets to the office later than he intended. He is particularly upset if Fabien's last-minute needs make him late for a meeting. Whether or not he stays and discusses the issue, this repeated scenario sets a bad tone for his day.

Blasts

Luis, twenty-four, is a jock. He is trim and proud of it, and wears tight shirts that show off his bulging muscles. He earns those muscles, in part by playing a lot of baseball. He plays two nights a week at the local field during the season, plus working out and practicing batting at an indoor facility when the season is over. Luis is so proud of his team that he wears his team shirt or cap to bars and even to parties with friends. He is also active in raising money for the team for travel expenses and new uniforms. Luis was the person who got a local pub to sponsor their team; they have shirts that they wear off the field that show a cartoon of the whole team raising glasses of beer at the bar, toasting the bar logo.

Luis and Leticia have been living together for three years. He loves it when Leticia joins him after practice for dinner. But although Leticia admires and supports Luis's passionate commitment to baseball, she finds it embarrassing to be with him after a game because his buddies are all so boisterous and uncouth. His teammates are loud. They swear. Some of the guys flirt outrageously with women at the bar. She can hardly stand to be next to them because none of them showers before they go to the bar and sometimes the smell is unbearable. She has mentioned this particular fact to Luis, who takes it as a compliment! "This is what real men smell like," he jokes. But Leticia is seriously put off by it.

Leticia could forgive some of the rude behavior that happens right after an important game, but what she can't forgive is that Luis has picked up some bad habits from his friends. Unfortunately, even when Luis and Leticia are out on a date alone and he's had a few drinks, he can be just as crude and loud as the worst offender on the team. When Leticia pleads with him to behave better when they are out alone together, he acts defensively and tells her that other people are "uptight" and that he is just having a good time. Sometimes if she presses her case, he gets mad and turns on her when she asks him to quiet down or not use certain words. He tells her she's being a "Bar Nazi."

The Doctors' Advice

Each partner in the relationship wants and needs to feel special. Couples want to feel a cut above others. Good manners send the signals: I hold you in high regard; I honor you; I respect you; I love you.

A lack of manners is eroding the emotional well-being of each of these couples. It's important for the partner who is upset to do the following: first, let his or her partner know what the true cost of these behaviors are, and second, make a request for a different way of handling the offensive behavior.

Here's how this could help Robert and Fabien:

First, Robert should set the scene. He needs to arrange a situation in which he can be calm and Fabien can listen. Bringing home a gift and inviting Fabien out to go for a walk, or sit down for a cup of coffee or tea, would be a good start.

Then Robert says, "I like to be involved with you in making plans and family decisions. At the end of dinner, I'd like to talk about upcoming events, what's new with you, and what questions and decisions we need to make. It's just not a good time when I'm about to leave the house. Having our conversations after dinner would help me be engaged."

Fabien agrees and is fine for a couple of weeks, and stops grabbing Robert at the door. But over time he slips back into his old habit of creating last-minute diversions for Robert about household issues.

When he does, Robert smiles and says, "Honey, I'll look forward to talking about it at dinner." He blows him a kiss.

Leticia has a different kind of problem. She has already told Luis to tone it down. Even though Luis admits that he can be boisterous, he doesn't get why he should change.

He is not taking her embarrassment seriously. But he should, because it is lowering her opinion of him, and it wouldn't take all that much for him to tone it down.

Luis is confused by Leticia's nagging. He believes going out and having a good time is supposed to mean cutting loose and being a guy. He explains to Leticia, "Guys get together, have a few drinks, and we are supposed to be loud and crude. It's like a vacation from normal life for a few hours." But Leticia has stopped coming to most of his games. He likes her being there and supporting his hobby and his passion. Plus, he doesn't want her to be mad at him.

An effort to compromise might sound like this:

LETICIA: *I am worried about how separated I feel from you. I know you want me to come to your games, but I don't like the way I feel when I am there.*

LUIS: *Leticia, it is important to me that you come to my games when you can. I like you being there and you almost never come anymore. I don't know what you want.*

LETICIA: *Do whatever you want to do with the guys, but when you're with me, I'd like you to treat me the way you did*

when we were first dating. You talked to me in a kind and
gentle voice and you seemed to always want to please me. I
know you love me and I love you—but this behavior that
goes on at the bar is making me feel like the guys are more
important to you than I am.

LUIS: *The guys are just the guys; you are my girl. So you want*
me to hold your hand? Open doors, and check in with you?

LETICIA: *Yes, I want to feel that I am the center of your atten-*
tion when we are out together.

LUIS: *So, when you are not there you don't care what I do, but*
when I am with you, then you want me to be a gentleman. I
get it. No worries.

The next time Leticia came to his game and after-party, Luis was
quick to greet her when she arrived, he thanked her for coming and
gave her a big hug. He found them a table and sat with her. He
got up and got her drink, and when he went to talk to the guys he
asked her to come with him, and he kept his arm around her. Leticia once again felt special and important to him, and that her being
there was important to him. Luis found it easy to focus on Leticia
because the ground rules were simple: When he is with her he is to
act like a gentleman, period.

One of the most common ways of being rude with a partner
involves technology. It is so easy to pick up your phone and check
email while waiting for the food to come, or take an important call
when your partner has seated everyone for a dinner party. It's not
uncommon for one partner to be checking his or her email while
the other is left alone to drive the car without any conversation
going on between them.

We believe that manners convey a level of high regard for your
partner, and that you want to honor them on a daily basis. Talk to
each other about what makes you feel honored; make it a point to
honor yourself and your partner. Doing so sends a message that can
cement goodwill and trust throughout your lives together.

Chapter 11

Careless Love

Loving relationships are fragile; give them tender loving care.

A Closer Look

Loving relationships are the most fragile and vulnerable relationships we have with other adults. Couples are more emotionally aware of and affected by each other than people in any other adult relationships. Communicating care, concern, or lust and love should start from the minute you are in one another's presence.

A clear focus on giving and receiving those signals at first contact can set the mood of the day, the night, or the entire relationship. In contrast, communicating disinterest, being too busy, turning on the TV, or talking on the phone all say, "You are just not that important to me." The feeling of connection has to be the mainstay of any long-term loving relationship; when it is not, divorce or infidelity is usually not far away.

Taking a minute, really one minute, to hold each other and exchange a kiss or whisper "I am glad to see you" when you first encounter your partner says, "YOU are first and most important in my life. I am here just with you, now."

Couples look to each other's signals to be sure "we" are O.K., so if you make sure that message is sent frequently throughout the day, neither of you will be checking or double-checking to figure out how you are doing. Make it clear, anytime. It takes a minute to really look at your partner and communicate, "I am with you, you are with me, and we are the center of our relationship—no one else. Our relationship is the center of my world."

The Situation
Ripples

Nolan is a respected surgeon and he is pretty sure he is the smartest person in the room. He has developed a conversational style that is rapid-fire, making it very hard for anyone else to talk. He will give long, pedantic lectures on what is "really" the truth about any subject. As difficult as it is to live with his ego, what is even worse is that he interrupts.

He interrupts just about everyone, but he is particularly guilty with Anika and their two teenage daughters. The girls are in high school and he insists on supervising their homework. If he disagrees with the instruction, he gives them a different way to do their work, and if they insist that not following the instructions will get them in trouble, he stops them dead and tells them not to follow "stupid" assignments. Anika tries to step in, but he shuts her down too. Anika and the girls look at each other with empathy because they all know there is no use trying to argue with their father when he gets into this kind of a snit. The girls' reactions range from just getting quiet to getting so mad that they have an outburst and rush out of the room. Anika tries to moderate the situation when it's about something that really needs a resolution, but if Nolan is being particularly full of himself and unreasonable, she too just gets quiet and tells the girls that she will do what she can later.

Anika realizes that she has started to tune Nolan out. When he goes on one of his diatribes or interrupts a lot, she starts thinking about other things: her To Do list of the day or what she will say to the girls later. Nolan has noticed Anika's lack of attention and it make him angrier. Neither one of them feels that conversation is productive; they are quite frustrated with one another. Sometimes it is hard for them to make even a small decision together, such as which movie to see. Anika will just say, "You pick."

Blasts

William and Violet are in their mid-fifties and newly married. Violet is an Internet blogger and freelance science writer. William works regular hours directing programs at a community center run by the city and comes home about six o'clock every weeknight. When he comes home, Violet does not acknowledge his presence. She never gets up from her desk to greet him, even though he knows she can hear his car come up the driveway of their small home. When he comes in, a wave of loneliness often engulfs him. The house is dimly lit and it feels like an alien environment. He can see the light from Violet's desk in the bedroom, but the door is shut. He feels like Violet is not really "into" him in the way he felt she was not even two years ago. Sometimes he will announce his presence with a half-joking, "Honey, I'm home," but usually there is not even a verbal response from Violet. He wants to at least be noticed and responded to, but Violet is always writing with the door closed. She hears him come home, but she's immersed in her work and doesn't get up. She feels that if she disrupts her train of thought she might lose valuable insights or language. She might yell, "Hi!" but she doesn't stop what she's doing.

This absorption in her work doesn't happen only when he comes home. When William goes to bed, Violet often shifts to her desk in the living room and so many nights he falls asleep alone. When he confronts her about this situation, she thinks he's overreacting and doesn't understand how often she is under strict deadlines. She says, "I said *hi.* I did greet you! But I need you to understand that I have to work. If I'm in the middle of an assignment, I've got to concentrate. You often go to bed pretty early, too, and I do some of my best work after nine o'clock." He says, "You could at least get up and spend a little time with me." She says that of course she would like to, but that getting up would disrupt her train of thought. William thinks she doesn't want to know how really unhappy he is. He feels unimportant in her life.

The Doctors' Advice

Love, plus physical, social, and emotional trust, are all part of intimacy, and this is what leaves us open and exposed. It is all these vulnerabilities that require we treat each other and our relationship with the utmost kindness, care, and protection. If our vulnerabilities are not protected, there is no intimacy, and soon, no love or trust.

We can see that both couples are not being careful with their relationships; in fact, their behavior is harmful. Intimate relationships require TLC (Tender, Loving, Care), and being out of communication, whether because of abrupt speech patterns or by simply not being available, is one of the quickest ways to destroy an intimate relationship.

Nolan probably has no idea how much he interrupts Anika or what a really bad habit it is. Even if she tells him, he still won't get it because he doesn't know how it feels to be cut off in the middle of a sentence. Since Anika has stopped trying to interact with him, and he is sulking over unfinished conversations, the situation is getting serious. It would help if Anika would ask for a moment in which he will agree not to interrupt. Then she can tell him, at length and with emotion, how dispirited she feels and why she no longer enters into conversations. However, she has to tell him in a way that doesn't make him into the bad guy because he will immediately become defensive.

The trick is to get ahead of those responses so that they never emerge. She can tell him, for example, "When I'm interrupted, I withdraw. It's not because I'm angry, but because I feel hurt." She can ask him to give her a little more time to finish her thoughts. If he interrupts, she can simply say, "I would like to finish telling you what I think." Harville Hendrix, author of *Getting the Love*

You Want, has an exercise that he gives some couples to solve the problem. Hendrix suggests that one person be given a piece of "floor" that he or she holds while speaking. Then the other partner speaks until he or she "gives the floor" back. Unwieldy, yes, but a good way to begin mending what has eroded the couple's communication.

By not acknowledging her husband when he comes home or when he gets into bed, Violet is showing disdain for her relationship. By not "being there," she is shutting off communication with the man who loves her. Not all communication is done with words; deeds matter too. Violet obviously doesn't realize that she is sending such a strong message about her priorities, and she is not hearing the true distress her partner is expressing. Perhaps her inability to take it seriously shows how reluctant she is to establish a new work pattern. But she will have to make some changes.

There are limits to what any person should have to tolerate. William is not delusional; he IS being treated as if he is unimportant, and Violet needs to decide if her husband is important or not. Maybe she doesn't think of it as an "either/or" decision; she probably feels her husband can adjust to her passion for her work. But over time her preference for using time to work rather than to be with him is changing his commitment to the marriage. He simply is not getting the attention he needs when he needs it.

Violet needs to ask herself some hard questions. The most central one: Is he more important than her flow of concentration and her work of the moment? If he isn't, there's a bigger problem here. But if he is, she had better show it. She has to communicate love, caring, and sensitivity to her partner's need for her presence at a time of his choosing, not just a convenient time for her. This is a question everyone should ask themselves: How important is your relationship in comparison to your work, your hobbies, your friends, or even your extended family? If it is the most important part of your life, that has to be demonstrated.

The more intimate the relationship, the more it is both strong and fragile. It is strong in the sense that you are connected, trusted and trusting, and sure of the love between you. It is fragile for the same reasons. Love and intimacy have to be fed, nurtured, and protected. Be careful, gentle, connected, and present to protect the vulnerabilities you share.

Difficult Conversations

When you have something important but difficult to say, script it.

A Closer Look

Make an important conversation short, and front-load it with your most precious, heartfelt message. One of the greatest challenges facing any couple is attempting to understand and help each other under intense stress. It is normal for people to have their own way of experiencing, understanding, or denying problems. When situations arise that require teamwork, stresses can divide you. The more emotionally difficult the topic, the more likely it is to lead to confusing, rambling, and alienating conversations.

We have found that most couples can ease these awkward conversations by following a formula to help them understand each other. Writing out what you want to accomplish during the conversation helps separate your thoughts and feelings and sidebars so that your message doesn't get lost. In order to keep on track, think about what you want to say without explanation, emotion, or justification. Then write it out and practice delivering the message to your partner. Success is most likely if your speech is 50 words or less. We know that it is hard not to explain, justify, or even blame, but shorter is sweeter, more powerful, and precise and much easier to understand, resolve, and move forward from.

There are hard conversations in every relationship. We think preparation for "the big issue" can make it possible to have a breakthrough. Would you ever go in to any important meeting without thoughtful preparation? When you feel strongly about something and you think your partner doesn't get it, or doesn't want to get it, your frustration and anger may cause you to say things you wish you hadn't. Or your first presentation of the issue may be so impassioned that your point of view gets disorganized, mangled, and lost in the torrent of words and feelings that come out. In that case, the real issue may never surface and no negotiation or understanding can proceed. The more important the issue, the more care that has to be taken with its presentation.

The Situation
Ripples

Hanna and Clan are two professional people in their late forties who travel and work hard. Hanna is a visiting mental health counselor for a rural county and often travels all over Idaho. She sometimes has to stay overnight for her work, but mostly gets back home in time for dinner. Clan works for the federal government, evaluating aid packages to underdeveloped countries. Most of his travels are to faraway, exotic places, many of them with dubious political climates. He feels perfectly competent in maneuvering his way around the world, but Hanna worries about him, particularly when he's uncommunicative about where he's going, what kind of transportation he will be using, or exactly whom he will be working with. He spends a lot of time in Asia and there is a big time difference, with only a few hours of overlap during reasonable times to call. Those are often midday, when he is in the middle of meetings or traveling to another destination without any Wi-Fi or cell reception. Even when there is a possible time to text or call, he tends to get immersed in what he's doing and forgets to follow through. They've had several fights about this issue. Here's the way it often goes:

HANNA: *Last time, when you went to Croatia, I didn't hear anything from you for eight days. I was so upset I couldn't sleep. It interfered with my work. I called your sister and mom to see if they had heard from you. I even called your assistant at the office, and no one knew anything. How do you think that made me feel? Do you care? I am not being unreasonable. Eight days is really a ridiculous amount of time to be out of touch. I can't help but take this personally. Do you even think of me when you're gone? I asked you before you left to just shoot me an email and tell me what's going on. And you said you would. But you didn't.*

CLAN: *O.K. But there was a big time difference and the hotel had a surcharge for the Internet so I had to go some place else if I wanted to get online. There were no online cafés close by and I was in meetings from 8:00 A.M. to 8:00 P.M. When I got back to the hotel, which took about an hour, I was exhausted. So yes, I thought about you; I always think about you—but it was just too complicated. I don't understand why you get so wigged out! You knew where I was going and you knew my hotel, so what's the big deal? It's not my fault you don't sleep. If anything had happened, someone would have called you.*

Blasts

Maria and Tim married when Maria was twenty and Tim was twenty-five. Now, Maria is thirty and Tim is thirty-five. They met when they were both backpacking around Latin America after high school graduation and they married two years later. They had a lot of fun as a young couple and there was plenty of money to live the life they liked. Maria took a job as an assistant manager of a restaurant, and Tim started at the ground level in a large corporation as a quality control person calling back customers to see if they were pleased with their purchase. He is a conscientious person and has been promoted several times. They weren't rich, but they had an inexpensive apartment and enough money to go out and have fun exploring the city together.

Ten years into their marriage, they now have two children, both in elementary school. The money situation has changed. Maria left her job at the restaurant because she did not want to work evenings. After a few job changes, Maria settled into a part-time position as a school bus driver. She loved being around kids, and liked the hours. This worked fine when Alexander, their first child, was born and Maria's mother could babysit while she drove the bus, but it all had to stop when their second child, Selena, was diagnosed with childhood diabetes. They were both crushed since they knew this would be a lifelong challenge for their daughters and they also knew that someone would have to be there to help with shots and medications on a regular basis. So Maria quit her beloved job and became a full-time mom.

Selena's illness really changed the family dynamics. First, Maria was no longer bringing in money. Second, Selena's illness brought unanticipated extra expenses. Some of the medical expenses were covered by Tim's health insurance through his newest job with a national coffee franchise, but that only covered about 80 percent of their medical expenses, and then there was all of Maria's travel back and forth to the doctors which emptied their gas tank a lot quicker than before. They fell behind financially, and they are terribly worried about sinking into debt and never climbing out of it. They are both so tense about expenses that whenever Tim broaches budgetary issues, Maria freaks out. She ends up shouting that she is doing the best that she can and starts to cry. Tim, a firm and controlled kind of guy, cannot handle her emotional outbursts and his response is to leave the room, get a beer, and turn on the TV. This is what they sound like:

TIM: *Maria, I've just gotten this month's charge card bills and we're in big trouble. Your spending is out of control and you're killing me. I told you last month that we're already paying interest at 15 percent and it'll go higher if we don't get down to a zero balance. What part of "Do Not Spend Money We Don't Have" do you not understand? We were a thousand dollars over last month and we could not pay everything last month, or the month before. We're going deeper in debt every month.*

MARIA: *You've no idea what things cost and what we, and our children, need. There is so little left after Selena's expenses. I want you to know that I'm a careful shopper. I look for deals, I go to Wal-Mart, and I use coupons. But the kids need new clothes and shoes. And let's face it: You bought a new TV because it was on sale. You seem to find the money when it's something you want! But when the kids or I need something, it always costs too much.*

The Doctors' Advice

These conversations are not unusual. Each member of the couple blames the other; neither sees the other's point of view. No one has even started to look for, much less find, a solution. But we can solve this.

1. PREPARE YOUR STATEMENT. Think about what you want to say to your partner ahead of time so that you avoid inflammatory remarks, criticism, and threats. It doesn't matter whether you use a journal or index cards, as long as you write down your brief, clear message in the simplest words possible.

2. HONE YOUR MESSAGE. Start with the one sentence that best describes what you want to happen. This statement cannot be more than twenty words. It is often hard to hone in on your central action point. You might need to do some thinking, and it is often necessary to do multiple revisions. Do not deliver this as soon as you have finished

it. Let it sit for at least twenty-four hours, so that you are sure you have written what you want to say.

3. SHARE THE EMOTIONAL IMPORTANCE. Use words like "critically important" or "deepest need" to help your partner understand that this situation has profound meaning and consequence in both of your lives. Add a word or two to show the emotion you are feeling. For example, "I feel scared" or "hurt" or "sad," but not all three.

4. USE TWENTY WORDS OR FEWER TO DESCRIBE WHAT YOU WANT TO HAPPEN. Be concise and brief, telling your partner what you're willing to do and what you'd like your partner to do to change the situation. Use these same words every time your partner counters or becomes defensive, and do not add to them.

Your entire message will be under fifty words. This word count is essential to being successful because your partner needs brevity and clarity to keep paying attention. Leave out the history and proceed to the problem.

For example, Hanna could make a simple request of Clan, asking for just enough information: "Would you email me every other day and tell me you are O.K.? One sentence is enough." (She said this in fewer than twenty words.)

Her message is short and clear.

Clan may just stick to the "letter of the law," but Hanna will get what she needs. And indeed, he wrote, "Arrived. All O.K." Not poetry, but enough to stem her fears.

The same approach will help even in our Blasts situation. By using the scripting method, Tim wrote down his worries and ideas in a brief, to-the-point, rational letter to Maria. He wrote three drafts before he managed to meet the four Snap standards.

He asked Maria to go have coffee with him on their deck Sunday morning. He knew it would be quiet and they could sit on the bench and talk while the kids watched TV. He said, "Maria, I want to go to a financial adviser because I am at my wits' end, and I'm scared" (fewer than twenty words).

Maria was touched when Tim admitted he was scared but she responded in the old way, arguing about how much she had already cut back and using the same rhetoric as in past arguments. Tim responded, "I know you have tried, but it isn't working, You have to . . ." Tim stopped himself and got back on task. He asked her to just listen, assuring her that he is not mad at her and that she has done nothing wrong. He went back to his clear set of short statements: "I am scared and I want to go to a financial adviser."

After he read the letter a second time, Maria started to cry, saying she was so sorry. Tim held firm, saying, "Maria, come with me to a financial adviser."

Maria agreed. She started to say more, but Tim hugged her and said, "We will be o.k. Thank you. I'll find someone and make an appointment. I cannot talk anymore right now."

When you use your script, the hardest thing to do is to stay on topic. It'll be tempting to go back into the old defensive dialogues. But keep your piece of paper in front of you and keep to your main point, using the same words you used in your script until you can focus on the present problem (and not how you got there). Then your partner will be clear about what you're saying, what you want, how you feel, and what action you want to take to solve the problem. Use four Snap strategies—Prepare, Hone Your Message, Express the Emotional Importance, and Use Fifty Words or Fewer—to describe what you want to happen to bring you together as a couple.

Chapter 13

Build Intimacy

THE SNAP

Compassion is the pathway to intimacy.

A Closer Look

Intimacy, a deep knowledge and acceptance of each other, is one of the most desirable and complicated connections we seek with a partner. Compassion for your partner will help create intimacy more quickly than any other pathway. We define compassion as learning and then understanding the sources of your partner's distress or disability and showing that you care. Part of the way you can show that you notice and care is to express a desire to relieve their suffering, or not put them in a position in which that distress, suffering, or even just discomfort is likely to occur. Compassion is different from empathy; you feel the latter when you have been in the same position as the person for whom you have concern and sympathy, but compassion is felt even if you have never "walked in your partner's shoes." Compassion is a primary pathway to intimacy because it allows the focus of attention to be completely on the other person, not yourself, making your partner feel understood, accepted, and protected. A person who believes that he or she has a compassionate partner usually feels able to be vulnerable and open, which is another way of saying that compassion allows the relationship to be intimate.

Intimacy is a modern requirement of successful relationships. It may not have been essential in past generations, but it is today. It allows a couple to trust each other enough to explore past and unknown territory with one another. They can talk about painful parts of their personal histories, as well as present difficulties, and expect loyalty and respect. In order to do this, each person has to feel that real vulnerabilities such as a physical disability, a tendency to "put her foot in her mouth," or a reactive temper stemming from a damaged childhood, are understood and factored into the relationship with kindness and care. Being a compassionate partner sometimes requires putting yourself, your emotions, and your thoughts aside and taking care of your partner when he or she is weak, hurting, or fearful.

Keeping your own emotions in check while being fully available to see, hear, and touch the one you love takes skill and discipline. Learning to be fully emotionally present and receptive can come naturally, but sometimes it is a learned capability.

Interestingly, research on brain scans reported in the *Psychological Science* in 2013 has indicated that one way people become more compassionate is to meditate. After twenty minutes a day of meditation, individuals in the study found themselves more able to focus more intently and kindly on other people. The Dalai Lama says, "The more we care for the happiness of others, the greater our own sense of well-being becomes."

Compassion comes without judgment, either good or bad, without advice (definitely not criticism), and without "Why?" questions. Compassion encourages confession, revelation, exploration, and self-knowledge that you can share.

The Situation
Ripples

Kevin and Fiona grew up in the same neighborhood and played together as kids. When they went off to college, they lost touch with each other, but met again in their thirties when they went to work for the same tech company. They have been together for five years now and usually get along really well. But they have a hot button issue: religion. Kevin grew up Catholic and had a terrible experience with it throughout his childhood. He went to a school that used corporal punishment. He was a rebellious little kid, so he was hit a lot. When he got old enough to enforce his own beliefs, he vowed he would never enter a church, any kind of church, again. He has no tolerance for any praise about organized religion. He can be viciously critical when someone is, in his mind, "snookered by all that mumbo jumbo." His attitude is hard on Fiona, who has had an opposite experience with her faith. It was a nurturing and helpful part of her childhood and her adulthood. Her brother is an activist for social change, very active in, and much beloved by others in his parish. Fiona belongs to a church that does a lot of social outreach and she feels close to her priest and religious community. If she says something about the good they are doing, Kevin makes nasty comments and they quickly fall into a heated argument. Fiona would like him to enjoy listening to her talk about church activities and be supportive.

Blasts

Mark, a fifty-one-year-old hospitalist, and Petra, forty-two, an artist with an established reputation doing oil portraits, have different politics. But that's not their problem. The problem is how they discuss their differences. Mark's nature is to question what other people think and go after them when their "facts" are shaky. He gives no quarter to anyone in any part of his life and his relationship with Petra is no exception. They both have strong opinions about politics, but Petra finds it almost impossible to talk to Mark about issues because Mark challenges her on her views in a way that shreds her. Politics are a flash topic between them. Here's the way it goes: It is primary season and there are ads about the candidates everywhere on TV, in the mail, and on the Internet. Although there is precious little talk about most issues, one of the issues that has gotten some press is that the two candidates have a different position on welfare payments.

Petra is supporting the Democratic candidate's position of increasing payments for school lunches; Mark, a Republican, feels there is so much waste that there would be other ways to fund lunches if the school system was better run. Plus he believes that too many "entitlements" undermine individual responsibility of the people who should really be paying for the lunches: parents. Mark and Petra get drawn into arguments similar to this one:

> **PETRA:** *It is hard for me to imagine that in this country children are hungry. Now they are cutting food stamps, poor kids.*
>
> **MARK:** *Right, Petra, let's give everybody free food, free health care, free transportation, free everything. Since you are so damn generous why don't you move to Sweden and pay two-thirds of your income so you can be sure everyone gets services they didn't earn.*
>
> **PETRA:** *Every child should be fed. It's ridiculous for a rich country like America to not feed children.*
>
> **MARK:** *So do you know how much it costs to provide free meals? Do you want to feed them breakfast, lunch, and dinner? How much would that cost? Do you have any idea? What do you think it costs to feed these kids, $5 a day, $10 a day? What are you willing to give up to feed them every meal?*
>
> **PETRA:** *"I don't know, but—"*
>
> **MARK INTERRUPTS:** *Before you have an opinion, why don't you get some facts.*
>
> **PETRA:** *Facts don't tell the whole story. What matters is that every child should have enough to eat.*
>
> **MARK:** *There's no point in talking to you about this. You don't know what you are talking about. You are just a typical knee-jerk liberal.*

By this time, Petra is tearing up. Mark feels that tears are an unfair strategy so he leaves the room with a disgusted look on his face.

The Doctors' Advice

The overarching question here is: Do partners have to accept each other's point of view on issues of importance to them? We think not. But intimacy is cut off and even extinguished by challenging each other, demanding explanations, or expecting our partners to provide reasons for what they think, feel, or believe. Compassion creates a safe zone to reveal yourself and explore each other, learning to develop a deeper love between you.

Fiona frequently brings up the topic of her religion, hoping that Kevin will see that Catholicism or, for that matter, religion in general, is different from what he has experienced. She not-so-secretly hopes that he might come back to the faith or at least come to some of the church's events. It's understandable, but Kevin has deep emotional scars and he doesn't want to go there. He has found a way to deal with his past that works for him, and talking about it just brings up bad memories and pain.

If you attempt to change your partner's feelings or positions, as Fiona has, it's going to harm the relationship more than improve it. She can't change Kevin's history and memories and he needs her to accept his feelings. Using compassion, Fiona can ask Kevin to help her understand his feelings toward religion. She can make it safe for him to talk to her by honoring and accepting his experience, his emotions, and his conclusions. She has to put herself and her feelings aside and just seek to understand and know him better. Listening with compassion takes a single focus: Only one person is sharing, while the other is exploring, learning, and accepting. Fiona will have to create a time, place, and setting in which neither of them is distracted, and then she can carefully delve into his inner world.

FIONA: *Kevin, I would like to know more about the pain you feel from your religious experiences as a child.*
KEVIN: *There isn't that much to tell. I just hated it.*
FIONA: *Is that because of the spankings?*

KEVIN: *No, it was more that I didn't understand what I did that was so bad that I was being hit.*

FIONA: *I am so sorry, Kevin. That must have been so frightening, to be in trouble and not know why.*

KEVIN: *Yeah, and I didn't know what to do to stop the punishment, so I decided I would never have anything to do with church again. That way, someday it would stop.*

FIONA: *I wish I could take that pain away. I can see it still hurts and now I understand why. It is so awful to feel unfairly punished.*

KEVIN: *O.K., so that's why no church for me.*

FIONA: *I understand, Kevin. I won't push you about church again.*

You can see that when Fiona truly wanted to have a deeper understanding of Kevin's feelings he opened up, and she could see the pain he still carries. That is the way to build intimacy. Fiona now knows it is not for her to judge, but rather to accept and love him, and ease his pain.

In Mark and Petra's case, the topic is not as important as the intensity and deprecating quality of the interaction. Mark wants to prove Petra wrong more than he cares about what he's doing to her in the process. He truly thinks she's misinformed and he is disgusted that she won't inform herself.

Petra cannot figure out how to stop her husband's attack mode. She has tried everything she could think of. Most of the time they get along so well, and this level of tension and emotional battering doesn't make sense to her. She is wise enough to know the only person she can predictably change is herself, so she went to see a relationship coach to get some advice. The coach suggested she probe a little and find out what is behind Mark's drive to have to "be right" and to become so hostile.

Mark is likely to pontificate, often with some interesting perspectives and what he believes to be fact, and Petra found that her best strategy is just to listen to him when he gets all riled up about something that he just heard on the news. She doesn't like who he turns into when she is being taken to task for some random comment of hers on the political situation, and in order to avoid that unflattering aspect of her husband's character, she has chosen to take her own comments elsewhere and not get involved when the news prompts some tirade of his. Fortunately, he does love and respect her, and so giving up on battles about politics does not cut out other positive conversations they can have about home, family, friends, travel, and many other topics. This is one problem they can solve by agreeing to disagree rather than arguing their opposing positions that bring out the worst in him.

We believe you can have an emotionally intimate relationship, strengthening the bonds between you by gently and lovingly creating a compassionate relationship. It is a lifetime process, getting past the outer layers of self-protection and fear of judgment we all have, to get to the tender inner layers of the vulnerable soul. Like an onion, each layer is a part of the whole, each layer important.

Chapter 14

Insults

THE SNAP

Don't insult your partner in any way, ever.

A Closer Look

Silent insults do damage. This is especially true when we are interacting with our partners. We use all of our senses—touch, smell, sight, hearing, and taste—to consciously and unconsciously gather information, and when they tell us we are unsafe we retreat, and intimacy and trust are compromised.

All types and levels of communication between couples are monitored by the senses. Our senses have no off switch. They are always on, even during sleep. When you have a feeling that something is different or not quite right between you, that is your senses sending you a warning. We refer to this early warning system as intuition or sensitivity.

Tones and gestures speak as loudly as words. Frowns, snarls, pitch, volume, glares, eye rolls, and hand movements all can communicate contempt. Insolent or bored body language can make polite or warm conversations impossible. Even worse, a constant barrage of negative facial expressions can create fear and distrust that lasts. Your partner will feel that he or she is walking on tiptoes and withhold honest exchange for fear of being treated as if he or she were dumb, uninteresting, annoying, or unworthy. Intimacy can only happen when couples feel safe opening up to each other. Harsh tones and negative gestures extinguish trust.

The Situation
Ripples

Harley, thirty-two, and Christina twenty-nine, have lived together for three years. Harley was temporarily out of work and taking some yoga classes to keep him fit and upbeat. Christina was in the same class and he noticed her right away. One evening she substituted for the teacher and he was impressed with her grace, beauty, and wonderful temperament. She has an inner sweetness and peacefulness that pervaded the room, and Harley started falling in love with her before they had exchanged any real conversation. Finally, he got up enough nerve to ask her if she would like to have a cup of tea with him after class. She was not interested (she was dating someone at the time), but that relationship fell apart, and when she continued to see Harley at class, she warmed up to him and indicated that getting a cup of tea might be a nice idea. They started going out and within six months they were a couple. Harley found a job as a web designer, and shortly thereafter, they moved in together.

Christina loves to teach. She continues to teach yoga part-time, but her main mission is the education of young children. She teaches third grade and finds the kids very entertaining. When she gets home, she is happy and energized and wants to talk about her day. She is especially excited when one of her children who hasn't been doing well has a breakthrough. But when she brings these stories home, Harley makes his disinterest clear by looking away while she's talking or settling into his favorite chair with his arms folded and his body language saying, "Can you get this over with?" What really frosts her is that he denies this behavior and says he's listening. He says he can repeat every word she said, but she feels he barely tolerates her download of her day.

Blasts

Vince and Callie married in their mid-thirties and were eager to have children. So, they had two kids in their first four years of marriage. Callie worked for an insurance company and made a good salary, but even though it would be a financial sacrifice, they agreed she would quit and stay home with the kids.

Money is tight and so when Vince recently got an opportunity for a better job, Callie was initially excited. He announced he would be working for BMW, which sounded great. But then he told her that the job involves taking classes in order to learn the cars, processes, and standards he had to know to be a certified BMW mechanic. She was not so thrilled then because there would be a time lag between training and earning more money, something she thought was a very bad idea. Vince tried to calm her fears and pushed on to take the classes. Now he's in the middle of training and is very excited about what he's learning and proud of the company he's working for.

Callie didn't have much say in the matter and she's unhappy that Vince has compromised their present budget by reducing his work as a mechanic at a small shop to take this other opportunity. Furthermore, he is now chatty about what he's learning each day and Callie is totally uninterested in cars. She really doesn't want to hear about it; she's at home all day with their one- and three-year-olds and the last thing she wants is someone else talking at her and asking for approval or even her concentration.

So while he's talking, she is smirking and rolling her eyes. When he lauds the company, she chuckles as if he were a simpleton. She is mad at him because his extra education is costing them money and time right now, and she was against it. So as he sees it, she's punishing him for trying to get ahead, and what's worse is she seems to be getting meaner all the time. He understands she is overwhelmed by taking care of the kids, but they agreed to have kids right away and she is living the life he thought she wanted. He wants to be excited about his work and he's proud of himself for getting ahead and into a position in which he can be paid what he's worth. He knows that their future will be better after he is certified and getting paid a terrific hourly rate. He really feels lonely and unloved because this is the most exciting thing he has ever done and it is being trashed by her. He is beginning to think his wife is a bitch.

The Doctors' Advice

We know that in today's world couples exchange emotional messages in many ways. People are communicating in person, over the phone, or by text, Twitter, or Facebook, but still, when it comes right down to it, the most intense and immediate communication are the messages we send when we are looking at one another. When these messages contain an insult, intended or not, they damage the fabric of trust in your relationship. Your eyes telegraph your emotions and your judgments, and you are accountable for what they telegraph. In fact, studies have shown that eye rolling, an indication of contempt, can predict divorce—that's how insulting and damaging a glance can be!

Sometimes our emotions pick up on these signals even before our brains have classified them, and so we can feel hurt, angry, sad, or generally upset without knowing why. Later on, we often realize what we were picking up—body language or facial gestures that made us feel discounted and unloved.

It drives Christina crazy when Harley goes stone-faced as she tells him about her day at school. Harley's face shows disapproval. She can see that he's only pretending to be present. It is true that he can repeat what she said, but he's not really thinking about it— he's thinking about when she will stop talking so he can turn on the news. Harley desperately wants a period of calm (a quality of Christina's he fell in love with) from the time he comes home until after dinner. He needs an interim period of just hanging out quietly, even though she needs to express herself. His body language is telling her the truth, and it would be better for the relationship if he stopped being verbally dishonest, but then giving her body language to show that he is not interested in thinking about her day at this time. It's better for him to tell her when he's can't pay attention to the topic than to have her notice these not-so-subtle signals. So, for example, he could say, "I am so dog-tired right now. I just want to hug you and watch a bit of TV and zone out. Then I'll help you with dinner, and how about we talk about the kids during dessert." Christina deserves a "good face" from him, and his time and interest. But if she is asking for it at a time when he's unable to give it, he needs to tell her, and they need to synchronize their timing better.

He also has to be honest that there is only so much detail he can take. He wants a lighter, breezy account from Christina. If they could agree on how long her review of her day would be, then he could agree to stay engaged. It wouldn't take much for her to get Harley to really listen if she would just hit a few high points and save the rest for a time when he is more receptive. Let it be up to him to ask for more information, if he's interested.

Callie is exhausted and thin-skinned by the time Vince gets home. All day, little people have demanded every bit of energy and attention she has. She'd do a lot better with Vince if he took care of her a bit when he first came home. He is full of enthusiasm that has nothing to do with her or the family, although he thinks he is doing it for them. As much as he thinks it is their joint success, he is really just putting himself first.

Callie may not even understand it that way, but she knows she's not getting the support she needs. So she's fighting back by going after him about something he loves because he thinks what he's doing is so important, and obviously if he thought what she was doing was important, he'd be full of questions about her day and eager to see the kids.

Although Callie is presenting all the wrong gestures, faces, and tones, she's actually expressing what she's feeling; we would recommend that Vince look at the true nature of her days and try to make them better and more of a collaborative effort. He could come home with flowers or with takeout food, or a toy for the children. Then she might feel more generous about his life and be a nicer person. For her part in this, Callie has to use words to tell Vince what he can do to help her, telling him that when he gets home she would like him to grab the kids and play with them for half an hour while she takes a break. Vince could also start transitioning into family life on his drive from work to home. He could listen to music in the car, think about the family, and enter the household ready to be a dad and a husband. Callie could gather herself up, maybe take a shower, and unwind. We believe that Vince actively helping her as soon as he arrives would diminish or eliminate those destructive gestures. She might even be happy to hear about his work once she gets over feeling isolated and unappreciated. If she is feeling more protected and loved, she is going to be happier for him and show more gratitude for the additional income his new work will provide.

We believe it is important to allow your senses to guide you, making you aware of potential insults that you are sending or receiving. If you are the one sending the insult, you know in your gut that you are being mean. So you need to hold yourself accountable and stop it! If you are on the receiving end of an insult and your stomach aches, or you are depressed or feel like crying, speak up and tell your partner so that these messages can be nipped in the bud.

Chapter 15

Overreacting

THE SNAP

Resist your gut instinct and keep your first reactions to yourself.

A Closer Look

Knee-jerk reactions usually come from protective rather than proactive instincts. Presume your first reaction is soaked in fight-or-flight hormones and resist your reaction. We know that knee-jerk reactions, like walking away immediately or blowing up, are wired into us and that they are a primitive and unconscious survival tactic. They are part of our autonomic nervous system and not mediated by the cognitive part of the brain. Unfortunately, they don't suit modern life very well. Researchers have identified four major defenses that are part of our earliest evolutionary history: fight, flight, freeze, or surrender.

During our cave-dwelling days, a charging mammoth meant it was a good idea to run (flight); if the marauding tribe was set on stealing your food, it was time to fight; and when the odds were against you, freeze was a good option—perhaps the enemy wouldn't see you if you didn't move. These responses bypass the thinking part of the brain and go right into survival mode. Realistically, your partner is not a charging mammoth, marauding tribe, or any other kind of enemy. You partner is your friend, your lover, and your mate and not a threat to your life. It isn't easy to resist these first urges and behaviors, but even taking a few breaths when you feel your temperature rise or your heart beat faster will keep you from making some bad mistakes.

The Situation
Ripples

Ines is a perfectionist and has been that way for all of her forty years of life. She likes to make sure that everyone in the family is dressed appropriately for cold weather. Ines and Ryan have been married for ten years. Ryan is an independent guy who is self-employed. Mostly he ignores Ines's obsession with everyone being "nice and warm, and dressed for the weather." He wears what he wants and doesn't say much when she is bundling up the kids so tight they can hardly move. One winter night, they were going out into freezing weather, and Ines said in a disdainful tone, "Ryan, where's your overcoat?" He calls this her "you stupid idiot voice." This time it was too much for him and he went ballistic. He said, "God damn you, I'm sick of you bossing me around. You tell everyone what to do, when to do it, and what to wear. We're all sick of you being the know-it-all. I think I can dress myself."

Ines's response? Understandably, she burst into tears, and Ryan felt bad.

Blasts

Marla likes to drive fast and aggressively, whether she's on her way to work in the morning or headed to the gym on the weekend. She weaves in and out of traffic and pushes ten miles per hour above the speed limit pretty regularly. Diego is scared silly when he's in the car with her. He grips the console and goes white. He has a much more cautious driving style and he thinks she's going to kill them both someday. One day, while they were driving, Diego nodded off, but he woke up suddenly, startled by the speed she was traveling. A truck slowed down and when she passed the truck driver, he waved his fist and started yelling at them. At this point, Diego lost it, and started screaming too, "Are you trying to kill me? You're a psychopath!"

Marla was angry and defensive and distracted; she careened the car to the side of the road, slammed on the brakes, and jumped out. After exchanging a few more seething comments, they froze each other out for the rest of the six-hour drive. The driving incident didn't get discussed and they were icy to each other the rest of the vacation.

The Doctors' Advice

We recommend taking a couple of deep breaths before opening your mouth to say anything. Even if you feel attacked, remember that your survival is not at stake. Adding fuel to already heated emotions is likely to create an inferno that is hard to contain.

Raw emotions, those coming from our primitive brain, are usually more intense than the situation merits. It is very difficult to explain these intense emotions because they are not based on present reality. When Ines started crying, Ryan felt like a heel. He knew that she was just trying to look out for him and he really didn't mean to be that nasty; it just came out that way. He apologized, but she was really hurt. Then she kept asking him if everyone really felt that way about her, and if he felt she was always too bossy.

Ryan found that Ines did not really believe his reassurances. This had a lasting effect on their relationship and that is why we really want you to take a deep breath and stifle immediate reactions, even if there is something valid that happened. In this case, the response was disproportionate to the crime, partly because Ryan's emotions had been building up about the way Ines talks to him at times.

So first, if something is annoying, face it. Ryan needs to tell her, in the nicest possible way, how her "mothering" voice annoys him and why. He can tell her that he interprets her tone as indicating he is stupid.

This is a good model for other issues that spouses or partners "sweep under the rug." Things don't stay under the rug. They build up and this frustration results in explosions that are generally not commensurate with what happened at the time. Ryan will have to be careful and not fight this battle immediately because it will be a very sore point for a while. Once she has healed from his assault, he can tell her what his sensitivities are. And they can agree that if she makes the same mistake he should say, "Thank you for your opinion," which will be a mild but effective reminder to her to back off.

Diego has a valid fear. Marla's behavior would cause anyone to be afraid and may, in fact, threaten their lives. But obviously, the explosion wasn't a good idea: It put them in more danger. You don't want a furious and upset person at the wheel. Moreover, it became a personal attack as opposed to an answer to a real problem. Something had to be done, but he could have said, "Slow down. This is scaring me; please stop."

They could have stopped, had a cup of coffee, and calmed down. Perhaps they could have worked out a plan that included a comfortable speed limit, staying in one lane, and no texting while driving.

Rather than demonizing Marla, Diego could make this dilemma about his comfort zone. Later, he could initiate a serious conversation that stresses his fear of losing her (not to mention himself) and makes her feel touched and concerned, rather than pissed off.

We want you to recognize that neither your emotions nor your partner's are always reasonable or rational; they are basic instincts that just spill over now and then. Moderate or suppress your knee-jerk reaction by taking a couple of deep breaths to slow down your reaction, and then de-escalate the situation with a gentle touch to the hand.

Chapter 16

Taking Each Other Seriously

What may be trivial to you is not trivial to your partner, so take it seriously.

A Closer Look

Whenever your partner takes a stand about something that's important to him or her—even if it's over how a steak should be cooked—listen. Any meta-message that says "This is important to me" should be important to you. A good rule to remember is a simple one: Know what is important to your partner and allow it to be important to you, no matter how trivial. We all have things that are important to us that may not seem like such a big deal to someone else. It is a mistake to think that your partner can always know the significance of these things to you, yet it is also incumbent on a partner to learn what is significant to you. Part of being a couple is remembering that there are two of you.

If you go to Starbucks, you know that every customer has a very specific way he or she wants coffee, and it seems sometimes like no two are the same. Each person wants a particular type of coffee and a specific type of milk, with or without froth, at an exact temperature, with the right flavorings. Oh, yes, and how many shots of espresso do you want for this particular order? Is it all really important? YES. Just watch if a customer's coffee is not precisely what he or she ordered. All these details *matter* to people.

Think of it another way: If your partner only likes steaks really rare, and you will only grill them well done, what does that say? Yes, it's "only" a steak, but not knowing or caring about the details of your partner's life and desires says a lot of unflattering things about the relationship. Let's reverse that observation and put it in a positive frame: Making your partner's preferences a priority and giving your partner what he or she wants communicates that you care enough to remember what matters and do your best to provide it.

Learning all the little things that matter to your partner is more than service or a peace offering. It is an act of love, and most partners recognize it as such. When you remember that she likes a bouquet of sunflowers rather than roses, you are saying, "I love you, I think about you, I know you well and, based on that knowledge, I try to please you." The added bonus is that you feel great because you know you are being loving, using the knowledge that is only acquired over time in a very intimate relationship. It is a gift to both of you.

This last point is one we wish to underline. Giving is, of course, part of being in a good relationship: It is part of bonding, of creating the "you and me" couple identity. When the gift is one that comes from knowledge that no one else knows because no one else loves this person as much as you do (besides, maybe, his parents!), it develops the feeling of being truly and deeply mated. Remember, it might seem trivial to you, but it's not trivial to your partner.

The Situation
Ripples

Hana is sentimental. So sentimental that she cries when she reads an especially effective Hallmark card. She tears up when she sees a particularly cute picture of a baby or puppy. So Hana always remembers events that are important to her friends. She always remembers her friends' birthdays, but she even remembers her friends' anniversaries and almost all holidays. Even though she works full-time in a sometimes very stressful job, she finds the time to buy perfect presents for people and create memorable events. She made her own forty-fifth birthday a huge celebration and she likes to do the same for her wife,

Phillipa. In fact, for Phillipa's recent fiftieth birthday she planned a masterful surprise party. Trained as a mechanical engineer, Phillipa loves cars and tinkering with them, so Hana said they should go to the new car museum about forty-five minutes away for her birthday. Phillipa loved the idea and was happily bowled over when a hundred people were there to yell "Happy Birthday!" As an added touch, Hana had rented an expensive sports car for her for the month.

Phillipa and Hana have been together for thirty years and married for three (when it became legally possible). Over time Hana has learned that Phillipa doesn't have a talent for doing the same kind of imaginative parties or surprises that she does, so she doesn't expect Phillipa to duplicate her extensive efforts. Phillipa does romantic things from time to time, but she doesn't know how to make them "pop." Her idea of the ideal romantic evening is renting a romantic movie and watching it in bed while drinking champagne from flutes. Hana likes these evenings a lot, but she'd like some different and fancier gestures. Hana likes to be romanced, so the one day she expects Phillipa to step up to the plate, at least a bit more than usual, is Valentine's Day. This one day is particularly important to her.

She has said as much to Phillipa, and reminds her a week before Valentine's Day and again two days before. Phillipa hears her, but she more or less shrugs off Valentine's Day as a commercial scam. She also feels put off that Hana has bought into the whole thing. So on Valentine's Day Phillipa makes what she thinks is a compromise effort: She swings by the grocery store and looks for a nice bouquet, but she has to settle for whatever bouquet is left. She also remembers to buy chocolates, but her last-minute attempt to make a dinner reservation failed. There's nothing available at the last minute, so it's hard for Phillipa to hide the fact that the reservation was remembered at the eleventh hour.

She is aware that this will not look good to Hana and apologizes, but Hana is visibly disappointed. Phillipa does her best to make up for it and get in a romantic mood. She says she will make dinner and she retrieves a special bottle of wine they have been saving for special occasions. Hana wants to lose her dark mood, and she sees that Phillipa is being very nice, but she is getting madder by the moment. In her opinion, she asks little enough of Phillipa and then Phillipa can't even do that! So by the end of the filet mignon and the bottle of wine, she loses control and lays into the woman she loves. "Yes this is nice, but no, it's not what I wanted. And it's not like I haven't tried my very best to help you remember that this is my special holiday!" Initially, Phillipa apologizes again and tries to humor Hana, but ultimately she feels she is being beaten up too much and she raises her voice and says, "This is unfair. You have read too many Hallmark cards! You are making too big a deal out of this!"

Blasts

Nora and Emmett have been married for seven years, and the marriage is still going through growing pains. Emmett, sixty-two, has just sold his sportswear business and he is feeling good about it. Nora, fifty-three, is working in marketing for a custom home-builder. Nora is self-confident overall, but not so much when it comes to personal safety. She is a beautiful woman who has been in some scary situations with men flirting with her and trying to grab at her.

Her father and mother had a great marriage and she always saw how protective her father was of her mother. She loved it when her dad would watch out for her mother whenever they were out as a family. Nora expects no less from her man; a man, in her opinion, should be looking out for her safety and comfort.

This feeling comes to a head when she perceives a threat. A few weeks ago, she and Emmett were coming home late from a movie and they had to walk through some unlighted, fairly empty streets to get to their car. They encountered what she perceived as two men who looked tough and capable of accosting them. She asked Emmett twice to please cross the street and twice he blew her off, distressing Nora to no end.

This hit a nerve in Nora's psyche. She was scared and hurt. It was clear to her that Emmett was oblivious to her fears or vulnerability and that if he was aware of them, he didn't love her enough to make her feel safer. When she thought about the fact that he wouldn't even do an easy thing like cross the street for her, she got really sad.

Her second reaction was anger. She yanked her hand out of his and stomped across the street. Emmett was so ticked off at her behavior that he refused to go after her and kept walking on his side of the street until they got to the car. When they got in the car, she burst into tears and he just turned to her, mystified about the strength of her reaction. She couldn't stop crying. She felt betrayed and deserted and left to fend for herself. He was bewildered and thought that maybe she was having some kind of hormonal reaction.

The Doctors' Advice

The simple pleasure that can be taken from pleasing the one you love with some minor gesture, or the memory of a trivial preference or an experience, are some of the little things that count.

Hana has tried all of the usual methods, year after year, to tell Phillipa that she really wants a great Valentine's Day. At this point, since it is so important to her, she needs to sit down and have a real conversation about why this means so much and why, as a favor to her, Phillipa needs to put away her antagonism toward the holiday and do something for Hana on Hana's terms. She can ask directly, "Will you take this seriously to please me? I know it's commercial, but I still want to use this holiday to be close to you. Can you do that for me?" Chances are that approach will really affect Phillipa because she does love Hana. Hana can also make it easier for both of them by suggesting something Hana thinks would be romantic or fun. If Phillipa does better at home than at dinner in a restaurant, they can play with home celebrations, for example, inviting another couple over for a special feast or having it catered and brought home to an especially pretty table setting. Or, if Hana needs to go out, Phillipa and Hana can make the reservation together ahead of time at their favorite restaurant a night or two before Valentine's Day so that they can have a lovely experience without Phillipa feeling annoyed about paying twice as much just because it's Valentine's Day. Although it might be fair to expect Phillipa to do the planning or get the right gift, it's not her talent and she's not mindful about these kinds of things. Ideally, your partner will learn what makes you happy and do those things, but he or she might need your help. Showing your partner how to please you is an important part of relationships. The crucial point is to learn how to succeed with each other, and sometimes that takes a lot of tutelage. Phillipa may have an allergic reaction to Valentine's Day, but if she just can't put this holiday together, she needs to make sure that Hana's romanticism is fulfilled in other ways.

Blasts

Nora and Emmett's circumstances are serious. He is really disconnected from her sense of vulnerability. And to make it worse, he actually belittles her. Even when she gives him instances of times when men have tried to grab her or made sleazy comments, he has brushed it off as no big deal. He doesn't understand that she has experienced many threatening experiences because she attracts more attention than most women get. So when she had a meltdown in the car, he still didn't get what it's about.

We don't want to send people to counseling all the time, but Nora now believes that he doesn't love her enough to protect her. Because he has not stepped up to protect her several times now, she is living in fear. Not only does he refuse to protect her, but he actually puts her in harm's way. Intimacy cannot survive if she doesn't feel safe with Emmett. Since she is unable to make him understand that feeling safe is critical to the survival of their marriage, he may have to hear it from a third party. If they don't get this kind of intervention, Nora will most likely start distancing herself from the marriage.

Fortunately, they did go for help. Over three months, the relationship coach helped Emmett understand how alienated Nora had become. Emmett had no idea how much his lack of concern for her feelings had left her feeling bereft and disappointed in her marriage. In therapy, Nora talked about her father and how much she had wanted someone who made her feel the way she thought her mother felt: precious and protected. Emmett had no idea that Nora did not feel that way with him and he was really shocked to learn how physical that protection needed to be. Nora is a very competent, strong person in many ways and it never occurred to Emmett that Nora could feel so vulnerable just by walking down a dark street.

By understanding Nora's idolization of her father, her mother's idolization of her husband, and her own need to not feel totally in charge, Emmett could begin to understand how deeply ingrained her fears were. He realized that even though Nora was a strong woman, there was this part of her that had to feel protected to feel loved. He asked what it would take for her to feel that he had her back. She said, "Simple things. If I don't like the look of someone, indulge me and help get us away from them. If I move closer to you, move closer to me. Help me remember little things like wearing a safety belt and locking the door." Emmett was touched by how little it took and how important it was to her. He resolved to do those things more and try to be consistent about them. And he did. The couple pulled together, stronger than before.

When we say the word "trivial," we often mean more than "small"; we sometimes just mean "ordinary," the little things that make up our day-to-day life. We believe the ordinary, day-to-day moments are the building blocks of love, and they can become extraordinarily memorable by the simple acts we have described in this chapter. We think that one of the most touching things you can say to a partner is that "every little thing about you is important to me." And back that up by observing and responding to those little things. Any relationship that truly observes the saying "It's the little things that count" is going to be special itself.

Chapter 17

Discovering Love Languages

Give what your partner wants, not what you want to give.

A Closer Look

Gary Chapman's best-selling book *The 5 Love Languages* is an important read for partners. The general idea is that people, like countries, use different "currencies" to represent a precious commodity. It's important to make sure you've got your partner's emotional currency right. Because once you understand that your partner may need a different expression of love than you do, and you start speaking your partner's primary love language, you'll see how quickly emotions can turn positive.

A love language is the way you express your love and also how other people express their needs for love. If you are speaking French and someone only understands English, your words of love may not be understood or have their full impact. If you are showing love in a way that another person does not understand, they may feel falsely unloved. Showing love in the way your partner wants it shown and translating your own needs for love so that a partner understands how to fulfill them are of fundamental importance. Sharing a love language means that you may alter how you send your partner signals to show you value him or her, and that those signals are received and understood for what they are by that person. Dr. Chapman identifies five easy ways most people attempt to give and receive love, and we feel they are valuable enough to repeat them here. They are not in any hierarchy of importance.

★ QUALITY TIME: For some people, love is expressed in the amount of time you spend with your loved one. It can't just mean co-presence, the casual sitting together watching television. It can be a variety of activities—a romantic vacation, a long talk over dinner, a walk every morning, date time no matter how long the marriage has lasted—but what is prized is time for just the two of you without distraction.

★ GIFTS: In most people's minds, this means presents. What is a present? It is a token of affection, of love, and, if it has been well thought out, it is a symbol of intimacy. The person who gives to express love wants his or her gift to be accepted as a sign of love, and the person who is given the gift should understand that the giver is expressing love. If the receiver sees gifts as important, then the act of love is understood for what it is. If he or she does not, it is just a thing, or a nice thought, or perhaps totally misunderstood as an apology or a ritual. Some people believe that a lack of gift giving at times like anniversaries and birthdays demonstrates a lack of love. The cost of the item or trip matters for some people, and they might feel the preciousness or the scarcity of something demonstrates how deep the love is. For others, even the smallest remembrance would make the point.

★ ACTS OF SERVICE: For many people, love means doing things for their partners and/or having things done for them. Love could mean doing a job for your partner that she hates to do, or relieving her of a responsibility. It could mean cooking, cleaning, or maintaining the house, or keeping a job you didn't like so that your partner could stay home and take care of the children, or write, or create songs. Your love language would be an action, and you would feel loved if someone did something touching for you.

★ WORDS OF AFFIRMATION: For some people, there is no substitute for hearing "I love you," and saying "I love you" is the only way to show their highest emotional feeling for someone. When words are the love language, certain specific words may be the best present you can give. Your partner may want you to use words like "handsome," "smart," "talented," "sexy," or "cute." Find out what these words are and use them, and they will hear your love. They need the words, the compliments, and expressions of emotions.

★ PHYSICAL TOUCH: For many men and women, the thing that differentiates love from other types of feelings is sexual contact. It is hard to think of lovers not touching each other, but the salience of touch, stroking, sex, and body contact may be the most important language of love for some of us. If it is a partner's love language, nothing will supplant the need for sexual contact, and if it is yours, the withdrawal or lack of sexual contact—whether just walking hand in hand, or snuggling at bedtime (or at other times), will be a sign to you that you are unloved in the way that you need to be loved.

The idea that there are languages of love speaks to all of us—which is why Dr. Chapman's little book, written in 1995 and updated since, became an instant classic. It shows us that we are not all the same in the way we love or need love and that we should make no assumptions that how we show love is accurately perceived or valued as we would have it valued. We have to understand that our languages are probably not the same, they may even change over time, and one language is not better or worse than another. Complex, yes, but since we want to succeed with the one we love, our challenge is to learn how to give and receive love in the way that nurtures each other and the union we are trying to protect.

The Situation
Ripples

Terrell, twenty-seven, and LaRonda, twenty-nine, bought a condo this summer, and now they have a second bedroom and a patio. The place has potential, but it needs work. When they bought it, they made plans to fix it up. Then they discovered LaRonda was pregnant. They were delighted, but the remodel would be slower than they had hoped because her pregnancy made it harder for her to do all the things she had planned. LaRonda understands that Terrell has a pretty inflexible schedule, particularly since he was recently promoted to manager by the department store where he works. She is busy, too, as a paralegal at a small law firm. She is overwhelmed these days.

Terrell is an affectionate husband. He tells LaRonda he loves her every day, and he often remarks how pretty she is and how talented she is. Of course, she loves to hear this, but the fact is, he's not showing his love in the way she needs it. For LaRonda, love is what Gary Chapman refers to as "acts of service." For her, actions speak louder than words. Love to LaRonda means getting the house ready for their growing family. Terrell is happy to get groceries, help make dinner, and clean up after dinner, but he doesn't get around to bigger projects. He has good intentions about repairing the condo, but he goes to basketball practice and hangs out with his friends from high school on Saturday mornings. He says that is the only time he feels like he can have some fun. He also uses the weekend to check in with his mom and dad, both of whom have health problems. It's not that LaRonda begrudges Terrell his sports, friends, or family, but she is in her sixth month and exhausted, and she wants him to take care of things at home to get ready for the baby. The way she sees it, Terrell is MIA and if he really loved her he would see how overwhelmed she is and fix up their place no matter what it took.

Blasts

At thirty-five, Lara is a success story. She grew up in a financially unstable home with a single mom who worked two jobs and who ultimately was able to put together her own business. Her mom was her role model, so Lara has worked hard all her life as well. It has paid off. She is a senior associate with a major telecom firm and she works with corporate clients on million-dollar deals. She has risen quickly, and now she is on an airplane almost every week and sometimes gone for a week at a time. When she is home, there are plenty of details to take care of for the company and she also uses the time to catch up with friends, continue her volunteer work with the Unitarian Church, and go to yoga and tai chi classes. She loves her fiancé, Nico, whom she met when he chaired a workshop on social justice sponsored by the Unitarian community. They moved in together last year. Nico works for a foundation that gives seed money for small-scale farming, including farming in urban neighborhoods, and he does some traveling too—but not nearly as much as Lara. Lately, although he is generally a stoic type of guy, he has been complaining about not having enough time together, which surprises Lara because she thought that moving in together would solve the problem. But Nico doesn't see it that way. Yes, he sees her more, but she is always on the run, never, as he sees it, focusing on him and not giving the relationship quality time. Nico's and Lara's ideas of quality time are quite different. She counts nights spent out with other couples; Nico does not. Nico wants more hanging out, more doing things together, and more thoughtful conversations—not just a quick lunch with one another a couple of times a week. Nico believes Lara's friends and activities and work are far more important to her than he is because of the amount of time she spends on these parts of her life. He has become angry and sullen and is wondering if she is really the person he should be with.

The Doctors' Advice

Loving your partner involves more than a feeling. The love you feel may not be the same as the love your partner sees, experiences, or needs. That does not negate your feelings or your partner's, but you need to take your partner's love language very seriously. Relationships can go under unless you learn to express your loving feelings in a way that works for both of you.

This is trickier than it seems because how we give and receive love can change over time. Things you used to do that hit the mark may not work quite as well as they once did; so updates are important. When you were first together your love language may have been singularly sexual. A disproportionate number of young lovers would for sure say their love language was primarily based on physical love. However, things can change over time. Libido becomes less preoccupying, building a family takes up a lot of energy, building a career takes up more, and friends and everyday life sometimes make people need a different love language. It may be time to review the five love languages and see if you or your partner has new ways in which you want to show, or be shown, love. In fact, we suggest you make it part of your anniversary celebration.

Unfortunately, these two couples are unaware that they are not speaking each other's love languages. LaRonda gets words; she wants action. Nico is getting a delightful companion, but not enough of her. It's often the case that what we give is not what the other person appreciates. We have to spell out what makes us feel loved because it's the path to rekindling emotional connection. With a "full love tank," as Chapman puts it, "a relationship is capable of much more intimacy and growth." If you feel securely and richly loved, conflicts go down, and when they pop up, they can be processed more quickly and in a more positive manner.

These couples need better communication about what makes them feel loved. Terrell is very expressive, both verbally and physically—and for some women, that would be perfect. But LaRonda takes those expressions for granted and although she likes them, they don't touch her heart that much. LaRonda has to tell Terrell what makes her feel loved and close to him. She needs to impress on him how much it would mean to her if he did house projects right away. Terrell needs to take a look at how much time he is spending out of the house and know that more lavish "I love yous" will not replace getting the crib done and the condo painted. If he wants a grateful and connected partner he has to provide acts of service rather than words of affirmation. Talk about getting a bang for your buck: If Terrell helps get that baby room done, he is going to have one smitten wife.

Nico and Lara also have different love languages. Nico wants time with Lara, when she can be fully present and focused on him. When she buzzes in for a quick dinner, she counts that as real time together—he does not. He respects that she can pack so much life into every minute, that she is getting enough quality time for herself, but Nico feels as if he's getting the crumbs, not the loaf of bread. He gets the time available, but not prime time. In the beginning he shrugged it off because he was impressed with her vibrancy and energy, but now he just feels unloved and unimportant. Nico needs to make it clear to Lara that nothing will substitute for time spent together for him—not gifts, not acts of service, not words of affirmation, not even sex. He will have to pin her down for an extended and difficult discussion about how much time and energy he needs for her to devote to him. He needs to be clear with Lara about specifics: how much time, when, and how often he needs her full attention with no one else around. If he is vague, she is bound to fail, because she has no idea that the way she is spending time with him is not meeting his needs. This is one of those situations in which a correction can save the relationship and replenish it, whereas ignoring the problem could end the relationship. Here's the way the conversation might go:

NICO: *Lara, I need your undivided attention.*

LARA: *Sure. I have twenty minutes before I go to yoga.*

NICO: *No, that's the problem. It's twenty minutes here and there. I am not getting enough quality time.*

LARA: *Sure you are. We had Saturday night out with Barry and Virginia and we will have our usual Sunday morning.*

NICO: *That may be enough time for you, but it's not for me. I am feeling distant and lonely and wondering if we really can make this relationship go the distance.*

LARA, SHOCKED: *I love you, Nico. Don't say that.*

NICO: *Well, I love you too. But I have to feel loved and the only way I can feel loved is with a lot more time than I'm getting, ALONE with you.*

LARA: *I didn't know you felt that bad.*

NICO: *Well, I do.*

LARA: *Well, you tell me what you need. We can put together a schedule and we will work it out.*

NICO: *That's what I needed to hear. Let's go over the schedule and figure out how to get enough time together so that I feel you really put me first and want to be with me.*

LARA: *I would love to do that. I do love you.*

Love changes over time and our lives change too, presenting us with new experiences and situations. We have to keep track of whether or not our partners know what we need, and if those needs have changed. We have to check in with them too. Update and use your love language, and learn new ways to succeed in making one another feel loved.

Chapter 18

Delayed Decisions

"Let me think about it" has to have a due date.

A Closer Look

Big or small decisions need to be discussed, not postponed, to keep the relationship alive. "Let me think about it" can be a simple, thoughtful comment that seems to say, "I would like to have some time to think it over." It seems an innocent enough request.

In our experience, it is often not used for positive reasons; in fact, it is used as a delaying tactic, meaning, "I don't want to think about it now or anytime soon." Or, "I disagree, but I'd rather keep pushing the issue away as long as possible so we don't have to confront one another." This delaying tactic is not innocent and not without consequences for the person who wants a real answer. It leaves the person waiting for a resolution "on hold." We all know how much we like being put on hold on the phone—not so much! It's never a good experience, and neither is waiting for a decision without knowing when it will be made.

We think the use of "Let me think about it" as a way of saying "No" is rather cowardly. You might think you are avoiding conflict, but instead you are setting yourself up for a bigger confrontation because your partner is either going to keep pestering you or is going to make his or her own decision without your input, leaving you out of the process. One of you is bound to be mad.

This tactic is also a power play for control. Shutting your partner out of the conversation is the same as shutting him or her out of your life. If you don't want your partner to have a voice in your life as a couple, then you are likely to get what you want: a life in which you are in control and alone.

If "Let me think about it" is meant as a simple request for some time to think, then it has to have a due date so you both know when a decision or a discussion will happen. If there is a due date, then neither of you is waiting, wondering, or resenting the other. In fact, then you are functioning as a couple.

The Situation
Ripples

Gabe, thirty-one, and Sebastian, forty-three, have been together eight years. Their attraction was immediate: Gabe was the handsome bartender and bar owner and Sebastian, tall, blond, and very good-looking himself, had come in to get a job as a waiter while he was finishing his undergraduate degree in the hospitality business. They laugh about the fact that Gabe didn't want to give Sebastian a job because he wanted to date him and Gabe told him so. Sebastian got a job elsewhere and they started seeing one another. They are a very happy couple and they think that the cornerstone of their relationship is the fun they have when they travel together, for a few getaway days or on longer trips.

However, they get into arguments about weekend getaways because Gabe is often noncommittal about Sebastian's suggestions for their trip. It annoys Sebastian to no end when he brings up an idea and Gabe says, "Let me think about it." When that happens, Sebastian's idea usually gets shelved and Gabe comes up with an alternative in the last hour, which is not the way Sebastian likes to run his life. He likes to anticipate where they will be going and what they will be doing. He likes to reserve nice places at a good rate, which is sometimes impossible with last-minute decisions. He's pretty irritated with this pattern.

Blasts

Riley, thirty-one, has always wanted a large family the very large Irish family in which he grew up. He was the second oldest of six kids and had an idyllic childhood. He knows he can't afford to have that big a family on a primary school teacher's salary, but he considers three kids the absolute minimum. He has been married to Julia, thirty, also a teacher, for four years and when they started dating they both agreed that they wanted kids, just "not now." Julia loves kids, but she finds teaching very demanding and she felt she couldn't handle both teaching and being a mom when she was learning her profession. "Not now" was three years ago, and Riley is ready to be a father. Moreover, he wants to be a young father so he can have lots of energy for his kids and time to have a good-sized family. He is dismayed when Julia keeps saying, "We will, but not now," because he feels he is running out of time to have a family as a young man. In fact, he is beginning to feel that "not now" means "not ever."

The Doctors' Advice

"Let me think about it," or words to that effect, can be a genuine request to be thoughtful. Unfortunately, that is not typical in our experience. Instead, these words can be a bad habit or they can spell the beginning of the end of your relationship. It is important and really not that difficult to set a due date. The due date is the time when you will have a discussion or your partner will tell you his or her decision. If your partner just does not like to make decisions and simply stalls, this approach actually gets both of you off the hook. The precise time is set, the duration is determined—probably around five to ten minutes (really!)—the place is established, and it's done.

For most decisions or discussions, one day is plenty of time. If there is new information to be gathered, decide who is going to do that, and by when. But set the due date as soon as possible after the time of the request.

If you or your partner don't like to say no because you are afraid of conflict, trust us when we say that you are only building a smoldering fire that will burst into bigger flames later. Again, the due date is the answer. The longer you put if off, the more tense you will become about starting a fight by saying no, and the more revved up your partner gets, suspecting you are going to say no.

Sometimes there is a simple fix, as in the case of Sebastian and Gabe. We think that when Gabe says, "Let me think about it," he is actually saying no. One solution is for Sebastian to call Gabe on his delaying and deflection of a decision when he really doesn't want to do something. So Sebastian can simply and lightheartedly respond to Gabe's "Let me think about it" with his own response, which is "I guess that means no." This opens up a discussion in case it really is a "maybe." But more likely, it creates a discussion about what Gabe does and does not want to do and allows time for an alternate plan. Another approach is that Sebastian could ask Gabe not to use that phrase and instead say how he feels about the suggestion. This way plans can be made, not delayed and changed if necessary (and costs can be kept lower!).

Riley has a more difficult task ahead of him because time is not his friend, and "I'll think about it" no longer suits his passionate desire to be a young dad. He needs a deadline. Julia may be honestly unsure of when, or even if, she wants children, and in that case she has to level with herself and Riley about her feelings. Her pattern of putting off any decision and the complications it poses for Riley are starting to have an increasingly negative impact on the relationship.

Riley needs to know what Julia's timeline is, and it has to be soon. This is so important to Riley that if Julia can't reach a decision, they might need the help of a third party. If her decision is to have a child, there are a number of next steps to consider, like when exactly she would go off birth control. Riley decided to go this route and face this impasse head on. He told Julia that he wanted to start the baby discussion in earnest and work through it together with a coach. The discussion was tough for both of them, but it went like this in front of the coach:

> JULIA: *I don't want to be pushed about his. Having a baby is a very serious thing and I don't think I can manage it with teaching.*
>
> COACH: *Is that now, Julia, or ever?*
>
> JULIA: *Well, certainly not now. I need to think more about this.*
>
> RILEY: *You didn't answer the question, Julia, is that now or ever?*
>
> JULIA: *I honestly don't know.*
>
> RILEY: *Julia, I love you; you know that. But kids are a deal breaker for me. I am going to make it a three-month discussion here and then it's in or out.*
>
> JULIA: *I can't have that pressure.*
>
> RILEY: *I'm sorry, but it's been three years, so I am going to take a non-decision as a decision not to have kids.*
>
> JULIA: *That's not fair.*
>
> COACH: *I think Riley has reached the end of his rope with this, Julia. Be careful what you say next, and make sure it's something you mean.*
>
> JULIA: *I love Riley. I'm scared of having a kid. I don't think I'm good with really young children.*
>
> RILEY: *I think you will make a great mom. But now at least we are talking about what's really going on and we can come to some decisions together.*

Honest conversations ensued, and Julia decided to get pregnant. Riley did not want to push Julia into making a decision to have a baby if she did not really want one. He helped Julia by making some practical suggestions to ease her mind, such as taking a class together on raising young children.

Decisions and discussions are important in every relationship, and setting a time and place for them helps to make that happen.

Each person's happiness and sense of well-being requires having a voice in the relationship. Putting off important decisions effectively cancels that voice. Hold yourself accountable and face whatever it is that must be discussed.

Steamrolling

THE SNAP

Steamrolling your partner usually backfires.

A Closer Look

You might be able to talk over your partner, wear her down, or talk him into something, but you'll likely end up losing more than you win. Steamrolling your partner backfires eventually. It is entirely normal to lobby your partner for what you want. In fact, the Gottman Institute's research found that the ability to influence your partner and the willingness to be influenced is a hallmark of a healthy marriage. Each person has a point of view, a set of beliefs, values, and priorities. Part of being a couple is to add to each other's lives and perspective. Ideally, we make better decisions and choices together than apart. The cliché that two heads are better than one has merit, and a good discussion is the best way to arrive at more options and better choices. When we have open talks that allow for new ideas, new thoughts, and new learning, we are at our best as a couple.

There is a big difference between influence and steamrolling. Influence is the capacity to persuade someone to consider your point of view and perhaps change his or her opinions or behavior through discussion. Usually, viewpoints are shared back and forth and there is no foregone conclusion. Steamrolling is using personal power to metaphorically run over the other person and, like the machine whose name the technique borrows, "flatten" that person and leave him or her without the ability to contradict, argue, or protest. Someone who has been steamrolled has lost the argument, but not with a legitimate exchange of opinions. The steamroller leaves no room for the other person to argue a point or win the exchange. The other person loses the argument but may be seething inside because he or she never had a chance to be heard. They may do what they have to do, but it is because they have to—not because they had a choice.

When people have dominance in the relationship, they "rule"—they make the rules to suit themselves, and they are the only person in the relationship whose opinion counts. They are the authority and their authority is all that matters and they will prevail, regardless of what it takes. Their motto is "My way or the highway."

Healthy relationships are based on an exchange of ideas or thoughts. Steamrolling is dominance, eventually creating cycles of rage, agitation, depression, and often the desire to leave. One partner may submit to avoid conflict and aggravation, but if this if the usual pattern on all issues in the relationship, the result is almost always unhappiness.

The Situation
Ripples

Aurora, twenty-seven, works as an intake coordinator in a pediatric hospital. She is a very caring and attentive parent to two girls. Which preschool her daughters will attend is very important to her, and it is her habit to make decisions about the kids' schools and then inform Alexis rather than discuss things with him first. Alexis, twenty-nine, works in state government as a computer engineer and prides himself on the ability to use the Internet to find trustworthy information. When he tries to ask questions or raise the possibility of alternatives about schools based on his research, Aurora is more than ready with a torrent of reasons why the one she has picked is the way to go. Alexis respects her, but feels shut down, partly because he is not as articulate or quick as she is to formulate his point of view. Even though he's done research and is often more informed about early childhood education than Aurora is, he gets shut down. He is particularly frustrated because her sources are generally from her friends' experiences, television programs, and bloggers, and not as much from the literature or research he has gathered. More important than the source of information is that he feels shut out of important decisions about his children's lives and he has started to take Aurora on, but it turns ugly when he contests one of her decisions. She ups the ante and starts yelling and accusing him of not trusting her.

Blasts

Olivia is just shy of her fortieth birthday, and she has earned quite a bit of respect for her work in human resources in a major software company. She is no shrinking violet, but when she wants to talk about the family's investments or how to plan for long-term dispersal of funds, such as retirement or the kid's educational fund, she is met by a lecture that totally shuts her down. Her husband, Frank, forty-seven, is an accountant with a mid-sized firm and he believes he has the right and expertise to control their financial planning. He is willing, he thinks, to discuss investments and planning with Olivia, but it's really not a discussion. He lectures her on budgets and spreadsheets, and if she makes any suggestions, he grills her on her "data." He is often unwittingly condescending and insulting to her, and once he starts talking, she has to fight to get even a few sentences in.

At the end of a discussion, she has not only made no headway with her opinions, but most of her opinions on the matter have not even been fully voiced. She is really angry about his controlling behavior, his treatment of her, and the fact that this is about her money, too. He actually refers to their joint money as "my money" and he feels because he earns more than she does and because he considers himself an expert, he really doesn't have to respect what she says on the topic. He considers these discussions an annoyance and he gives the same lecture to her every time. He thinks she's willfully resistant to the good economic guidance he provides (he quips that she's his "worst client"), so he does what he believes is right on their discretionary funds and doesn't give it a second thought after that. She is steaming mad and hurt, and sometimes, she just hates him.

The Doctors' Advice

We know that sharing influence, or arguing for what you want, is normal and healthy. We don't think of power as a 50-50 game; we also recognize that power is fluid in a good relationship. Sometimes one of you gets your way and sometimes the other, and other times you come up with something entirely different from where you started.

When one person "rules" by steamrolling over the other, he or she is dominating the other person, and we have heard more than a few people say their partner "left me with no room to breathe." Sometimes that's a metaphor and sometimes it seems like an accurate description of someone sucking up all the oxygen in the room. If you feel your partner has not only sucked up all the air time in a "conversation" but also leaves you gasping for air, the relationship is seriously out of whack.

We have two very different levels of steamrolling here, but what they share in common is this: One partner is dismissive and totally ignores what his or her partner is saying and only allows conversation to take place that fits his or her point of view. By dominating the topic and your partner, claiming all expertise and not listening, you have denied your partner dignity and deprived the relationship of teamwork and synergy. What could be more contemptuous than thinking your partner has nothing to contribute to a conversation?

Aurora has claimed too much territory. Her husband is being cut out from having influence over his own children. She believes that she wants and values his opinion, but her rolling monologue leaves him no space to contribute. He needs to tell her, because she's not going to see what she's doing unless he does. Her style of argument makes it impossible for his opinion to be heard. His verbal style is slower and more intellectual and he needs time to get his thoughts out. Aurora needs to learn to slow down her response and if that's hard for her to remember or to do, then they can set a timer for each person's delivery of what they want to say. It could be five-minute segments (which is pretty long, actually) or whatever time frame feels natural. But they need to make time for BOTH people to contribute.

Frank is a bulldozer. He probably is like that outside of, as well as in the home, but it is having a deleterious effect in his marriage. His wife thinks he is an arrogant bully. She has been withdrawing from any meaningful conversation with him. Yes, he has expertise, but this is a relationship and Olivia isn't even allowed to vote her own "stock." Frank is making her feel like a lowly employee, not a partner. This is an issue of serious magnitude, both because of how it makes her feel about him and because it's her future too, she should have the right to contribute to its welfare. Olivia needs to tell him the truth: That even though she realizes he has expertise, she still needs to have a real voice in making choices about her money and her future. She can say she feels the marriage is in trouble, and that if they can talk differently to one another about this and other topics, she could retrieve her feelings of love and affection for him. She should write out a list of her understanding of their current financial situation and she should ask him to make a list of the information he has about their income, investments, retirement, and cash flow. Then they can talk about one item at a time for ten-minute sessions once a day so things stay simpler and it is truly a dialogue in which questions can be asked and opinions give by both parties.

The talk could go a bit like this:

OLIVIA: *I need to have several conversations with you about our financial life. I have tried to understand our investment strategy, our insurance policies, and a number of other things, and you shut me down. It's making me very angry.*

FRANK: *Well, you are getting yourself upset. It's my area of expertise; leave it alone—it's not an area of strength for you.*

OLIVIA: *Whatever your opinion is of my financial acumen, I need to understand how my money—our money—is being invested and what decisions are being made and I won't take no for an answer. I want to set out a list of questions and I want to talk.*

FRANK: *We do talk.*

OLIVIA: *No, just you talk. And I am so angry about it that it is hurting our relationship. I need to be able to contribute, ask questions, and agree to decisions without being interrupted or treated like an idiot.*

FRANK: *I don't treat you like an idiot.*

OLIVIA: *My perception and feeling is that you do—and I need it to stop.*

FRANK: *Can't you just let me do this?*

OLIVIA: *No, I can't, and if we don't start talking about it in a civil way we are going to need a marriage therapist because I walk around here sometimes just crazy angry after you have lectured me like I'm a three-year-old.*

FRANK: *O.K., O.K., if you don't like how we talk now, how do you want to proceed?*

OLIVIA: *I have some written guidelines for our conversation. Can we start tonight?*

There are power dynamics in every relationship. Influence is the best power-sharing style for couples. It places a high value on an exchange of thoughts and ideas between equals. Both people have room to breathe and grow, making each other and their relationship better.

Chapter 20

Learning to Engage

THE SNAP

Log in to life: Be present and engaged with your partner.

A Closer Look

Have connection without distraction. Connection is one ingredient that every relationship must have to be viable. Being connected is like being attached to each other. For connection to happen, couples have to link themselves through shared meaning, shared emotions, shared experiences, and shared values, among other possibilities.

Connection to one another and developing "us" means making contact on many levels—socially, intellectually, physically, emotionally, and spiritually. These connections grow and change and have to be rebooted now and then. Rebooting means staying close and engaged so you can make your updates regularly.

You'll see couples having dinner together, but really, they're on their phones, sending texts, or opening up websites to show each other. There is no exchange of the senses, no touch, no eye contact, nothing sensual at all. It is hard for us to imagine a lively, loving, sensual relationship conducted through surfing the Internet.

Connection requires talking, touching, smelling, hearing, and seeing each other; so far that doesn't happen over the Internet. We believe that technology is demeaning the person you love. Turn off the web and turn on your partner.

The Situation
Ripples

Helena and Caden, a young Seattle couple, are both well situated in the tech world. Helena loves all forms of technology, especially games she can play against herself like Sudoku and Spider Solitaire. Part of her job is to develop game ideas and that sometimes involves solving some technical puzzles or finding out if someone else's game can really be played. She loves the challenge and so she is usually experimenting with some kind of programming morning, noon, and night. That's all well and good except it has, according to Caden, started to cut into their available time.

Caden works in technology, but he is less obsessive about his work. He works on the business side of the massive firm that employs them both. He figures out partnerships that would be worthwhile for his firm to make. When he leaves the office at six, he puts it behind him until the next day and he would like Helena to do that as well. But just the opposite happens. Helena can't seem to stop thinking about, responding to, and actually doing her work no matter where she is.

She always has her tablet with her. Whatever they are doing and whomever they are with, she takes out her tablet and plays a game or makes notes. She will even take out her tablet in the middle of a dinner party. If Caden objects, she says, "Just let me finish this. You can all go ahead and talk." It didn't bother him at first, but now he considers her gaming obsessive and her treatment of him downright rude.

Blasts

Sylvia and Jack are fifty-five and fifty-eight, respectively. They have been together twenty years, but they never married. Jack lost a lot of money during a knock-down, drag-out divorce in his thirties and after that he had no taste for legal entanglements. Sylvia was sort of a hippie in her twenties and she never liked the idea of being trapped in a marriage mainly because it would have been too expensive to divorce. Occasionally they talk about getting married because they feel married. But they never quite get around to it.

They both travel for work. Sylvia is a sales representative for a commercial lighting company. Jack sells exotic cars and travels sporadically throughout the world looking for rare cars for his clients.

They often travel the world together, and in the "old" days when they only had home phones, no one could reach them. They both liked that because most of the time their idea of a vacation was to find sun and sand and have sex as much as possible. They have a similar libido and sex was daily, at least in the beginning of their relationship. Even today, they have sex almost every other day. Jack speaks fondly about Sylvia's "prodigious sexual appetite" and jokes that he had to be with this woman because "she was the only woman who could keep up with him." Sylvia and Jack both gush about each other and what a wonderful relationship they have, but there is one thing that Sylvia hates.

Sylvia hates, really hates, the way Jack uses his phone at home and when they're out together. If his phone rings, he answers it, whether it's in the car, in the kitchen, or in bed. He has answered his phone even when they've started making love. He often says, "It will only be a moment," but that's rarely the case. She feels insulted and she has told her therapist it makes her feel that she might as well not be there.

Jack feels Sylvia is being too harsh and too selfish. He has told her repeatedly that "high-end sales are a service job." After one extremely upsetting evening together when Sylvia felt insulted because of the number of times Jack took phone calls, he growled at her that he sells high-end cars to high-end people and those people expect service. He says if he doesn't respond to their phone calls immediately, they became disenchanted with him in a matter of hours and treat him badly or even go to another agency. He has tried to tell her that he really has to be totally present with these clients, and her comeback is often, "Well, just remember I also need you to be present!"

The Doctors' Advice

We are sure that to be a couple you have to have a connection to each other. Connection can happen socially, emotionally, physically, sexually, mentally, or spiritually—the more areas where you find intimacy, the better.

Caden has a point about being disconnected from his partner. When technology interferes with couple activities he feels unimportant, and that her valuing their relationship less than her gaming is disrespectful—and it is. Caden needs to tell Helena how her intense gaming makes him feel invisible. He can tell her that he wants her to be more available to him in all ways. He can remind her of all the fun they have had, and how much they enjoy dining out and playing cards with friends.

When he reminds her of all the positive experiences they have had, she will feel wanted rather than criticized, which would make her defensive and maybe even drive her further away into her obsessive gaming. Getting someone to stop doing something they find pleasurable is not easy, but the best bet is to have them move toward something else that is pleasurable (eating out, seeing entertainment, etc.) rather than feeling punished by having to give something up (gaming). Couples can work toward change but should not police one another. That kind of oversight is insulting and demeaning and would likely create resentment or deception.

So Caden can tell Helena that he would like to schedule some activities together and put them on the calendar. For example, he would like to take a walk with her after dinner so they have a chance to catch up on each other's days and what's happening. He can also tell her that it is important to him that she banish the phone from the bedroom. He wants to go to bed together, rather than fall asleep long before she is through with all her emails. He misses the feeling of contentment he used to feel when they cuddled before falling asleep. Also, he worries about her personal sleep patterns because she stays up so late. Even when she stays up until all hours of the night, she still gets up at the same time in the morning that he does.

If she went to bed with him, he would know how much sleep she is actually getting. That would reassure him because he worries she is not getting enough sleep.

In the case of Sylvia and Jack, Sylvia has to feel empowered to solve this problem—and she can be. They usually have breakfast together in the morning, so this is a good time to tell him what she wants.

> SYLVIA: *When we have time that is physically or emotionally intimate, I want your phone turned off. That means if we're out to dinner together, or with friends, the phone is off. I'm not alone in these feelings: Most restaurants suggest that people shouldn't use their phones while dining. And I really want the phone off in our bedroom. I feel like that should be self-evident.*
>
> JACK: *Sure, that's just fine, I'll turn it off and miss a client, lose a sale. Then we will really be intimate. That's a great idea, Sylvia, just great.*
>
> SYLVIA: *I want the phone off when we're out to dinner and when we're in bed. I think that's reasonable.*
>
> JACK: *It's not about being reasonable. If I turn it off, I forget to turn it back on, and you know, a lot of these calls are business and they are time sensitive. I have to protect our income. I don't know if I can do that.*
>
> SYLVIA: *O.K., you can do what you want. But I don't want to be subjected to this and I want you to know that it makes me think that you'd rather talk to the person on the phone than talk to me, even when it's our intimate time.*
>
> JACK: *Well, I don't want you to feel that way. But I'll try it. You've got to help me remember to turn the phone back on, though.*
>
> SYLVIA: *Agreed.*

Although this might seem like a small infraction in his relationship with Sylvia, it is actually a deal breaker. It is an insult to Sylvia and to their relationship. Beyond that, we think it is sad that Jack is missing out on being with someone who really enjoys him and wants to have a good time with him. In fact, we could argue that his business might actually be better if he were happier and having more fun in his life.

Sylvia can make it clear to Jack that this phone is a threat without threatening him. She can remind him of what great lovers they have been, so he knows he is not about to be attacked, which would only make him more argumentative and likely to "forget" his commitment. His cell phone obsession has cooled her libido, but it would not be difficult for her to reignite it. She can tell him, "There are a lot of new toys and I would like to try some, but we have to allow time to read the instructions." We can nearly guarantee he will be eager to remember his commitment.

Technology has added much to our lives, but it has also taken a heavy toll on lasting relationships because it is increasingly difficult to resist distraction. There are so many things that phones do these days: check the weather, stocks, the score of the soccer game, the airplane gate location, or email from friends; let you play a game; even ping you when your 2007 Rhône wine is perfect to drink. Many people cannot bear to put their cell phones down, and sneak a peak almost any time. They probably could resist the siren call of email, but they don't. But resist you must. Cell phones, laptops, cameras, tablets, and other gadgets vying for attention tend to mount up and collectively compete with a relationship with a real person. Our future will most likely include more distractions, but even though we are curious animals, we need to guard our allocation of time. Otherwise, we can be more engaged with our cell than with our partner! Don't let them take you away from the most important people in your life.

We believe most people are motivated to do something positive like have fun together. It is best to offer incentives that inspire and engage each other, and make that connection something desirable.

Chapter 21

Using Touch

> **THE SNAP** ....
>
> Touch your partner before you talk about anything important.
>
> ....

A Closer Look

Touch has the power to lower blood pressure, strengthen the immune system, calm the brain, and give you a feeling of connection. That's because a touch sets off your endorphins. Endorphins are hormones that lower your risk of heart disease, strengthen the immune system, repair cells, relieve pain, and counter the affects of aging. Endorphins are created by what we do, like dancing, singing, biking, exercising, kissing, or laughing. They are also generated when we think positive thoughts and give or receive compliments.

Endorphins are nature's miracle drug for repairing both brain and body. They counteract steroids, the toxic hormones we create when we are frightened, angry, or full of anxiety. Steroids are part of the body's defense system, wired into us to create an involuntary defense when we are threatened. But they exact a cost for the sudden energy, bravery, or strength they give us. High levels of steroids every day has been linked to heart disease, cancer, stroke, accidental death, diabetes, obesity, and so on. In general, we want a life that produces steroids only under extreme conditions (flight, fight, or sometimes extreme sports) and endorphins daily!

Most important to us is how endorphins affect your relationship. Recent research by Matt Hertenstein M.D., shows that they lower your levels of cortisol (a stress hormone) and increase oxytocin, a bonding hormone. Endorphins give us a natural high. We need endorphins as part of our daily life as well as during trying times. When we keep up our endorphin levels, we are ready for whatever comes our way.

The Situation
Ripples

Jerome, thirty-one, is an assistant professor of African American studies at a small religious college. He is an intense guy, very organized, and fastidious about all parts of his life, from his clothes to his car to his orderly approach to daily tasks. He expects a lot from himself and others. His disciplined approach to his goals has served him well in graduate school and in his career. He is doing great and is up for early tenure. These same qualities, however, cause some aggravation in his relationship. For example, he gets truly annoyed when Stacey, his twenty-seven-year-old live-in girlfriend, acts less responsibly than he does. Stacey is in a demanding program in culinary school and she is pretty wiped out when she comes back to their apartment. She usually arrives home before he does and casually parks her car over the line of the parking slots that are allocated to them by their building.

Jerome's car can fit in the slot, but he can't get out of the car very easily. He has been reduced to crawling over to the passenger side and squeezing out that door a few times. He sees her lack of consideration as a character flaw, and it makes him have doubts about their relationship. Even more worrisome to him is the fact that he has mentioned it to her before, and even though he is averse to arguments, the discussion has always devolved into a series of defensive and angry accusations about which one of them is more thoughtless or has more bad habits.

Stacey, a petite and beautiful woman of mixed ancestry, has a temper, and even though Jerome prefers to base an argument on the facts and the present, not the past, they both slip into bringing up old problems and losing their cool. Most arguments end in slammed doors, with Jerome retreating to his study and Stacey crying and depressed. She regrets her part in the argument, and he regrets his, but they don't seem to be able to do better. There is a lot of love and respect between them and both of them feel bad that they aren't solving their issue better. They know this bodes badly for the future.

Blasts

Holly, thirty-eight, and Raphael, forty, are passionate people who let their tempers get the better of them rather regularly. Holly, a slim, fashionable lady with a tattoo on her right shoulder that reads "Love Is All," is pleasant all day in her job as a hairdresser; she is chatty, warm, and funny and has many clients who have been with her since she started. No one at the salon has seen Holly's temper. Raphael, her husband, also has great people skills. He needs a great personality in his job as a therapist for returning war vets who have psychological as well as physical disabilities that he helps them conquer. In his job, he is a patient cheerleader for his clients and is proud of how many gravely injured men and women he has helped on their way back into civilian life. His clients see him as a supporter who totally believes in their ability to have a great life despite very significant injuries. But Raphael is like his wife: He puts away his anger during his work but at home, when the two of them disagree on something, sparks really fly. Over their nine years of marriage, Holly has been known to throw a few hairbrushes, and Raphael has turned over some furniture.

This scares them. This is a second marriage for both of them and they really want to make it work. So the fury that sometimes erupts makes them fear that they will destroy their relationship. A recent fight that could have been avoided by simply holding hands first was over her picking up their dinner at Whole Foods instead of a less expensive local grocery. Raphael thought that she was buying brand more than budget and chided her for wasting money. Holly perceived this as an attack on how she managed all money for the family and felt that he wasn't respecting either her time or her concern for providing healthy food for both of them.

Her instant retort to his wisecrack about her "total lack of concern about how much things cost," citing pre-cut fruit as the height of irresponsibility, was to snarl, through clenched teeth, about the "crap he eats" and the fact that he's getting a "spare tire around his middle" so his "tacky clothes" don't fit anymore. That was too much for Raphael, so he went after her weight and when he mentioned saggy breasts, it became a verbal free-for-all. The feud ended with Raphael throwing a whole carton of eggs against the wall and Holly stepping over the mess in her hurry to get to the door to go over to her sister's house for the evening. They don't know how to stop the escalating tirades, but we do.

This kind of fighting is not good for them—and they know it. So, how to avoid it? It's simple, really: Reach out and hold hands.

The Doctors' Advice

Touch, if it is gentle and reassuring, will act as an immediate mood mediator, changing the climate from adversarial to collaborative and considerate. It can stop your brain from building up those steroids that foster aggression, anger, and irrational behavior. Touch can be your guardrail, keeping you from going off the deep end. The right kind of touch will allow your brain to release oxytocin, which reassures and calms each of you, allowing you to connect and bond with each other.

We believe the power of touch will help develop trust and build a platform for positive communication when more difficult discussions are needed. If there is tension between you and your partner, first prepare yourself to be calm, loving, and conciliatory. Choose a time to talk when you feel good about yourself and your partner before you touch, so that your touch is soft and bonding rather than aggressive or perfunctory. Studies show that both men and women are very accurate in assessing the emotions felt by the person touching them. So if your touch holds tension, anger, resentment, or other steroid-creating emotions, your partner will also have a hormonal reaction, taking you farther away from peace and calm. You want to send and receive the message that, whatever the issue of the moment, this is the person you love.

Touch before an important talk should not be sexual, which creates a different type of hormone that actually makes it harder to pay attention to the conversation. After a talk that goes well and you both feel close, even a bigger dose of bonding chemicals that comes with sex is great, but only if you are both feeling secure and connected. If not, give it a bit of time because pushing your partner to be close before he or she is ready will backfire and you will get a real hit of hormones, and not the good kind.

We think Jerome and Stacey do have an issue to work out, but the strong arguments are unnecessary and harmful. Yes, Jerome has a valid complaint, but the way he confronts Stacey undermines her, prevents a possible solution, and threatens their solidarity as a couple. Here is a way that touch can modify the way this gets resolved:

Jerome might say, "I can't believe you've done this again. Do you realize how hard it is for me to get out of the car?"

Stacey responds, "I try, and you don't appreciate all the times I do it right. These are tight stalls and they make it impossible, especially when the car on the other side is over the line."

At this point Jerome would normally blow up. But not this time.

What Jerome is going to do is take Stacey into his arms and give her a big hug and maybe a kiss on the forehead. He will say, "I know you try—let's go down and take a look and see what we can do to make it easier for you."

Stacey is totally disarmed by the hug and is open to following his suggestion. She can see he is not attacking her; he is joining forces with her to solve the problem! They go out the door and down to the cars, and Jerome figures out a solution. Stacey can line up better after Jerome laces a crisscross of blue tape on the wall in the middle of the space. The hug completely changed the mood, making Stacey more receptive, less defensive, and more willing to please him. Rather than Jerome being involved in an angry storm, he could think creatively and come up with a solution to help her. Sound too simple? It is simple—but hugs and hand-holding are unexpectedly effective. It would be effective for Holly and Raphael too. They have got to stop going for each other's jugular when they are mad. Things said in anger are not forgotten just because they were said in the heat of battle. Holly had trouble taking off her clothes in front of Raphael after the fight they had in which he criticized the way her body looked. Since they are both mutually upset at their own and their partner's behavior, they need to make a pact: Never discuss something when they are really angry (see Chapter 6), and when they do discuss the problem, sit facing each other, holding hands—and don't let go. This will help them remember they are joined together, that they are not fighters in a ring, no holds barred.

Sometimes simple is what works. We have talked about the biochemical aspect of our emotions, and when we recognize those spontaneous reactions are real, we can do an end run around them. By holding hands or giving a hug, people reassure each other that they are safe, that they are a team confronting a problem rather than combatants confronting each other. This team concept has a powerful and immediate effect. When you touch sweetly, you are friends, not enemies. It is pretty impossible to be really nasty when you are holding hands. It creates a bond, so if you agree not to let go, it will change the way a discussion proceeds. And the bond between you grows even stronger. If you really want to feel bonded, try to intertwine your fingers and look into your partner's eyes. Then all things are possible.

Chapter 22

Giving Compliments

THE SNAP

Compliments feed loving relationships.
Feed yours daily.

A Closer Look

Compliments are a special currency to use in your relationship; they create positive emotions in the same way touch helps release endorphins and leads to feelings of goodwill, positive emotion, and solid bonds between partners.

In the early stages of a relationship we are usually love struck, adoring, and effusive with all kinds of compliments. Compliments seem easy and obvious; you want to give them and you feel wonderful saying something loving and seeing your partner beam with pleasure. When going through those early dating dances, we instinctively flatter, engage, pursue, and seduce our mate.

Over time, however, these mating hormones subside, and what happens next is up to the thinking part of the brain. Thoughts lead to feelings and feelings lead to action. The more positive thoughts and feelings you express the better you feel, the better your partner feels, and the stronger the bond between you. But of course, feeling good about giving and receiving compliments takes some practice. Most partners want to sound and be authentic. A compliment can sound cheesy if it sounds as if it is being given for effect rather than from the heart! When compliments are given wholeheartedly, however, they usually work well. The problem is that over time, partners forget to give them often and sometimes stop giving them at all. As human beings we can decide whether we think about something in a positive light or a negative light. It is what you choose to think that determines what you feel. Think negative thoughts about your partner and you will have negative feelings. Think positive thoughts and you will have positive feelings.

Knowing how to give a compliment does take practice. All compliments are not created equal. There is a skill set you can use to learn how to give a compliment that will keep you both connected and sizzling. A compliment is a great aphrodisiac.

The Situation
Ripples

Bruno has always been an "old soul." He has been very goal oriented, even in childhood, and now he is totally committed to getting his union card in the plumbing industry. He came from a very poor family and always had to do some work that would bring in a little more money. So, from an early age, he was serious, and never had time to date. He met Shay, his wife, on her twenty-third birthday at her father's paint store, when he went in to buy some paint for a home project and she was working. He thought she was so beautiful and sweet, and he proceeded to sweep her off her feet. Three years and one baby later, Shay still works part-time at the paint store, but has started a small online discount paint shop that is producing some significant income. The twenty-six-year-olds seem to be finally paying off business debts and building a firm economic base, and that makes them both start thinking about having another child.

Some problems interfere, however, with Bruno moving forward on, as he calls it, "project new baby." Bruno is afraid that one more child will take up even more of his wife's focus and attentions, and he will get even less than he's getting now. And in Bruno's opinion, he is not getting the hugs, kisses, and admiration he needs now—and in no way does he want it to get worse.

His Philippine heritage has given him a warm and expressive personality. He is used to giving lots of compliments, and he regularly tells Shay how lovely she looks and how impressed he is with her energy, style, success, and mothering skills. Shay, however, came from a family in which compliments were far and few between, and she never learned the habit of conscientiously complimenting her husband. Actually, she feels a little uncomfortable with all the compliments he is constantly giving her because she knows she should be saying something back, but it feels inauthentic to her. She feels she should remember on her own when to compliment Bruno, except she just doesn't. Although she accepts all the nice things Bruno says to her, she rarely reciprocates and almost never initiates.

Bruno is pretty happy in his marriage. He knows Shay is a good person, but he hears her say all these sweet and flattering things to their two-year-old and is kind of jealous that the baby gets more compliments than he does. He would really blossom if she complimented him too, even just now and then. He would feel much more comfortable having another child if Shay said things to him that made him feel more important and loved.

Blasts

Zoe and Darren, both in their fifties, are in their second marriage. Zoe is a dental hygienist who has worked in the same office all her life, and Darren is a dentist. They met at a lecture at the state dentistry meetings and there was a strong attraction. They all sat around a table and talked shop and it was clear that Zoe had eyes only for Darren. They stayed together and talked all through the meeting. Both of them are cautious people, but they come from families with at least one dentist in them, and so they shared a lot right from the beginning. They fell in love pretty quickly, and she moved in with him after a couple of months. When they become a solid couple, they decided to work together, and she moved into his practice. This turned out to be a mixed blessing. The problem is that Darren is highly judgmental.

Darren is a perfectionist, and when Zoe has a different way of approaching a patient or if she takes less time than he thinks she should take with someone, he takes her aside and tells her he thinks she is taking shortcuts, or, somewhat paradoxically, spending too much time chatting with the patient instead of working steadily. What really upsets Zoe is that he rarely tells her anything good about what she has done. He considers his comments to Zoe to be objective and professional, but in Zoe's mind he is critical, and in a personal way. Zoe is upset, feeling unappreciated, and craving some recognition.

After one long day in which it seemed nothing went right, she got upset enough to knock over a tray and broke a mold of a patient's teeth. Darren chastised her in front of a long-time patient about the accident and she had to fight to keep her composure and not cry. She behaved professionally for the last two hours of the day, but when she got home she called her old office and said she wanted to go back to work there if they had an opening. She told Darren about the call when he came home, and he was flabbergasted. He couldn't believe she would leave him and his state-of-the-art office for her old position at what he considered a second-rate place. He told her, "You are letting your hypersensitivity hurt my practice, our patients, and our marriage." He gave her a short speech about how she needs to learn to develop a thicker skin. In truth, he actually thinks she is a talented and valuable hygienist and doesn't want to lose her, but he doesn't know how to keep her either.

The Doctors' Advice

The study that informs *The Normal Bar: The Surprising Secrets of Happy Couples* (coauthored by Dr. Pepper Schwartz) shows that there is a shocking shortage of compliments in American society. Only about a quarter of couples regularly compliment each other.

This looks even worse if we look at how giving compliments differs by gender. Men are far more likely to tell their partners that they love them every day than vice versa. And most men have never been complimented on how they look or dress. In addition, American couples give far fewer compliments than French, Italian, or Latin American couples, which is detrimental to their relationships.

In the case of Bruno and Shay, Bruno, is used to hearing constant compliments in his extended family and he passes this tradition on to his wife: He loves to say nice things to Shay. Shay doesn't realize that her generous behavior with her son—that does not include Bruno—makes him feel deprived and even less loved. He is embarrassed that he feels jealous of his own child, but he does. Bruno tells Shay what he's observed and that he would like some nice, flattering words said to him. He is, after all, having great success at work, is a good father, and keeps himself fit and sexy for her. She says she knows and appreciates these things, but it has never occurred to her that he needed her to say it to him. So, now she says "I love you so much" every day and then once a day thinks of something good to say, such as "You were so patient with the baby" or "You look hot today, honey." Very simple stuff, but it has made them both a lot happier.

Darren has a harder task to correct his situation because he doesn't know how to compliment Zoe or how to withhold criticism on a daily basis. He is used to saying things like "That uniform makes you look slimmer," with the implied criticism that she looks heavier in general. When she's working, he is likely to say, "You're running behind," rather than "I know you are juggling a lot and doing as well as much as humanly possible." He notices problems, but he rarely notices successes, and when he does notice, he just thinks that's the way it should be and says nothing. He is totally unaware of how harsh his responses to her can sound.

Darren is going to lose his best employee—and his wife!—if he doesn't figure out how to make her feel respected and valuable. Since he is a tough customer (nothing in this realm will come naturally to him), we have him look on the Internet for examples of compliments. Just searching for "the top ten most appreciated affirmations for couples" will give him an idea of what he should be saying.

He should take the list and say, "I am lucky to have a beautiful wife, beauty and brains in the same package," or "I am a better person because of you." He should pick two compliments that he will deliver each day. It will help him to remember to start giving her some affirmations each morning when both of them are getting ready, and pick an activity (such as when he shaves) to tell her how good she looks. He can simply look at her and say, "Wow." In the afternoon, after lunch, he can compliment her on something she did in the office. He is not being encouraged to lie; to the contrary. We want him to remember to tell her the truth, and that truth is profound: He appreciates her being in the office, and he depends on her and the high quality of her work. He can say something simple, with real gratitude, such as, "The office runs so much better now that you are here." Even if this feels artificial—which it will in the beginning—it is the only way Darren can repair the damage he has done in previous interactions when he withheld compliments but not criticism (see Chapter 9).

Darren may even have thought he was just teasing at times. Couples sometimes become more like siblings than lovers, bantering, teasing, even provoking. Although these behaviors may be fun for kids, more than a rare quip at your partner's expense will undermine intimacy with the one you love. Staying emotionally connected as lovers and equals in the relationship is far more important than creating defensiveness and anger by deciding to "mentor" your partner or hold him or her to impossibly high standards.

We highly encourage learning to compliment your partner as your lover, your friend, and your helpmate. It is fine for some compliments to be repetitive, but don't get lazy. Look at and listen to your partner in a warm and loving light. Look for what is right about them to you. Here are a few of the most popular and treasured compliments:

★ You have beautiful hair.

★ You deserve a promotion.

★ You make that sweater look great.

★ I appreciate your style.

★ You are like a spring flower, precious and beautiful.

★ I am utterly disarmed by your wit.

★ I really enjoy the way you think.

★ You make me laugh.

★ I love the feel of your skin.

★ You are looking good.

★ You smell great.

★ You look so youthful.

★ I like the way you move.

★ I am proud that I am with you!

★ You are my inspiration.

★ I like how athletic your body looks.

★ Thank you for being my best friend.

We encourage you to borrow from our list and then think of others or ask Google.

Chapter 23

Being Grateful

A Closer Look

Gratitude is the best gift you can give yourself and everyone around you. Recently, scientists found that the inward and outward expression of thankfulness leads directly to happiness. And since we believe it takes two happy people to make one happy relationship, it is important to learn how to be grateful.

Gratitude *is* a skill you can learn to increase your happiness and your partner's. And happiness is a goal the world over. So if simple acts of gratitude lead you to happiness in yourself and in your relationship, why wouldn't you make the effort to practice it?

Gratitude is another opportunity to create endorphins for your partner and yourself. In the late 1990s, psychologist Martin Seligman, University of Pennsylvania professor and author of *Authentic Happiness, Learned Optimism*, led studies focusing on happiness as something to be learned, not something people are born with. Seligman has said, "As a professor, I don't like this, but the cerebral virtues—curiosity, love of learning—are less strongly tied to happiness than interpersonal virtues like kindness, gratitude and capacity for love." Gratitude, or being thankful for your life and for those around you, leads to happiness, and all you have to do is learn to be grateful and intentional and practice thinking of yourself as grateful and happy.

The Situation
Ripples

Every morning Liam, a sixty-eight-year-old retired Air Force pilot, gets up early to take his dog, Maggie, to Starbucks and gets not one, but two coffees. It is his habit to bring one cup to Abigail, and he times his own coffee and walk so he can get her coffee to her at precisely the time she gets up. Abigail, sixty-three, is still working as a high school counselor, and she appreciates the gesture, knowing it is a way for him to show her he is thinking about her. She has told him that what she really wants is a non-fat latte. But since Liam doesn't approve of what he calls the "ridiculous prices they charge for a latte," he brings her regular coffee with milk in it. Abigail appreciates the coffee and realizes this is a gift from him, but would really like a latte once in a while.

Blasts

Antonia, forty, and Manny, forty-one, have been married twenty years, and during that time their work life has changed a lot. They first knew each other in high school and got married the year after high school graduation. Antonia initially wanted to go into medicine and now enjoys her job as a nurse practitioner in a hospital. She doesn't mind her demanding schedule, even though she works long days and, sometimes, long nights as well. She is proud of what she has accomplished and so is Manny.

Manny is a quite successful stylist. He and Antonia agreed that because he can control his time more than she can, he should take care of household tasks when her career doesn't allow her to do her fair share. They have shared values about housework: They try to divide jobs according to who has what time available. Since Manny has a flexible schedule with frequent gaps, he is happy to make sure there is food in the refrigerator and that the cats are fed. Over the years, this division of time and labor has meant that the shopping and cleaning are mainly Manny' s responsibilities and he has learned how to efficiently manage most of the household's practical needs. Antonia helps when she can. But Manny has begun to feel that the division of their labor has become unbalanced over the years. Antonia has done less and less and now rarely spends even 25 percent of the time that he does on household maintenance. Manny understands that her job has become even more hectic since the hospital is so understaffed. But still, it has been a long time since Antonia really took care of the house, shopping, cleaning out drawers and closets, and attending to the various things that make a house a home, and Manny feels like he is now the sole reason their daily life together functions at all.

Manny is usually happy to create a nice environment for both of them, but he thinks Antonia has lapsed into taking his work for granted. He notices that she seldom gives him what he considers to be heartfelt thanks. Sure, she says "thank you" now and then, but it seems lightly tossed off. He thinks she doesn't remember what it takes to manage the house and he has a suspicion she is seeing him as less than an equal partner. He was kind of shocked recently when he got home early, unloaded the dishwasher, cleaned up the kitchen from the night before and prepared a special dinner for them (her favorite, stir-fried shrimp and cashews), and set a nice table, only for Antonia to come in and barely notice how clean and neat everything was and only briefly comment on how good the dinner was. He had expected some lavish praise and maybe some romance, but instead he thought she acted as if she were "entitled" to this kind of treatment. Then she made an announcement that she was taking on more hours at work.

He feels she no longer understands what it takes to do his "second job" and that she has become spoiled and self-important. He doesn't want to do any more housework than he is doing already; in fact, her attitude is making him want to do less.

The Doctors' Advice

We recommend prioritizing happiness as a way of life. And one very direct pathway to happiness is gratitude. Expressing gratitude comes naturally to some of us, but unfortunately it is not always instinctual. That said, the ability to show and feel gratitude can also be learned as a skill—and it needs to be. Giving gratitude is so important: It adds warmth to the emotional climate of any household. Giving and receiving it can make your own heart expand and your partner's expression glow. Sometimes it really is as simple as a few words and a grateful look, and those endorphins start flowing.

Liam and Abigail's story is very instructive. Liam is a sweetie, but he wants to get Abigail what he wants to get her. He knows Abigail wants a latte, but he thinks coffee is good enough and that it's ridiculous to spend the extra three dollars for some foamy milk. So he ignores her requests, but he likes doing a favor for her in the morning and he wants her to know that he is thinking of her. Because she prefers lattes, she is disappointed. But should she be? We might be divided on this one. Dr. Pepper feels she is entitled to get the damn latte and be the princess that she is. Yet Dr. Lana feels that she should be grateful for his gesture and the fact that he is being thoughtful. Dr. Lana wins. Why? Because if Abigail's "standards" keep her from appreciating the gesture Liam can give, there is less overall gratitude being shown. And we both do agree that anything that helps create more gratitude is helpful to a relationship.

When your partner is making an effort to please you, that's more important than getting exactly what you want. If your partner brings you coffee, but not the latte you wanted, smile and say "thank you." It is the thought that counts. If you really have to have a latte, get it yourself, discreetly.

In the case of Manny and Antonia, Manny is right. Saying "thanks" is not enough when a partner puts out extraordinary time and effort. If something becomes very routine, it is easy to discount it or expect it, but that's not the way to make a partner feel appreciated. Just because someone does something for you all the time doesn't diminish its importance. This kind of day-in-and-day-out effort requires a complimentary paragraph every so often, at least every week. "Thanks" feels perfunctory, and no "thank you" should feel that way.

What Antonia should say to Manny is the following: "It's so nice to come home and find the house so clean and food in the refrigerator and a handsome husband in the kitchen. What would I do without you?" There are many ways to give a worthy compliment, but it must always be proportional to the effort; anything less won't do. All it takes is thinking ahead and surveying the situation so your comments are sincere and have depth.

It's surprising but true that if you practice being lavish with appreciation, your verbal acknowledgments of great treatment start to get mirrored by your partner. Your partner will thank you more than before, and pretty soon there is a significant increase in mutual praise, making a real difference in the culture of the household. Gratitude then begins to be a core value in the way you both approach the world, which has a terrific impact on overall happiness. You start to see the gifts of everyday life more. You are more likely to remark on the sunrise or sunset, your partner's smile, or a small act of kindness, or just express gratitude to be together for another day.

If greeting the world with gratitude is hard for you to do, a great tool is a daily gratitude journal. The first step is to take five minutes to write three good things that happened in the day, and the next day tell your partner. (Tip: Include something they did as one of the three good things!)

Do this same exercise each day with your partner: Make notes on your smart phone when you remember a moment that made you smile or something your partner did that made your day better. Then get used to saying something about it out loud. The recognition of gratitude is the first step; the second step is expressing it. Say specifically what it is you are grateful for, and how it pertains to you: "Thank you for cleaning up the dishes; that meant a lot to me. Your cleaning up the living room gave me a chance to recover from a hard day. I feel much more relaxed now." Notice this is a paragraph, not a sentence.

Expressing gratitude is a form of giving back, especially to your partner. For example, if your partner put gas in your car, a "thank you" is necessary, but take it a step further and offer to do something special for him or her. Just highlight your feeling of gratitude and your pleasure in giving back. These exchanges of gratitude and reciprocity endow you, your partner, and your relationship with a new level of kindness and well-being. It becomes easy and automatic with practice. We know it feels awkward or artificial in the beginning, but it won't feel forced when those endorphins kick in and you both feel loved and treasured.

Chapter 24

Forecast Your Future

THE SNAP

If you see the present well enough, it will tell you about the future.

A Closer Look

You don't need a crystal ball, a fortune-teller, or a therapist to know what is going to happen next in your relationship. If you are aware of yourself and your partner, you will know that most future outcomes are predictable given past behaviors.

There are ways in which we can change and other ways we cannot. We all have some personality characteristics that are the bedrock of how we think and act in the world. Although we are capable of behavior modification over time, our personalities are rarely totally redesigned. There are characteristics that don't change at all for most people. For example, some research has asserted that the need for order, a state in which everything is in its correct or appropriate place, is an inborn personality characteristic; that is, it is hardwired in the brain. A person with a high need for order may want the bed made perfectly everyday and all clothing hung in the closet with all the hangers facing the same direction and each color segregated from the other. A person with a low need for order may not even see or care whether the bed is made, and the clothing can be in the closet or not. If two partners are on opposite sides of the continuum on this characteristic, each person can make modifications to accommodate the other, but the root difference will still be there.

The Situation
Ripples

Monika, forty, is an environmental engineer who's happily married to Soren, an architect. They get along well, except for one subject: guns. Soren, forty-two, grew up hunting with his father in Sweden and these are happy memories for him. He is comfortable with guns, has shot in competitions, and has a hobby collection of different kinds of rifles. He likes the fact that there is constitutional protection for the right to bear arms. His defense of the right to carry a gun makes Monika crazy. She hates the idea of hunting animals, feels that guns cause harm rather than provide protection, and wants guns to be highly regulated. When some crime spree is reported on TV, which is often, there is a predictable blowup. Monika says, "See, that's what guns are doing to our society," and he goes into a lecture on the importance of the Second Amendment, the prevalence of responsible gun ownership, and why you wouldn't want only criminals to have guns. This same conflict happens regularly.

Blasts

If you met Susanna, thirty-five, you'd first notice what she was wearing. She is always experimenting with high-concept clothes, and being a tall, dark beauty, she always looks chic and attractive. She works part-time in a high-fashion clothing store downtown, and she can't entirely control which days and what time of day she will be working. These irregular hours are inconvenient, but she loves her job and her customers. She is working hard to advance her knowledge of fashion, marketing, and design, and hopes to have her own store someday. When she doesn't have a customer, she is researching trends, suggesting what to order, and calling customers whom she thinks might like something she has just gotten in. She can get so focused on what she is doing with a customer, or reading industry magazines, that she completely loses any sense of time.

This makes her life even more complicated. She lives forty-five minutes away from San Francisco with her partner of seven years, Norris, thirty-nine, who is a successful entrepreneur. Norris is a gregarious guy who often wants to entertain people who are interested in investing in his computer programs. Although he and Susanna have been together seven years, he is undecided about whether they will make it long term because her repeated lateness makes him worry about her ability to be responsible, and it also embarrasses him.

There have been a few client dinners that really created a crisis between them. Susanna had promised to bring home wine and vodka, and when she was very late, there was nothing to offer the guests. Norris thinks of himself as something of a wine expert and normally he would have had a supplementary stash, but they had just moved and he didn't have a place for wine yet. People were gracious, but he was really upset about it and then, when time dragged on and he had to do all the prep work by himself, he worked himself into a really angry mood. By the time Susanna arrived she was a full hour late, and everyone was through the first course. Of course, she was her usual visually arresting, sweet, and entertaining self when she joined the party, but Norris was so mad that all he could see was that she was a flake. Since then he wonders if he is wasting valuable time with Susanna because even though he loves her, he has lost a lot of respect for her and he worries that she doesn't have it in her to be a responsible life partner. He also wonders if her lack of responsiveness to his request for a timely entrance is in some way an attempt to undermine his career. He is undecided about whether or not this behavior should be a deal breaker.

The Doctors' Advice

You're predictable. Your partner is predictable. And your exchanges have their own patterns and rhythms. Sometimes they are intractable patterns and rhythms, and you both know it. Personality characteristics don't change much, if at all.

So if you know what's going to happen and it isn't good, why are you testing it again? Do you really want to go down a road that's a dead end? Why do you insist on finding it out again and again? If you are doing this, don't you realize it's a bit insane?

Of course, you see your partner's patterns that annoy you as something you would like to change, but most of these qualities have an upside as well as a downside.

For instance, a person with a high need to be part of a group or organization can benefit the relationship by creating experiences with other people, but if your need for affiliation is low, you will feel overwhelmed by the sheer volume of opportunities. It is not likely this need is going change for either of you, so there is no point in fighting it.

Recognizing that such things are, for the most part, wired in, let's assume that at least in some areas, you can predict with a high level of accuracy what each of you will want in the future. With that knowledge you can create a plan that allows both of you to get your needs met. You know a lot about your partner; you know what brings out the best and what brings out the worst in each other. So use what you know to avoid pitfalls and make life smoother and happier.

Soren and Monika should just stop talking about guns. Whether it's hunting or gun control, their dialogue is going nowhere. They know their positions, and they aren't going to change. They don't really need to have this discussion ever again. It's O.K. to disagree on something, and it's appropriate to leave it alone. They do not have children, so there is no need to discuss a gun cabinet or a household gun policy. They don't have to personally resolve the debate—and in fact, there is no chance that they can do that. So keep the family peace and pleasure on the myriad things they do share and like about each other.

Susanna's lateness is no fun for either one of them. To Norris she is out of control and obviously doesn't know how to fix it, and despite his many complaints she continues to be late. Susanna is passionate about her career, so much so that she gets completely absorbed when she is at work. Building a clientele and creating a brand are both hard work, and she may be well suited to the world of high fashion. Norris can either accept this as something that enlivens his partner's life and keeps her creative or he can rethink whether or not he wants someone who is deeply immersed in her career.

If Norris really loves Susanna, he has to accept the fact that she's closer to being a workaholic than a housewife and plan accordingly. So if he's hosting a client dinner during the week, or even on Friday nights, it's better for him to do that alone. Trying to do something during the week, when she is working, is setting them up for failure and ultimately that is proving drastically dangerous for the relationship. As for friends, Norris can suggest that they get together for something informal, like ordering pizza. If that proves difficult, then Norris and Susanna can do things with friends that are already in progress, like a cocktail party. Norris loves Susanna, and he has to decide if all that is a trade-off he can make. If so, then he has to accept the whole package.

There are some qualities your partner can change but typically cannot change who they are. We have not seen many people who are chronically late become punctual. It's even less likely that messy people become highly organized. (Unless they hire someone to do it for them—that is not a bad idea!) We all have patterns—some reflect the way our brain is wired, and others come from life lessons—but we all have our predilections. You can reduce conflict and increase affection and intimacy by being aware of and practical about your partner's habits and personality and planning accordingly.

Chapter 25

Argument Escalation

THE SNAP

Escalating an argument is a bad habit;
nip it in the bud.

A Closer Look

Don't up the ante and increase the risk of damaging your relationship by escalating an argument to the point of causing pain. A conversation that starts off as mildly adversarial can fall quickly into a battle or full-blown war because one or both of you start building your case, using past misdeeds as ammunition. An accusation on one side leads to an accusation on the other, and pretty soon harsh, ugly words are flying back and forth. It can happen in heartbeat. The angrier you get, the more your entire hormonal system goes into gear and sends you into fight mode. At this point you are incapable of going back to square one, which was much less angry and far more rational.

It is inevitable that when one of you ups the ante with furious words or threats, the charged atmosphere will trigger your partner's emotions. This is the mirror image of triggering your partner's response in a positive way by your smile, support, or physical closeness. At times, aggression happens suddenly; a partner is silently stewing about something and suddenly explodes. You will feel like you stepped on a land mine without warning when your partner goes off at you. The "natural response" is to reciprocate: anger met with anger, hurt met with hurt, fear met by fear. We suggest you use the thinking part of your brain instead to take you in a better direction.

156

The Situation
Ripples

Amelia is a tiny, very slender young woman who initially trained to be a ballet dancer. When dancing eventually became too stressful for her, she went into teaching and is very happy that she did. She is twenty-four now, working as a tutor at a private school and living with Oliver, twenty-nine, who works for a head-hunting firm. The two of them care very much about their small but stylish apartment and both dress very carefully and very well. Looks matter to both of them and they are proud of each other's fine appearance. They recently bought a dog together, a Havanese, and Oliver took the puppy to the groomer and without much instruction asked the groomer to get rid of the mats and give Zorro a trim. The groomer gave the Havanese a poodle cut. When Oliver brought Zorro home, Amelia flipped out. Her masculine little dog now looked like a girl poodle, and she was beside herself.

"How could you do this to him?" she snapped at Oliver, tears running down her cheeks.

"What do you mean?" Oliver replied, aghast at her attitude.

"You made him look like a different dog. I can't stand it."

Oliver thought Amelia was just being dramatic and that she would resign herself to the cut, but Amelia just kept getting sadder and madder, even after hours had passed. Every time she looked at Zorro, she got more upset. Oliver really thought Amelia had gone off the deep end. Finally, he lost it himself and said, "Take care of your own damn dog." Amelia had whipped herself up over this "catastrophe" and couldn't let go. She continued, "I will—because I can't count on you to do even a simple thing like getting the dog the right haircut." Oliver stomped off, slamming the door. Sundown did not improve the situation. They slept in different beds that night, Amelia and Zorro in the bedroom, and Oliver on the couch. The next morning was frosty, too.

Blasts

Ines, fifty-one, and Noah, fifty-two, have been married for eight years. Ines has her own green business that involves hemp; she has been a hemp enthusiast since college days and she is excited about finally doing something real with her conviction that hemp could be used for multiple products. She and Noah work out of their home. They own a small building and Noah makes and sells fine furniture on the street-level part of the building, and they live in the two other floors. They spend a lot of time together most days, and that suits them just fine. They really enjoy conferring about their business issues and taking breaks and having conversations. It's surprising that people who like each other's company so much could get into such hot-blooded fights, but they do.

The problem is that both of them have mothers in their mid-eighties and both of their mothers are quite combative. During the most recent holiday, the mothers came to visit at the same time and the scene became inflammatory. If one mother said it was a nice day, the other said it was going to rain. And each mother subtly and not-so-subtly indicated why her precious child could have done better. After the mothers left, the couple sat down with glasses of wine, intending to recuperate and relax. But that didn't happen.

Noah said, "Your mother always has to be right."

Ines was immediately miffed—she didn't know why Noah had said something so incendiary. She took the bait and replied, "Are you kidding? Compared to your mother, my mom is a saint."

Noah laughed, "What? Are you crazy? Your mother is an absolute terror. I think she pocketed the change I left on the table."

At which point, Ines really felt insulted and said, "How dare you! She probably thought the money was hers. Perhaps you're forgetting that your mother wet our bed and I had to change the sheets."

Noah asked, "Why are you being such a bitch?"

Ines, "Bitch? You called me a bitch! I promised myself I would never endure that kind of name calling again. My mother said you would be like this. I'm done."

Noah said, "So leave if you don't want to be here."

At that point, they both exited the room and Ines cried in confusion. *How did we get here?* She wondered.

The Doctors' Advice

One of the most important talents that a couple can learn is how to argue. There are a few simple instructions that can go a long way toward keeping things fair, balanced, and constructive. The most important rule is to stay on topic. The second most important rule is to handle the topic without insulting or offending the other person. Amelia was shocked at the dog's appearance, but she should have just stayed in that moment of shock, taken a deep breath, and asked for a minute to regroup. She should not have jumped to blame. Instead, she should have asked Oliver, "What happened?"

Asking for more information when you are upset is always a good idea. "What happened to our dog?" is better than "What did you do to him?" Oliver also could have stopped the escalation by saying, "He does look pretty funny, doesn't he?" If that attempt at lightness failed, he could apologize to her—and probably to Zorro as well. At the very least he could have said, "You have a right to be upset. I just didn't know what to do about it." Or he could say, "You know, I didn't do this—the groomer did." In other words, he could deflect her anger and stop the escalation.

Ines and Noah are in a more precarious situation, having just managed a difficult visit. They were more emotionally raw than they recognized and adding a glass of alcohol might not have helped. If you up the ante in an argument by throwing in threats and innuendo, you're likely to make your fears come true. We create our fears by making threats, promises, and punishments. You know what you are saying is probably wrong, and your anger is screwing things up even while you are doing it, so stop it!

In this case, Noah threw the first punch by insulting Ines's mother. Under other circumstances, she might have agreed with him, but now she feels the need to show her loyalty to her family. How could they have stopped this escalation?

For starters, don't discuss tough stuff when you are tired. When Noah brought up the first barb, Ines could have said, "I don't want to talk about this now. I'm exhausted and I just want to wind down and have a nice evening with you!" Deflect by changing the subject, or change the tone with a smile or a touch, even an embrace. Communication might not be in order when feelings are tender, so suggest a movie or something that is totally unrelated to the past week.

Noah could have salvaged this argument, too, as soon as he realized he had said something inflammatory. Research indicates that a quick "Let me take that back" or "Honey, I am so sorry I said that" is generally effective at stopping a battle from starting. Whatever you can do to avoid escalation, do it—even if means leaving the room for a while. It's fine to make up a reason to cool off, as simple as, "I have to use the bathroom." This gives you the chance to get back in charge of your emotions and have a civilized conversation with your partner. Your goal is to have a conversation that ends on a friendly note.

We also want to remind you that reaching an agreement is not the point of an argument. There is a lot of research, as well as our own experience, indicating that people in relationships have to reframe what they expect out of a disagreement. You are NOT looking for agreement; you are looking for an understanding of each other's thoughts, beliefs, values, or emotions. Arguments should ultimately help you know your partner better, giving you the opportunity to find ways to work together and to work around the areas where you don't come together.

Chapter 26

Protect Your Partner's Flank

THE SNAP

As a couple you are a team. Look out for each other.

A Closer Look

Being part of a couple has similarities to being part of a team; it comes with responsibilities. As a team member, you look out for the good of the team, you behave in ways that enhance the team, and you do your best at the job you are assigned. The same is true of being a partner. Being part of a couple with someone you love comes with obligations, and one of those responsibilities—perhaps the most important one—is looking out for each other. This is part of your marital vow (or its equivalent in a nonmarital but committed relationship). Regardless of what you think or feel at any one time, you, as the popular saying goes, "have your partner's back." That is true regardless of who is present, even if it is other people you admire and are close to. You never knowingly embarrass your partner. You never publically side with a close friend over your partner, except perhaps in trivial ways, such as preferring one movie to another. Your partner should never have to worry that you will undercut him or her in front of strangers, friends, coworkers, or family, or anyone else.

There are two especially sticky parts to this commitment to protecting your partner's flank. First, when you don't agree with your partner, when you think he or she is dead wrong, or maybe inappropriate, it can be hard to have your partner's back. We recognize this is tough, but the right call is to back your partner, your

161

teammate. It is perfectly appropriate and necessary that you talk about what happened at a time when you can both be calm and listen and understand each other's point of view. You can disagree on what's important and what happened, but you do it in private.

The second sticky part is the "who." You might think your partner is fair game if he or she is being teased or ridiculed by siblings or a parent, but no. Always, always put your partner first.

In fact, families and friends can be most cruel in bringing up the past in a way that is humiliating, and no one wants to be humiliated, even if they may try to laugh it off. More subtle but perhaps more harmful are labels from the past, such as "She was always the crazy one" or "He always had two left feet." These labels are ancient history and have no merit in the present and no business in your relationship. They do harm. Be loyal to the one you love; everyone else is an outsider. These are important boundaries that define you as a couple.

The Situation
Ripples

Summer is a forty-seven-year-old party planner, and her husband Sean, forty-eight, is a police officer. He is a "guy's guy," and he and his buddy are always kidding with each other in an aggressive fashion. They like telling stories about each other's screw-ups and they all find it hysterical to embarrass the friend who is the butt of the jokes. Sean takes the same approach with Summer; he is always joshing around about various events in their past and sometimes he goes too far. One of his favorite story topics is how she is always losing her keys and getting hysterical about it when she is in a hurry. Summer was O.K. with it for a while, but it's begun to grate on her, especially when he tells these stories in front of clients. She has told him nicely but firmly that she doesn't want her clients to think she is disorganized or inept. She has been clear about her discomfort, and she has resorted to bluntly telling him to cut it out—but that hasn't happened.

Blasts

Katie, sixty, has been married to Harry, sixty-six, for two years. Katie works in a hospital as an ultrasound technician and is very comfortable talking about body parts and sexuality. She has quite the colorful sexual past, which Harry knows about and accepts, but he doesn't really want to hear about her past lovers and husbands. In fact, Harry is not so comfortable about sexual topics in general. He grew up in a conservative, religious household where talking about sex would have been considered extremely bad manners. Most of his professional life was spent as a military logistics officer, and he is used to keeping to himself. He considers people who openly talk about personal issues as both weak and, actually, somewhat dangerous. He admires discipline. He knows Katie is very different from him, but he suffers through her verbal overshares because he admires so much else about her. But if she gets really outrageous, it distresses him greatly. It really upset him when, at a dinner party, Katie merrily informed the group about how happy she is that Viagra was invented since otherwise Harry wouldn't be able to function after prostate surgery, and now he's better than ever! Harry just about died. He went red in the face and very quiet. There was distinct discomfort around the table.

When they got home, he abruptly went back out the door to take a long walk. When he came back, he said, "I cannot believe you said that in front of those people. Why would you humiliate me like that?"

Katie protested that these were old friends who talked about these kinds of issues openly and that it was not her intention to humiliate him, but he didn't buy it. Hurt, angry, and disillusioned with Katie, he checked into a motel that night.

The Doctors' Advice

Telling tales out of school about your partner is a disloyal act. When you talk about others' private affairs behind their backs, or even in front of them, it's hurtful. Loyalty is a cornerstone of a healthy relationship and you are obligated to look out for your partner's vulnerabilities, particularly in a public domain. We don't care if your partner talks about very personal issues to close friends—that is your partner's privilege, not yours. If they want to tell an embarrassing story about themselves, it's their story to tell, not yours. Even if you have heard your partner tell how they fell into the hotel's lily pond a hundred times, you have no right to tell it the next time. Other people get to pick the time and place they choose to say something potentially or obviously embarrassing about themselves.

Sean doesn't realize his joking is truly hurtful to his wife. He thinks she's just "being a girl" and being too sensitive, and so he isn't paying enough attention to her complaints. He may think it's funny, but if she doesn't think its funny, it's not. True, she has not blown up at Sean, but that should not be the litmus test for when to stop teasing. A partner should not mistake toleration for approval. It's important to note a partner's discomfort even if he or she doesn't make a bigger deal out of it. Sean should apologize and stop doing it. That story should get lost. Permanently.

Harry has a right to be really mad. His new bride violated his right to privacy in a very public way. He probably feels that he could never face those people again, and worse than that, his trust in his partner has been severely diminished. This is particularly dangerous in a young relationship, no matter how old the people are. Katie willfully ignored Harry's very real boundaries, and if she's not careful, it could cost her her marriage.

Clearly, what she might feel comfortable with is not what Harry is comfortable with. When this kind of boundary has been breached, a serious and heartfelt apology should be delivered as soon as possible. In Katie's case, this is such a severe blow to the relationship that she needs to repair it as soon as he will let her. She should apologize deeply, and promise never, ever, to say anything about their personal life together or his private life. If she wants to tell a story, she should keep it about herself and not impinge on his right to privacy. If she is at all uncertain about a topic, they should develop a system in which she checks in with him with her eyes and he signals to her by smiling or frowning about how to proceed. He has to feel that she has his back or this marriage is going to be a nonstarter.

Katie and Harry's story is extreme, but let's face it, every relationship has boundaries and each individual has boundaries. Not only do partners often have different levels of need for privacy or discretion, but also feelings about what to say or not say can change over time. Something that was a big deal five years ago may not be a sore spot anymore. But you can't know for certain unless you ask: Is this a story that can be shared? Is there any part of this incident you want me to skip or spin a different way? Good partnerships err on the side of discretion if they are unsure what would or would not protect their partner. If there is a story that might be O.K. to talk about now, let your partner tell you when privacy is no longer necessary. Don't guess.

By the way, it is also important to preserve these boundaries when your partner is not present. Talking about your partner behind his or her back, especially if it is an area in which he or she feels vulnerable, is relationship suicide. Never mind any excuse about trying to help, or trying to understand through someone else's perspective, or, worse yet, trying to get the whole story. This is just plain betrayal and abuse of your partner's love and trust. If you have done it, apologize profusely and never do it again, unless, of course, you want to end the partnership. We are pretty black and white on this issue. To expect protection from our partners and to desire to protect them from whatever harm could come is basic human nature that evolved from learned experience. People who could protect each other's flanks lived to fight another day. People who could be part of a well-functioning team would be more successful in life's challenges and were likely to be able to live to have families. Collaboration and trust were everything. They still are today. You and your partner are at your strongest and most deeply bonded when your loyalty to each other is solid and inviolable.

Chapter 27

Neglecting "Us"

THE SNAP

Think of it as a threesome: you, me, and us.

A Closer Look

An intimate relationship between partners is something bigger than each of you as individuals. Who you are, what you do, and the things you say—all of this changes when you commit to a partner. It is no longer just your own beliefs and experiences or just your partner's. Now there is "US," and us has to be bigger than you or me. As Euclid wrote, "The whole is greater than the part," and that concept applies here. Together you are more than you are separately; that is what the "us" does. It creates synergy, or the increased effectiveness that results when two (or more) people work together.

As you probably guessed, creating the "us" is neither quick nor simple. Couples sometimes think that once they are married they are a couple and automatically they have "us." We agree they have an "us," but it is a seedling that needs care and nurturing, and lots of time to grow and change. They will need to engage in continuous dialogue about the boundaries between "me," "you," and "us." That's the fun of a threesome.

The Situation
Ripples

Lila and Caroline, both thirty, started dating in college. They met sophomore year in a women's studies class, and worked on a class project together. That began a comfortable friendship that morphed into a passionate relationship. They moved in together their junior year. After graduation, they both chose to work in health care. Lila now works in a clinic for street youth that she helped create, and Caroline is an RN. They have an extended community of gay friends and not too many straight friends, except for family and a few colleagues. They belong to a softball league and have other activities in common. But one place they have kept resolutely separate is their money. Basically, they split day-to-day bills and have a kitty for small expenses. Neither one actually knows how much her partner makes and they have no savings or investments that they share. They rent the place they are living in now and each of them has resisted any intertwining of their financial resources. They don't even talk about it, but lately Lila has begun to feel uneasy about this arrangement. In the beginning, she felt that economic independence was the key to staying in a relationship because you wanted to and not because you were economically dependent on each other. But as her relationship with Caroline has deepened, she feels that they would be more of a couple if they saved for a house together and if they shared a financial future as well as some expenses in the present. She is unsure if this is the right thing to do, so she keeps her thoughts to herself.

Blasts

Daniela, thirty-two, is a hotel concierge, and Ruben, thirty-four, owns a sports bar. They met at the front desk of a hotel where Daniela was working eight years ago and Ruben was so playfully flirtatious that she accepted a date with him. It all went very quickly after that and they eloped when she was twenty-four. In the beginning, it was very romantic. Rubin had just bought into the bar and Daniela helped make it look cool. She worked there after hours and pitched in when an employee was sick. Even though she was often working both jobs simultaneously, she loved the fact that they were building something together.

Ruben doesn't need her help anymore. The bar is doing great and Daniela has been promoted into a job she loves that takes more of her time. But that lack of need for Daniela's help is part of the problem now: Daniela just doesn't see enough of Ruben.

Ruben is no longer the ardent, romantic lover. It seems that his love of sports has taken over his life. He loves to watch sports, talk about sports, and play sports. He is especially obsessive about golf and soccer. He is glued to the TV during major tournaments, and he plays soccer on Saturdays and golf on Sundays almost all year long. He knows he is not ever going to be a professional athlete, but he is good enough to drive himself hard when he plays at the club level. He was a champion golfer in high school and he got a scholarship to college based on his golfing skills. He's also an excellent soccer player and was one of the few people at his college who made the team as a walk-on. Sports are still at the center of his life.

Daniela always understood how important sports were to Ruben, but she used to feel that she was even more important. Now she is feeling that he simply won't make time for her. To be fair, she has a complicated schedule and her own valued hobby. When Daniela isn't at the hotel, she loves to play bridge, and she plays tournament bridge as often as she can. Those tournaments can take up a weekend, and she has signed up for more of them because of Ruben's frequent absence or near absence. She has also programmed more time for friends and has gotten into the habit of having brunch with friends and maybe taking in an afternoon movie.

Although Daniela likes her friends and bridge, she would rather spend some of her time with Ruben, but she can't seem to pry him away from his sports. Worse yet, when he comes back from the games, he doesn't feel like doing much. She will try everything. She will bring him a cold beer and a snack plate and cuddle up to him, but instead of turning toward her, he is likely to snooze or watch more sports on TV. She will suggest taking a shower together and "playing around," but he says, "Let's do that later," and falls asleep. Daniela remembers the good old days—and how long ago they seem. Lately she confesses that she wonders, "Is this all there is?" Sadly, she admits, "I don't think my life would change much if Ruben and I were no longer married."

The Doctors' Advice

Creating "us" requires being intentional and conversational about who you are as a couple and who you are as individuals. It becomes even more complex because each partner is changing, and the "us" is in a continuous state of growth. The arrangement between Lila and Caroline was perfectly reasonable and appropriate the first year they were together, but ten years later it is obsolete and undermines their moving forward as a couple. Either way it is a conversation they need to have, as a team, developing synergy to build something more than the two of them as individuals.

An important part of being a couple is helping each other create a better financial future. Couples are an economic unit and to act as if they are not undermines each individual's future and the potential strength of the relationship. We believe that couples must talk to each other about money. If a couple truly plans to be together for a lifetime, they need to think about all kinds of economic considerations, for example, wills, budgeting, and how they will handle their debt-to-savings ratio. Both members of a couple should discuss what they are saving and investing in order to get each other's counsel and wisdom so that better decisions can be made. Even if a couple is not legally married, the welfare of the couple has to include their financial welfare, and if there is no consultation or cooperation, their economic success and stability are less likely.

Money is really the last bastion of privacy between people. It often seems to be a more closely held and taboo topic than sex. But true intimacy and trust means that no issue is off limits to a couple planning a lifetime together. That doesn't mean that every couple has to be financially fused. It is understandable that spouses also want some economic independence and we think that's a very good idea. Many successful marriages and long-term relationships have separate investments, savings, and checking accounts. Building "us" in this case involves answering this question: "Who we are as financial partners as we look toward our future?"

We believe that part of being more than you and me means planning together for the future. Independence is necessary—to a point. If the individuals in the relationship start living totally parallel lives they can, like Daniela, wonder, "Is this all there is?" The relationship loses its centrality, even its meaning. We think that if a partner feels that life would be unchanged if the relationship disappeared altogether, then something is terribly wrong. If it doesn't feel like a huge hole would be created if the marriage disappeared, then the "us" is not being nurtured or prioritized.

That seems to be what has happened between Ruben and Daniela. Ruben has pretty much taken himself out of the marriage. Even if his message is unintentional, it is real. He's not trying to starve the relationship, but famine is coming. This is the kind of parallel living that causes one or both partners to go along obviously until one day they realize that their marriage is empty. Then they are vulnerable to another person stealing them away for an affair or new relationship or just being so disconnected that a crisis (economic, health, or family) could easily tear them apart.

Ruben and Daniela need to reserve some of their individual time for each other. They need routines that anchor them to their marriage, such as reserving Sunday mornings for the two of them and Wednesday nights with friends. They need mutual friends and they need a marital community so that there are some things that happen through the marriage, not outside it. Since Ruben seems to be unconscious of his impact on Daniela, she will have to tell him how she feels, without any sugarcoating. She should tell him that he still loves him, but that he is virtually out of her life and she wants him back in it. Fortunately, although this marriage is devitalized, there is nothing more sinister going on. Ruben is not having a secret affair, and no one is really mad at the other person. Daniela is lonely and dispirited, but she would do a lot to rescue her marriage. When the conversation finally happened, it went very well:

> DANIELA: *Ruben, I need to talk to you about something very serious.*
> RUBEN: *Can it wait until tomorrow? I am totally tired.*
> DANIELA: *If we don't talk about it now, I think there might not be a tomorrow.*
> RUBEN: *What the hell are you talking about?*
> DANIELA: *I'm talking about the fact that I am sad and lonely and heartbroken. I love you and I am not sure you love me anymore.*
> RUBEN: *Of course I love you. What ARE you talking about?*
> DANIELA: *I am talking about being lonely. I need to see you more; I don't see you at all.*
> RUBEN: *Well, sure you do.*
> DANIELA: *Ruben, I want to go out with friends and have fun every week. I want us to have part of a weekend morning and a special date every week. When's the last time we did that?*
> RUBEN (STUMPED): *Well, I see what you mean. But that's hard to do with your schedule, and the bar and the games.*
> DANIELA: *I know it's hard, Ruben, but will you give me those times if we work on it together? Otherwise, I just can't go on.*
> RUBEN: *I will find a way. But you know I just can't drop everything.*
> DANIELA: *I know, but if you really mean you will find a way, and we do it, we can have our old relationship back and I miss that—and you—so much.*

Much kissing happened after that.

Your relationship is the three of you, and the "us" needs the help of the "me" and the "you" to exist. The "us" has to be nurtured, protected from all others, and guarded with good boundaries. Otherwise it is easy to lose "us" through neglect, erosion, or the intrusiveness of others. So protect yourselves as a couple, grow, learn, and change.

Chapter 28

Unwanted Advice

THE SNAP

Advice is rarely invited, seldom welcome, and usually resented, so unless asked, keep your opinion to yourself.

A Closer Look

Giving advice is very seductive if you are the one giving it. It can seem like such a good idea at the time. You can give your partner the benefit of your opinion on what you would do, or what he or she should do, because you are obviously far wiser and better informed. We hope you know that we are just joking here!

Advice is treacherous territory in an intimate relationship. It is often likely to be taken either as "I am better, smarter, wiser than you" or "I am superior in some way." There is also the other aspect of giving advice that signals contempt: "I don't want to hear what you have to say and I have no empathy or compassion for what you are telling me." Your "advice" can be seen as an attack, and nothing is going to go well after that. And as you know, when someone feels attacked the response is either to fight back, go passive, or get away, none of which is a desirable result. The best resolution when you get this response is to apologize quickly and resolve not to continue this kind of behavior. To be clear, there are a few times when it may be safe to offer your advice, and that is when you hear these exact words: "I would like your advice."

The Situation
Ripples

Taba, forty, is a translator for a federal government agency, and Amad, forty-five, is an urban planner. They have been married for ten years and together for thirteen. Taba is very interested in urban planning and the city politics that affect planning, so she often offers advice on Amad's projects. He appreciates her interest but not the flood of advice. He particularly bristles when she formats her question or advice in a way that he sees as a not too thinly veiled rebuke about something he has already done. She often talks about what would have been a better way to do something. Most recently, when Amad was working on a growth plan for the city that would have created some very high-density areas, Taba gave a lot of advice about why she thought he should get the plan changed. She thought the city had not adequately researched the areas that were delineated as future high-density neighborhoods and she thought some of them should be preserved as low-density areas. Since Amad was in on this plan from the beginning, he felt that her advice showed that she had no respect for his professional judgment. He was upset that she didn't like his plan and even more upset that she would give advice about changing it when it was really a done deal. That made him feel that the whole point of her advice was to show him that he had not done a credible job. He realized that he felt a lot safer not telling her about his work.

Blasts

Savannah and Parker's marriage is the second for both of them. Savannah, thirty-six, has two teenage boys that she had when she was quite young. She was barely twenty when she got pregnant with her college boyfriend. They married and he was a dutiful partner until the second pregnancy, when he panicked and urged her to get an abortion. Even though Savannah is pro-choice, she just couldn't bring herself to do it. He made it an ultimatum: "Either get an abortion or I am going to leave." She did not get the abortion and he left.

Savannah eventually got a job as a nanny in a home that would allow her to bring the boys and also receive a good salary. She started a small nanny service and she met Parker when she was trying to figure out how to incorporate her growing business. A former client referred her to Parker's law firm.

When they met, Parker thought Savannah was adorable but was understandably skittish about getting involved again. They did eventually fall in love, marry, and have a child together, a girl named Belle. With a toddler at home and two teenage boys, Savannah turned over the day-to-day operation of her nanny business to someone she had trained, and opted to stay at home as the primary caretaker of the children. Unfortunately, things have recently been rough at home because the two boys have gotten into a lot of trouble at school for drinking on school premises.

Parker and Savannah disagree on how this should be handled. Savannah thinks this is quite serious and Parker is making light of it. He objects to her desire to ground the boys and thinks that breaking the rules is what boys do, part of growing up. Savannah has been telling him in no uncertain terms to stay out of it and he is insulted that she doesn't want his opinion or his advice. He thinks he should have earned her trust and respect by now, and furthermore, many people have paid him a lot of money because they valued his advice. It frosts him that he is not getting the respect at home that he gets elsewhere.

The Doctors' Advice

No one should really give a partner advice, unless it's been requested. Granted, there are some things that affect both partners and so discussion is necessary. But if there is no shared risk or responsibility, it is up to your partner to ask for advice or an opinion—otherwise giving advice really is a provocation and to some extent, an insult.

Taba is definitely butting in, since she is not a professional urban planner and her husband has not asked for her opinion. Moreover, Amad has indicated that he is upset when the advice comes across as criticism of things he has already done. He might even agree with her that something could have been done another way, but post hoc advice is the least helpful and the most likely to be seen as criticism because the time for action is over. If Taba really has a burning idea that looms in the future or present, she can ask if Amad would like her opinion. Otherwise she should just listen to him with empathy and interest.

Savannah and Parker are in a common but difficult situation. There is no situation in which people are likely to be more resentful of someone else's opinion than one that involves their children. Parker has some rights here because he lives with Savannah's boys, but they are her children and she is territorial about their lives. When he tries to impose his opinion without asking, she is likely to resist what she sees as inappropriate meddling. He should remember that Savannah had been a single mom for a long time before he met her and she can (and should) take some pride in raising those boys by herself. She has had to make a lot of lonely judgments along the way, and even if she would admit that not all of them were right, she can still feel justified in following her own instincts.

Parker should realize that the most primal drive for us mammals is to protect our children, even more than our partner, our parents, or our siblings. He should realize that when a child is in trouble, a parent's most protective instincts kick in and virtually no parent really wants advice.

We suggest that Parker might ask Savannah out for dinner one night, just the two of them, and plan a conversation that affirms her parental primacy over the boys. He might say, "Look, I don't have any magic answers to this. I am just floundering around trying to be helpful. You are a great mom. I want to support you in any way I can. If you need more time to handle the boys right now, I can take some other stuff off your plate. I can run errands, cook, get groceries; just put me on it. I've got you, whatever you need."

Or Parker could say, "I apologize for being so flippant. I understand now that the boys could be expelled for this behavior and that would be terrible. I would like to know more about what you think should happen. Do you want to talk about what worries you about what the kids did?" Savannah will probably be touched both by his apology and by his offer to help, but what will really soften her up and make her trust Parker more is his sincere desire to listen to her and to accept her leadership on this issue. Parker's next step is to listen with empathy, understanding, and compassion. He has to resist giving any advice to make this supportive and respectful. He should only offer responses like "I know" or "I can see why that's important" or "That's scary."

Savannah will be grateful to Parker for taking the pressure off her rather than adding to it with his advice, because his advice creates stress for her, whereas his offers to help in other ways are empathetic suggestions. And, best of all, Savannah may say, "Actually, I do not want to talk about the kids. I want a night just with you." The reason we hope for this response from her is that it focuses on them as a couple, as a team that provides a safe haven for each other in a time of stress.

The art of the badly bitten tongue has to come into play at times. Parker's advice may someday become constructive and desired. But that time has to be requested rather than assumed and taken without permission.

Chapter 29

Overthinking Your Partner's Mood

THE SNAP

Your partner's feelings are not always about you.

A Closer Look

It is easy to mistake your partner's bad mood or anger as commentary about you, and react in kind. A pause button on your emotions would probably be a good thing to have, but since you don't have one, you will have to use the thinking part of your brain to stop from reacting.

Fluctuations in our moods, our emotions, our resilience, and our hormones are normal. Although the two of you may feel emotionally connected, that does not mean that everything you feel is related to your partner. Consider the possibility that your partner's bad mood, irritability, or out-of-sorts vibes may have nothing to do with you. Sometimes our early warning system is overly sensitive and we see storms heading for us from our partner that are just their inner turmoil or their anxiety about something else in their life—not, thankfully, at least this time, about us!

The Situation
Ripples

Leonardo was the sixth of seven children in a traditional Italian family. Tradition was important in the family and he was proud of his family's heritage. His father and grandfather and great-grandfather had worked in the Carrera marble quarries near Tuscany, Italy. When Leonardo was thirteen, his family of nine moved from Italy to Philadelphia. It was a confusing change for Leonardo, who did not speak English and was a tall, lanky kid, standing a foot taller than his classmates. They noticed, and called him the "Jolly Green Giant." At first, he didn't know what the teasing meant, but he knew it wasn't good. He became increasingly quiet and withdrawn as he continued to grow to a height of 6 feet 3 inches. He graduated from high school at nineteen and took a construction job immediately.

As an adult, Leonardo came into his own. He was tall, dark, and handsome and, much to his surprise and pleasure, women swooned over him. He went out with many women, but he was still lonely until he met Violet. He met her at his dad's restaurant when she came in with a group of girlfriends to celebrate her twenty-first birthday. He passed her a note asking for her phone number. She immediately sent it back to him with her number and the words "please call" underlined several times.

Violet grew up in a moderately liberal family with her parents and sister. She had a great childhood, growing up in the same neighborhood with many friends and relatives from birth until she was nineteen. Then she and two of her childhood friends went to a beauty school downtown. The three of them got an apartment together, and soon they all had full-time jobs. They worked days and played nights. Violet was the first one of them to have a serious boyfriend, Leonardo.

Violet loved Leonardo's quiet, sweet ways when they were first together. He seemed so calm and unflappable. She loved the idea of this strong, silent type of guy. And he was the most handsome man she had ever seen. She could not get enough of him. She was head over heels in love and so was he. They married after a year of dating and quickly had two children a year apart. When their younger son was two, the relationship hit the skids.

Leonardo, now twenty-eight, comes home, turns on the news or his favorite reality program about motorcycles, and tunes out until it's time for dinner. Violet, twenty-six, is also tired. She spends all day on her feet at the hair salon, but when she gets home, she wants to talk to Leonardo before his mother brings the kids home and the evening chaos starts. She wants contact with Leonardo. Violet realizes he's tired, but she wants to talk and he doesn't. He doesn't even want to have sex before the kids arrive. If he does talk he's monosyllabic, and when she presses him for a little more attention, he shows that it irritates him to have to talk to her then. Violet feels hurt and lonely. She keeps trying new ways to engage him. She does everything she can think of to please him. He is so quiet and withdrawn she worries that he doesn't love her anymore.

Blasts

Clare and Brody live together in Brody's house and are in their early fifties. Each of them has been divorced and neither of them wants to be legally married. Clare felt that getting married changed her first cohabitation for the worse and she doesn't want to repeat the mistake. Brody feels that marriage is for people who want children. Neither he nor Clare had children in their first marriages and they certainly don't want them now. What they do have are two beloved dogs, Bear and Sandy. They joke about Bear and Sandy being their children and to some extent they treat them as such. The dogs are Yorkies, weighing all of six pounds, and they carry them with them almost wherever they go.

They have been together three years. Brody and Clare enjoy a high standard of living, courtesy of their jobs in the large firm where they met and work. They started within a year of each other at an environmental engineering and architectural company in Kansas City, Missouri. Clare is in the graphics division, and Brody works at the architectural facility as a supply chain manager.

These two were attracted to each other from the start, but no matchmaker would have thought to put them together. Brody is a happy-go-lucky guy. Everybody likes Brody; he is upbeat and likes to do things to help others. He is the kind of man who will stop to help a stranded motorist in a heartbeat. Claire is a nice person, too, but quiet and shy. If someone was stranded she would call for help, but she would not want to engage with a stranger. People tire her out, whereas they light Brody up.

Brody is very sensitive to Clare's feelings and wants to make her happy. He knows she is quiet, but sometimes he is not sure if she is just quiet or she is unhappy. His first wife always seemed to be angry, so it was a relief to Brody that Clare was on a more even keel. But when she is quiet for too long, he goes out of his way to cheer her up.

Clare likes a lot of space to be alone. She loves graphic design because she can work by herself. She loves to read and once her Kindle comes out, Brody knows she can be gone for hours. Brody takes it as a signal that she wants him to leave her alone. Clare tells Brody that just wanting to be alone is not the same as being unhappy. In fact, this is some of the happiest time in her life. But he feels shut out and thinks she is either mad at him or something is wrong and she won't tell him. He often peppers her with ideas of fun things to do and interesting conversations of the day. Clare will often pick up Bear and say she's going to bed, leaving Brody and Sandy on the couch. Brody feels rejected. Brody loves their little foursome and fears Clare doesn't love him. He doesn't know what to do.

The Doctors' Advice

It's very hard to believe its "not about you" when someone rebuffs your attempts to engage. But in both cases, it's not about them. But Violet and Brody could make it about them, if they keep pushing.

Leonardo is an introvert, and being with people takes energy from him, whereas Violet gets energy from being with people, as most extroverts do. The very qualities that attracted them to each other are now getting in their way. Violet has needs that are not being met. Leonardo simply can't function the way she wants him to when she wants him to. He needs his recovery time to make the transition to home, family, and wife. He might just want to talk when he is not being pressed instead of during his own relaxation period. Taking it personally ignores the facts of his pattern and to some extent, disrespects it. Worse yet, Violet is turning herself inside out to find some way to get his attention, and that isn't being fair to herself. The way she can get the kind of time she deserves is to schedule it with him outside his transition period, when he is able to be more of a husband to her. The two of them might also get more imaginative about what will help him recharge his emotional energy. Perhaps that would be watching some TV with the kids or playing with them while she makes dinner. Or perhaps after dinner, they could take a walk around the block to help refresh him. Otherwise, if Violet continues to push without mutual collaboration on how they can both get their needs met, he will start reacting to her and not just be trying to carve out a zone of relaxation between work and family.

Brody is creating a situation that is precisely the opposite of what he wants. He wants to make Clare happy, but he is trying to make her happy in his way as opposed to the way she thinks of being happy. When he pesters her with questions and ideas, he is actually pushing her out of the room. She has an absolute need for private time that has nothing to do with him, and Brody needs to accept that. Clare has to let Brody know that she loves him dearly, but her need for alone time preceded him and that need is unaffected by having him, or anyone, as a partner. She needs to tell him very clearly that her need to be alone and quiet is not a criticism of him.

When Clare told Brody more directly and believably that she loves him deeply but still needs her quiet time, Brody finally was reassured. Now Brody jokes with her that she loves Bear because he doesn't talk.

If you watch your partner's every mood and often feel that you are being judged, rejected, or not loved, we suggest you step back and look at the situation from your partner's point of view. Do a quick overview before you jump to your usual conclusion. What is your partner telling you about themselves by their body language or perhaps by their lack of engagement? Do they seem generally stressed, tired, depressed, or unhappy at work? Have there been conflicts or crises with family or friends? What are all the things, besides you, that could be at the heart of the troubled or tense way they are acting? Before you venture into the eye of what may be their very personal storm, prepare yourself with a soft approach by calming yourself and starting with an assumption that this is probably NOT about you. If you have some anxiety, calm yourself with a few minutes of deep breathing, ten minutes of meditation, or a cup of tea. Understand that even if some of the anger or distance that you are sensing is aimed at you, you may just be in the vicinity of the problem, but not be the problem itself. Your partner may have snapped at you because you left the car unlocked, but the real reason they turned nasty was not the car, or you, but the fact that they hate commuting or the task they were just assigned. By not taking everything personally, and not reacting to what is sometimes a very pointed and critical shot at you, you can often calm your partner, save yourself from needless hurt, and create a more intimate bond by asking questions to discover the true source of what has upset your partner.

Chapter 30

Harmful Humor

THE SNAP

Humor is only funny if both people are laughing.

A Closer Look

A sense of shared humor is a wonderful gift in a loving relationship. Laughing, joking, playing around, and engaging in various forms of silliness produce a plethora of endorphins. And it is these silly, frivolous, laugh-inducing experiences that create deep and lasting bonds.

There can be a fine line between being funny and joking with your partner, or veiled emotions and a betrayal of trust. As Charles Churchill wrote, "A joke, a very serious thing." So the mood with your partner can go from hilarity to hurt in the turn of a phrase. If you hit a vulnerable spot in your partner's psyche, whatever you said or did is not funny, humorous, or witty regardless of your conscious intent.

We have seen humor used as a weapon to deliver serious blows to the heart of a partner, and the person launching the "humorous attack" can run for cover using phrases like "Can't you take a joke" or "Jeez, I was only kidding." These comments signal that your partner doesn't not want to own up to his or her hostility. We consider this a ballistic missile aimed at your relationship. It's important to keep your humor playful and funny, and be sure both of you are laughing. If both of you are not laughing, stop and comfort your partner.

The Situation
Ripples

Erin and Dylan married in their early twenties, during their college years; they were each other's first true love, and they married right after graduation. Erin briefly flirted with going to graduate school but, upon reflection, did not want to mix a career and motherhood. She took a temporary job as a paralegal while Dylan went to law school. As soon as Dylan finished law school, they had two children. Dylan joined a small firm in Denver specializing in real estate transactions. Erin stopped working and became a stay-at-home mom. All of these turned out to be good decisions for them: They have had a solid marriage, enjoying family, work, and each other. They joke that they grew up together.

Now forty, Erin is going grayer by the month. Dylan is a particularly handsome man and he finds it amusing to notice that she's getting gray and often says, "Hey, there's a new one, should I pull it out?" She doesn't like his teasing, but she laughs to cut the tension. She's not too happy about getting older and she hates going gray. It gets worse, because Dylan really is a funny guy and he has put together a whole riff on what happens when your wife finds the first gray hair. He has actually been doing what would be a standup comedy routine if he were on a stage. He leaves people laughing so hard they have tears in their eyes—but Erin isn't laughing. When she's asked him to stop it, he smiles innocently and says that he has really worked hard on this monologue and wants to write a column about it because he thinks it's such a crazy concern of women. He tells her that she can talk about his gray hair any time. He says, "You know I love you, including every one of those gray hairs of yours. Can't you let me have a little fun with this?" She doesn't call him on it anymore, but she is starting to think of him as insensitive.

Blasts

Ida and Emil met in their late forties. Neither had been married before, and they found each other to be the perfect match. They are most happy staying home together, watching movies and playing board games in the evening. They don't spend much time with other people; they are perfectly happy with just the two of them.

Ida is a master gardener. She spends hours each year planting a new garden of vegetables and herbs, and generally gives most of them to the neighbors. Ida has even created a communal garden, where everyone can plant and grow whatever they want and she takes care of it. Her flowers brighten the entire neighborhood, and they are there for the taking for anyone who wants a fresh bouquet.

Emil started a small plumbing business a decade ago and he works alone. The neighbors say, "Emil can fix anything that has moving parts." In his spare time Emil fixes everything from outboard motors to motorbikes for the neighbors. He has a knack for figuring out how things work and repairing them, at little to no cost. Both Emil and Ida feel blessed to have such a perfect life together. They express their wonderment at finding each other and being so happy. They love their life and their neighborhood. They consider themselves lucky to be able to contribute to the lives of others.

Ida just had her sixty-fourth birthday and is looking forward to retiring from her career as an independent real estate agent. She recently had to have a hip replacement but doesn't want to tell people because she thinks they will feel sorry for her, or maybe not want her to work in her garden. Emil is a few years younger and has no aches or pains. In fact, he rides his bike every morning at dawn for ten miles. He has always stayed fit and trim, and is a creature of habit. Emil has recently started kidding Ida about needing a TOTAL hip. He jokes, "If you need a total hip, what other parts can you get? Maybe I can get some spare parts just in case." He really sent her over the edge when he joked, "I'll have to become the garden boy pretty soon, because you can't get up once you get down."

Emil has his own aging issues, although he is only starting to realize it. His memory recall is not as good as it used to be. Sometimes he cannot remember the names of people when he has not seen them for a while. They have recently started exchanging barbs: He jokes that she is falling apart and she counters that at least her brain works.

She calls it out every time he can't think of a word or forgets a person's name or can't remember where he put something. Emil really doesn't like joking at all about memory issues. He is actually worried that his memory is degrading and so jokes on the subject are extremely unwelcome.

The Doctors' Advice

Being funny is sometimes a gift to everyone around you. We are all for laughter because it brings lightness and joy, camaraderie and goodwill. Self-deprecating humor can also be good for a relationship. Most of us enjoy people who can laugh at themselves, showing a humility and sometimes realism that helps us know they have insight into their own motivations and can see the humor in everyday life. It is intimate to share laughter together. There is a line, however, between real humor and veiled emotions, and it is a line that should never be crossed. If you accidently cross the line, you will know by reading your partner's face. Stop, quickly apologize, and then comfort your partner using his or her love language (see Chapter 17).

These couples are way over the line between humor and hostility. These jokes are insulting and are driving a wedge between them. This isn't the way loving partners act. In fact, they are hurting each other in areas where they are vulnerable, and we want them to stop.

In the case of Erin and Dylan, Dylan is being obtuse and seems to have forgotten how to empathize with his wife about this issue. He is unwilling to let Erin have her vanity, perhaps because her upset about gray hair irks him. Well, just because it irks him doesn't make it fair game for constant ribbing. Even if Erin wasn't sensitive about it before, constant attention to the topic is bound to make her feel irritated and oversensitive. Few women discover a growing number of gray hairs without an initial sense of dismay. Erin doesn't want to stop her husband from expressing his humor, but she'd like him to change the topic. She needs to make this dialogue more serious and not laugh it off just to keep the peace. She could say, "Dylan, my appearance is important to me and I am sensitive about it, so let's schedule ten minutes after dinner to talk about this. Seriously, I want to hear what you have to say, and no joking or teasing, o.k.?" When they talk, Erin can tell Dylan his opinion matters a lot to her, and she's curious whether or not he thinks she should change her hair. She can start by saying, "I understand that you have feelings about my hair color, and I don't want you to express them with jokes. I care about what you feel about how I look, even if it doesn't seem rational to you."

Dylan can also realize that despite Erin saying his comments don't bother her, she doesn't think they are funny. He should take the lead and say, "Erin, I am sorry I have been kidding you about your hair, and I know it is not funny to you. I am embarrassed to say that the gray does bother me a little. I think you would look more attractive if your hair was the color it used to be. But it is up to you, and I love you the way you are."

Humor can be a psychological defense protecting us from fear. Emil and Ida are on sensitive ground that all couples will get to sooner or later: increasing health worries. They are making jokes about something that is bothering them rather than facing the topics of aging, disability, and changes in mental acuity. They are trying to make light of it because they don't know what to do and are afraid to admit it even to each other. And they don't want anyone else to know.

This is a very poor way to deal with your fears about yourself and your partner. Ida is already worried about aging and now her very own partner is confirming her worst fears. His bantering makes her feel that he no longer considers her a desirable partner. Ida's kidding is a "right back at you" kind of repartee, and her quips puncture his waning self-confidence. They are misusing humor and they need to break this pattern.

They should have a serious conversation about their very real and frightening aging and health issues. Emil is worried about what's next and whether Ida's going to be o.k. or not. Some of it, quite honestly, is worry about how this will affect him and whether he'll be able to take care of her. And part of it is worry about her and if she will be able to have a healthy and enjoyable retirement. He knows she's been looking forward to it for a long time, and he wants her to be all right.

Ida is afraid that if Emil's memory gets worse or if he does develop Alzheimer's, they will not have the resources to take care of him. They used to joke about a "suicide pact" if either of them developed dementia. Now it's not a joke; dementia is a reality they are facing. But it can't be dealt with by teasing. It requires open, honest, sensitive, and direct conversation about what is going on and how it might affect their future together, physically and financially.

This is a time when they need to come together as a couple and get some outside help in determining which risks are real and what is simply fear. Then they can get professional help on how to manage their health, their finances, and their relationship.

Remember, humor is only constructive if both people are truly laughing. We want to make sure that humor is being used in a happy, playful way—not as a way of displacing fear or as a way to get a message across without having to take responsibility for it. We applaud humor in the service of happiness and we caution against joking about serious issues.

Chapter 31

Neglecting Appearance

Look good, especially at home.

A Closer Look

Our personal appearance is important. We want to like what we see when we look in the mirror. And we like to see our partner's eye's light up when we walk toward them. Attraction is another one of those hardwired drives that draws couples together or, if it disappears, pushes them apart. When two people send messages of mutual attraction to one another, the underlying message is "come closer." When personal appearance is relatively disheveled, when there is obviously no attempt to look good for the other person, the message that is sent is "go away." Thinking of home as the place you can afford to look your worst isn't fair to your partner or your relationship.

We are often perplexed that couples will spend enormous resources, time, energy, and money being attractive to each other while they are dating and then consider the mission done when the first few years of the relationship have passed (if not sooner!). Both men and women know appearance is very important, and yet it seems that reducing effort to keep looking good is one of the perceived perks of marriage. Beauty and good grooming are appealing both to men and women, and there is no reason to believe this priority goes away after marriage.

It seems that many people assume love is supposed to be so profound that appearance plays a secondary role in relationships. That ideology, however, may not work for every couple. Gaining a lot of weight or looking sloppy, unclean, or unkempt puts many marriages and cohabiting relationships at risk. As relationship experts, we hear many men cautiously complain about their partner's more casual approaches to appearance, saying, for instance, that the weekend sweats are a turnoff.

Men and women both turn off when their partner stops practicing ordinary hygiene and body odor, dirty hair, and dirty clothes become commonplace. Less obvious offenses are wearing the same clothes over and over, never dressing to please their partner, and wearing functional rather than seductive clothing. Of course, great weight gain (or occasionally, great weight loss) can radically change a partner's appearance, too.

We believe that giving up grooming is giving up producing a valuable kind of pleasure for a partner. In some ways it is irrational to dress up for outsiders (or a dinner in a nice restaurant, a party, or an event) and be less attentive to how one looks at home. Of all the people you want to impress physically, your partner should be first on the list. Research shows we are careful about our appearance when we are around people we respect, and sloppy and poorly groomed with those we don't. Partners will get that message. So we believe that putting some energy and effort into looking good at home is important for both showing how you feel about each other and also for relationship happiness.

The Situation
Ripples

Even as a kid, Cole, now thirty-eight, loved to go up to his bedroom and write. He wrote short stories, mostly science fiction. Cole just could not resist writing, so in college he majored in journalism and minored in computer science, a program his parents were willing to support financially They didn't give him enough to go to school without working, however, so he lived frugally, saving every penny he made working at the bookstore on weekends.

Gwen was in Boston attending an Ivy League graduate school when she first met Cole in the same bookstore. She found him engaging and attractive and she went back to the bookstore six weekends in a row before she got up the nerve to ask him out. He was surprised but said, "O.K." They went to a gallery opening and Gwen was impressed at the scope of his knowledge and his articulate descriptions of book plots and popular culture. She hoped he would ask her out for a second date, but she didn't hear from him. Gwen started dating the former frat brother of a friend of hers, but her mind kept drifting back to Cole. So, she went back to the bookstore to see if she could find Cole again. He smiled when he saw Gwen, quickly grabbing her in a giant bear hug, and said, "I have missed you so much. I thought I would never see you again." Gwen was shocked, since he could have called her and did not. But his enthusiasm was real and they stayed together from that night on.

Ten years later they are married with one child. Cole writes technical manuals for two software companies in addition to freelance journalism. He usually works from home. He likes his small office in their apartment and he has become attached to being a homebody. He will pick up their child, Marni, from school and run some errands, but he really doesn't have to dress up for anyone most of the time. So he doesn't. He is happiest in an old T-shirt or sweater, ancient sandals, and even more ancient jeans. He has favorites from his high school and college days that he wears no matter how tattered, torn, or faded they are.

Gwen, now thirty-seven, teaches American history at the same Ivy League college she attended. She loves her career and is grateful to be living in Boston, and she loves Cole. The rub between them is his appearance. She has tried to get him to put himself together better every so often—but he resists her pleas. She has given up trying to influence how he looks at home, but giving up doesn't mean that she is unaffected by his appearance. His uncombed hair, three-day stubble, and ratty clothes just turn her off. Sometimes they can solve that romantically by taking a shower together and having sex when they are both squeaky clean. But it's not just their private world that is affected by his dress code (or lack thereof).

She is extremely embarrassed when he wears the same old clothes when they go out to dinner, go to a faculty gathering, or get together with friends. She dresses up and looks well put together and he comes off as rumpled and careless which she feels is insulting to their friends and to her. Recently, they went to an evening reception hosted to recognize her work mentoring students. She was afraid of what he would wear to the event, and her fears proved correct. He was the only person there in Birkenstocks and without nice pants and a jacket. When she asked him to put something better on, he looked at her steely-eyed and said, "I will wear what I want. I don't tell you how to dress."

Blasts

Lulu, forty-one, and Kyle, fifty-three, have been married since Lulu was twenty-one. When they met, she was a cheerleader in college and he was a budding realtor who was well on his way to success. One of the things they liked about each other right away was their shared love of sports and the fact that they were both trim, physically fit, and active. They played tennis, went biking, rollerbladed, and raced sailboats with friends at the Yacht Club. And they usually won. They were a great team.

After they were married, Lulu and Kyle had two kids, and Lulu worked part-time as a salesperson in some of Kyle's condo projects. It was the perfect job for her. She loved sales and was good at it, and it balanced her time spent at home with some productive professional time. She loved her kids but she also liked getting away from them a couple of times a week, and during down times in the office she could read, and meet and talk to prospective clients.

Once the kids went off to college, Lulu decided to work full-time, and Kyle was glad to have her help. They were again a great team, loved and respected in their community.

But a central problem emerged as time went on: her increased size. When they were first married she was a babe. She kept her figure until she started working full-time, but now she says she doesn't have time. She finds herself eating from the trays of cookies set out for customers at open houses and frequently going out for wine and appetizers with friends. Then she goes home and makes dinner for the two of them. Slowly but surely, she's developed a very large tummy and a thick midriff.

Kyle has tried to get Lulu to drink less and eat less, and she says she will, but her efforts have been less than disciplined. Kyle loves Lulu, but he has lost sexual interest in her. He is simply grossed out by the way she looks. He even looks away when he sees her from behind.

Kyle has noticed himself ogling other women to the extent that one of his clients asked if he was available. He didn't answer for a moment before he stammered, "No, I don't think so." He was stunned and felt stupid. He did not want to have an affair and break up his family. He had friends who split up, and he had been very critical of them for not putting family first. Now, he wasn't so sure. He doesn't believe in extramarital sex and wants his marriage to last, but he is frustrated and upset that Lulu has let herself go.

The Doctors' Advice

We want you to think about what you did and how you looked when you were dating. Were you put together, clean, well groomed? Probably. You were in mating mode and you wanted to attract people to you. So you practiced looking good for the kind of person you wanted. That could be bohemian or preppy or exotic or basic jock . . . but you perfected your "look."

Gwen has found out that asking Cole to change what he wears has not worked. Instead, it turns into a power struggle. Asking your partner to wear clothing you find attractive on him or her sometimes works; your partner takes it as a compliment and you go forward. But that approach did not work for Gwen and Cole.

Cole does not really understand that this is a big deal to Gwen, and despite her efforts to tell him, it has become a power struggle in his mind. He has become defiant and locked into his position.

But there is a way out. Since it is important to Gwen, she can take the lead. She can look carefully at the color, texture, and fit of the clothes Cole picks out to wear every day and find a better but similar version she can buy for him. Then over time she can give him presents, one item at a time, that he will like and can wear without embarrassing her. Cole is no dummy; he will know what she's doing. But if he likes the stuff, he'll wear it and it can be a transition. And if he objects, she can simply ask softly, "Would you wear this for me?" However, she can't just come in one day and dump a whole new closetful of clothes on the bed. That would be a criticism.

Cole does love Gwen and he cares what she thinks, but it is hard for him to know or show his emotions, especially verbally. We think he will be delighted to please her by donning new clothing, one item at a time. Even if he's not delighted, he has no reason to reject the new clothes and Gwen can get a better-looking guy without a head-on power struggle over it.

Lulu and Kyle are about to be in trouble if they can't find a way to modify the way Lulu looks. Kyle can't help it if he doesn't find Lulu attractive at this weight. Yes, he could just be with her in a platonic relationship, but they are still young and it's unlikely that can last for the next forty years. Lulu knows that Kyle is not interested, but she tells herself it is just that he is tired, although we suspect she knows the real reason.

Kyle needs to tell Lulu what is bothering him and that he is looking at other women and they are flirting back. He can say, "This flirting made me realize that we no longer flirt with each other, and we used to be so playful together. I miss that part of our relationship." He can take responsibility for his part by saying, "I avoid being close and cuddling with you because once I feel your tummy, I am turned off. Your looks are important to me."

Lulu needs to know the seriousness of the situation. If he talks about his own feelings, she may still be defensive, but she won't feel attacked. Yes, she will feel hurt, and he should reassure her about how much he does love her and that he wants to stop looking at other women.

Lulu, like most people, will need to make her own decisions about whether she wants to change and, if so, how. So, Kyle can just share his feelings and wait until she comes up with an answer that will really change things between them. This is a risky situation for both of them, but it has to be addressed in an honest, straightforward way if there is to be hope for the future.

Physical attraction is an essential ingredient of a romantic relationship. That attraction is only sustained if the chemistry continues, and like it or not, looks are a big part of the chemistry. We are not suggesting cosmetic surgery or looking put together every hour of every day; we are simply suggesting you do what you did when you were dating. If you prefer sweats or other casual clothing, be sure they are clean, fresh, and attractive. Put some honest effort into taking care of your looks for your partner wherever you are, and especially at home.

Chapter 32

Celebrating Strengths

Catch your partner doing something right.

A Closer Look

The key to ongoing motivation is progress, not completion. This idea applies to you and your partner. Knowing you are making progress motivates you. We believe it is important to talk openly and specifically about what is important to each of you in your relationship, and taking the next step is important to keeping the good times rolling.

One way to motivate your partner is to catch him or her doing something right, at the moment they are doing it. Give it a good "Wow, I love that." Several things happen when you are "wowed" by your partner. The brain is surprised and the brain likes (good) surprises, so it wakes up and lights up. That jolts leads to endorphins. Voila. You are connected, having fun, and bonding all at the same time. When you express that to your partner, your positive words encourage him or her to do more of what you like. Of course, it goes both ways. The more you express being delighted the better you feel.

The Situation
Ripples

Phan and Bianca met through their families. Phan's parents left Vietnam when he was four and his sister was two. His parents had both been professors at one of Vietnam's leading universities and decided to accept a year's residency at an American university when the country seemed about to erupt in civil war. One year in the United States turned into two and the family petitioned to stay because of political reprisals they might experience if they went back. They were allowed to stay and ultimately qualified as resident aliens.

Phan was a very serious little boy whose conduct was courteous, quiet, and diligent. His grades placed him at the top of his class, but he was not integrated into the social life of the school. He had no friends. But that didn't bother him. He was happy to just be with his family.

Phan received scholarships and was able to graduate from college with a degree in business. He soon had a series of good jobs and worked sixty hours a week. He had no time for anything but work and his family. By the time he was twenty-seven, his mother told him that he should look for a wife, so he did. Of course, he had no idea how to make that happen. His parents asked their friends for names of a good girl from a respectable family, and finally an unexpected but good candidate was found: Her name was Bianca.

Bianca's father was Brazilian and her mother Vietnamese. When Bianca was seven, she and her mother left her father to live with relatives in Los Angeles. Bianca's mother worked evenings cleaning office buildings, so Bianca didn't see her mother very often, and her cousins were uninterested in her. Bianca had very few good child-hood experiences until she was about twelve. She had trouble learning English, which isolated her but also had some positive effect on her intellectual growth. In order to learn the language better, Bianca read several books a week and became a standout student.

Bianca's family was distantly related to one side of Phan's family, which resulted in one of these relatives telling Phan's parents about Bianca. Bianca and Phan were married a few months after they were introduced by their extended families. Now Phan is thirty-two and a successful bank examiner. He travels almost every week for his job and usually comes home Thursday afternoons. When he gets home, he goes first to the kitchen, and if his favorite food isn't there, he comments on it. If there are dishes in the sink, he complains. If the sun is still shining, he has a tendency to swipe a table and if there is dust, he complains again. Bianca, now thirty-one, is extremely annoyed at this behavior. She has one child in preschool and works part-time running lab studies on new scientific inventions. She also does their family's budget, cleans reasonably well, and takes care of their second child, who is three. She thinks she has the household under control, and it annoys the hell out of her that Phan does not. She has started to dread Phan's homecoming because he is always pointing out something she should be doing better.

Blasts

Samuel was always at the top of his class, the best athlete, the best looking, and the most talented in his high school and college days in a mid-sized town in Ohio. Now thirty-nine, Samuel is the managing partner with a well-respected law firm in his hometown. He enjoys his clients and the work he does for them. He met his wife, Luci, when they were both students in business school. They dated but it never got really serious. He got into a law school on the other side of the country and when he left, they stopped seeing each other. Meanwhile, she was off on an adventure of her own: She had accepted a job in London working at the business end of the operation for a worldwide upscale hotel chain. Luci eventually came back to Ohio for a family wedding. She and Samuel reconnected at a party that mutual friends threw for some of the reunion returnees. This time there was an immediate and strong connection. She was far more worldly now and was highly entertaining, telling great stories about life in London and her travel over most of Europe with a number of friends of diverse nationalities. Her world sounded exciting to him, but she also felt wonderfully familiar and comfortable. Even though their lives had taken different paths, they still had a lot in common with similar backgrounds in Ohio and huge extended families.

They have been happily married for about ten years and have two children they both love very much. But lately, Luci has become a critic. She comments on how simple her life is and how uninformed Samuel is about international events and she criticizes him for getting his world news on CNN. Because he doesn't like the conversation about world politics that always takes place when she has her friends over for dinner, he rarely speaks, and if he does, she criticizes his opinions. She makes it clear that she thinks he is unqualified to keep up with the political discussions at the table. She is finding him less interesting and thinks that she may have "outgrown him." On the other hand, she loves their kids and their extended family life, and she really doesn't want a divorce, but things aren't looking good.

The Doctors' Advice

There is a saying that is at the heart of this chapter: If we look for what is wrong in others, we find it. When we look for what is right in others, we find that. Take the time daily to think about those qualities you like in your partner and those things your partner does that are meaningful to you, and then jump on them with enthusiasm. Call attention to those golden nuggets of gestures and goodwill and applaud them. Some recent research shows whatever we pay attention to increases in importance in our minds. So, pay a lot of attention to what you see that you like, and pass over those that you don't like.

Research also shows that people who go to a type of counseling or coaching that focuses on their strengths are happier and healthier than those who go the route of traditional therapy, spending countless hours talking about what's wrong.

Everyone makes mistakes and in a marriage, they are going to surface sooner or later. The question is not, "Will I be disappointed with my partner?" Of course you will, at some point. But why obsess over that? Notice what you focus on: Is it your partner's mistakes or triumphs? Strengths or weaknesses? Do you notice the good things your partner does most of the time, or are your feelings based on when he or she falls short or gets it wrong? We are not excusing or overlooking bad behavior, but if you look for good things, you will find what you are looking for, and if you set out to find what's wrong, you will find that too. In a marriage, it helps a whole lot to look for the good.

Phan has made the quite common error of returning home and noticing everything that isn't to his specifications. It may be natural for him to see the dishes in the sink or the dust on the table or no eggs in the refrigerator for his breakfast. But he isn't noticing his daughter's neat room, the fresh sheets on the bed, or the fresh papaya and melon neatly sliced in the refrigerator for him. If everything good gets passed over and he notices only the disappointments, it is no wonder Bianca is starting to dread his return. That is not what you want a homecoming to feel like.

Phan needs to narrow his concerns to one or two that they can address together. We understand his need for predictability, since his early life was so uncertain and terrifying. Still, he really needs to change course: His negativity is infecting his household and his marriage.

Research done by the Gottman Institute states that if you make one critical remark, it will take at least five compliments to get back to a happy mood and an open and forgiving heart. We want Phan to give himself the task of looking for and telling his wife about all the good things she has done for him and their daughters daily. He will need to practice compliments acknowledging what Bianca has been able to do. He should pitch in and do a few dishes instead of carping about them. On the way home from the airport, he might call and ask about his favorite things by saying, "Do you need anything from the store—eggs, fruit, coconut milk?" Then we would like him to ask, "Do you need anything else?" This way, his disappointment will be averted. His wife will feel supported, not criticized, and she'll be happy to see him.

Luci has started to typecast Samuel as a small-town attorney in ways that are going to destroy this marriage if she keeps it up. There are always things that we wish were different about a partner, but the fact is, she is now building a case against him. If she wants to stay in this marriage, she has to build a different case and look for what's right. For example, this is a man who has now taken on very impressive roles in their community and is serving on the boards of several non-profits. He picks up their kids and cleans up around the house. This is a man who has a lot going for him and if she starts using that to frame her thoughts, she can get off the road she's on and head toward home and family.

It is easy to find what you don't like, but we are urging you to get out of that habit and learn a new one. Current coaching and cognitive therapy models emphasize looking for the good in life, feeling gratitude and forgiving others, and striving for your personal best. If you do these things, you will also find the best in your partner. A fine book on couples therapy by psychologists Tobey Hiller and Phillip Ziegler calls upon therapists to build couple strengths by having the couple describe their "good marriage" that may have big problems rather than their terrible marriage with some good points. Couples can likewise think of their good spouse with flaws rather than their spouse who is riddled with so many flaws that the appreciation never gets a chance to surface. We ask you to handle your issues within the embrace of a partnership that actually has a lot of things going for it.

This will, of course take some discipline. *We want you to catch your partner doing what pleases you so you avoid the slippery slope of negativity.* Think about what your partner does that makes your life better, richer, more fun, and easier, and write these things down. Now wait until you catch them doing one of those and pounce! You caught your partner doing something right. Good for you.

Chapter 33

Creating Desire

THE SNAP

Desire creates desire.

A Closer Look

Desire is a longing, a craving, and an appetite for one another that deepens the bonds between partners. In new relationships, hormones take charge and propel you into love and lust. But over time, the love and lust hormones fade into a nice friendly pace of life. Familiarity tones down those raging hormones and relationships can become comfortable, but boring. And boredom leads to discontent, and perhaps a wandering eye or a need to look for love and excitement elsewhere.

We want you to escape boredom by trying romantic and sexual innovation. Couples can spark desire in their relationship in a variety of ways. But there is one way that always works: Create new venues for novel experiences. Try a new sex toy, make love on a deserted (you hope!) beach, or talk each other into viewing a pornographic film.

Many of us feel like we get out of the habit or think our partner doesn't enjoy us sexually anymore—even if our partner does! Research shows that arousal is amplified by a partner's arousal, and that the feeling of being wanted is a critical element of intimacy. Losing that connection is depressing and distressing for at least one partner and usually both.

The Situation
Ripples

Abby's mother died when she was six, and her father was devoted to Abby and did not remarry until after she left for college. Abby thought she might be gay when she was ten years old. She told her dad, who simply said, "Yes, I know, does it matter to you? It doesn't matter to me." Abby said, "Good, I like me." She was out by the time she was a junior in high school.

Eliza's home was in a suburb outside San Francisco. She and her three sisters were pals. Eliza was the "baby" in the family. Family life was easy and fun until one day, to the complete shock of all three children, their parents told them they were getting a divorce. Fortunately, the divorce was friendly most of the time and civil all the time. The older sisters could drive, so they saw both parents several times a week. The sisters were almost always together and even when the oldest two sisters went to college, the girls still got together several times a week.

It wasn't until Eliza's senior year of college that she fell truly, deeply in love. She met Abby in the university bookstore and they went out for coffee and talked about their personal passage to claiming a gay identity. The conversation went on for hours and at the end of it Abby and Eliza each felt she had found her soul mate. They had a giddy period when they couldn't stop talking about each other to friends and their siblings. They told each other "I love you," even though it was way too early in the relationship to know if their love was going to have a chance of being permanent.

Eliza was so infatuated that she told her sisters about Abby before she told them she was gay. Their response was cautiously supportive. They were afraid she had fallen in love too fast and had almost no dating experience, and they wondered if she was sure she was gay. But the more they saw Eliza and Abby together, the more comfortable they became with the relationship.

In many ways it looks like Eliza and Abby have created a successful relationship by integrating their parents and friends into their lives.

But there is one troubling problem: Although they have a lot of hobbies that they share in common, and both have great jobs, they do not seem to be able to translate their general warm and cuddly approach to each other into sexual passion. Abby is feeling isolated and lonely, but she doesn't want to make a big deal of it because they are happy.

The part that is really missing for Eliza is affection and, much to her surprise, sex. She asks her sisters how often they have sex and they tell her two or three times a week. Eliza told Abby how often her sisters had sex, and all Abby said was, "Good for them."

Eliza convinced herself that she shouldn't put so much weight on sex. But she misses sex and the touching, cuddling, and kissing that come with it. Abby has no idea how deprived Eliza feels. She likes sex, but once every couple of weeks is enough for her.

Eliza comforts herself by thinking that Abby has a low sex drive; that idea makes her feel better because at least Abby's lack of desire and lack of initiation doesn't seem as personal that way. Eliza really does feel horny a lot of the time and doesn't know what to do about that. She tries to burn off her sexual energy in sports. And she masturbates when she's alone. The whole situation weighs on her, but it doesn't affect her love for Abby.

Blasts

Ada, forty, grew up in a big Irish Catholic family that was originally from New York. Her father moved the family to California and got a job as an electrician for a power company, where he worked until he retired. Ada was the middle child and the only girl among four brothers. Her mother was a homemaker and loved taking care of the family. That job, raising a big brood of children and being at the center of all of their lives, was the career Ada craved. When Ada graduated from high school, all she wanted was to get married and have children.

Patrick was the oldest of six kids and, like many children of alcoholics, grew up fast and became a caretaker of his family. Patrick was often the one to pull his dad out of the pub before he spent all of the family's money or got into a fist fight. His mother was overwhelmed with so many children, and she relied on Patrick to be the man of the house. After high school graduation, Patrick packed up his VW and headed for California. He got into aviation mechanic school on the recommendation of a friend, proved to be very talented, and was hired as soon as he completed his training by the company where his friend worked.

Patrick and Ada met at his friend's engagement party, and they hit it off pretty quickly and married a year after meeting. The first few years of marriage went pretty well for them. Ada was pregnant right away and they were both thrilled. Her second pregnancy however, didn't go well and she had a miscarriage, and it hit them both hard. They wanted a big family, so she immediately got pregnant again and had a second miscarriage. This time the doctor told them to wait a year before trying again. They did, and they had one more child. But that was the last child they were able to conceive. Both were disappointed, but they never talked about their feelings of loss or grief. They pretended nothing had really happened. Ada later said, "I felt like I was at my babies' funeral and I was the only one there."

Now, Ada cannot quite remember the last time she and Patrick had sex. They are both in their early forties, and it has been at least five years since they made love. They learned to be lovers together and they were very happy being affectionate and intimate in the beginning. Now their life continues to be pleasant, but there is no physical exchange between them of any kind. Occasionally, Ada gives Patrick a hug, or he kisses her on the forehead, but that's it.

Patrick thinks their sexual relations halted when he had a fight with Ada's mother and aunt at Thanksgiving and the whole dinner was ruined. People left before dessert and Ada was furious. She felt that Patrick knew how important this holiday was to her and how important it was for him to manage his resentments about her mom. She had told him to stay away from politics and religion that evening and he started it up within half an hour of sitting down at the table. That night, she didn't talk to him when they got into bed. When he reached over to touch her, she pushed his arm away. He got mad and slept in the other bedroom, which turned into a habit. When she tried to get him back in their bedroom, he said it had nothing to do with her because he slept better alone. But the outcome was the end of their sex life.

The Doctors' Advice

Desire is extended foreplay. It is flirting, playing around, and gently seducing each other. It is fun and exciting; the chase is part of the fun, even if it is not clear who is chasing whom. As a relationship matures, creating desire comes through thought and planning, not just chemistry. Most likely, many of the things you did while you were dating or early in your relationship will still work. Did you have a special look you gave your partner, a certain touch, a wink, a nod, a special name? We strongly recommend you be intentional about incorporating these behaviors into your everyday life. It may seem artificial at first, but over time it will become a normal part of life.

Regardless how hot or varied or vanilla it is, we do believe that sex is an important element for every couple to enjoy. Sex is soothing and healing. It softens the mind and body. Sex is not only about pleasure, or release; it's also about flooding the system with the endorphins that create kindness, forgiveness, and closeness. So we believe that you can never relegate sex to a minor or absent part of your life without serious consequences for your relationship. Numerous studies show that sexless marriages are more vulnerable to divorce and tend to be unhappier than marriages with an active sex life. Sometimes people lose perspective and don't realize that they are having sex rarely or that not having sex is unusual and dangerous. Most happy couples have sex a minimum of once a week, even those over sixty.

In the case of Eliza and Abby, no big emotional rupture has taken place, but daily life has made Abby more or less forget about how little sex they are having. Eliza is now feeling that loss but doing nothing about it because so much of the relationship is great and she feels it's just the way it is. It is understandable that this is an important need for her, especially since she had such a close and affectionate relationship with her sisters, who are no longer nearby.

Meanwhile, Abby is totally oblivious but not unresponsive. Eliza really needs to realize that she's entitled to an active sex life and that she will be doing the relationship a favor by bringing the subject up. She needs to know that Abby is receptive, and that even if Abby's lack of initiation of or desire for sex represents a lower sex drive, it's o.k. for Eliza to figure out ways for them to have more sex. Maybe, by suggesting a romantic weekend without their usual gaggle of friends, they could concentrate on their physical relationship and reestablish their sexual bond.

If romance doesn't do it, they could try some edgy sex. Eliza should come home with a copy of *50 Shades of Grey* and a riding crop. Or, if that seems way too edgy, she should bring home a few editions of *Erotica*, a very nice compendium of mostly nonfiction stories that are meant to be a turn-on. These and other parlor tricks really can introduce new forms of sexual play, which can help you see each other in a whole new light. You should not give up on desire until you have tried everything possible that might create sexual interest, and failed.

Ada and Patrick are in serious trouble. What started out as a bad fight has turned into a sexual stalemate. Neither one of them knows how to get back to a loving, sexual partnership. When Ada suggests that Patrick come back to the bedroom, he steadfastly refuses. We think he's still punishing her for her rejection of him; he felt she chose her mother over him and he's still wounded. This has gone on too long for them to solve by themselves. They need a sensitive counselor or therapist who is willing to talk with them specifically about sex.

The therapist can start by asking them to forgive each other. They can't move forward if they are locked into their past and still grieving the loss of the family they wanted. If they will agree to that and understand why each of them acted the way they did, they can start to rebuild. The first thing they can do is to go on a walk and hold hands. They should have a nice day and not talk about what they've been through. In this way they will relearn the pleasure of even a modest physical connection. Each day they can give each other a hello and a goodbye hug. The next stage would be for her to go to his bed and just snuggle with him. After that, if it fits into their value system, it would be good for them to watch some sexually explicit films.

Goodvibes.com usually has a curated list of sexually explicit films that are not objectionable to women. Most men and a lot of women will get aroused looking at these films and, indeed, that was the case for Patrick. Then things can take their natural course and a new habit can be created. If Patrick really does like sleeping alone, he can do that. But only after they have gone to bed together, snuggled or made love, and had the feeling of being in their mutual bed. Then, if he needs to sleep in another room, that is fine. We just want them to have the bond and balm of sexual pleasure . . . and at least a weekly dose of love hormones.

Recreating appetite or desire for one another has to involve a stretch beyond what you already know and have tried. Remember, this is not just about sex; it is about all the fun you can have before and after.

Chapter 34

Plan Sex

THE SNAP

Plan sex: You schedule everything else that's
important to you.

A Closer Look

Multiple studies clearly show that people who have active sexual
relationships that include orgasms are healthier and happier than
those who do not, yet sex can drift into the background of busy
lives. If it seems that Americans have less time for fun, you are
right. Studies show that citizens of First World countries like Spain,
France, Sweden, Norway, Italy, and Canada have nearly two hours
of leisure time a day, whereas Americans have less than one hour
a day. A study by NationMaster, shows that the United States
ranks twelfth in the world in the amount of leisure time available.
Americans have only 5 percent of their time for leisure. Citizens of
Canada, France, Sweden, Norway, and Finland, all countries with
strong workforces and strong GDPs, have over 8 percent of their
time for leisure.

We are sorry to say that one important aspect of a couple's leisure
life has been a victim of this busy lifestyle, and that is an energetic,
passionate, and dynamic sexual relationship. We believe it is essential
to schedule time in advance that is reserved exclusively for enjoying
one another physically. Scheduling sex does not cramp sexual desire.
What it does do is make sure that sex happens. Couples need to use
the times before sexual contact for seduction and anticipation. Foreplay has to happen way before two people get between the sheets.

The Situation
Ripples

Johanna's parents had a very affectionate relationship with each other and were married for more than forty years. She idolizes them as the perfect couple. One of the qualities she likes most about her husband Kieran is his kindness to others and his enjoyment of children. Kieran was the nicest guy she had ever dated, and in addition the most affectionate and the best lover.

Kieran's parents also had a long, happy marriage. He has one brother who is five years younger, and they are best friends. Kieran calls his parents every week just to chat and travels across the country from St. Louis at least twice a year to see them in Florida.

Johanna and Kieran are both thirty, and they just bought a beautiful new home in the suburbs, which requires almost an hour commute each way, sometimes longer. Johanna sells hospital supplies and travels a lot. Kieran is a finish carpenter whose work is highly prized, and he always has a waiting list. They are both busy and often tired, but it's not fatigue that's interrupting their sex life: It's the fact that they are aroused at different times of day. Johanna is a morning person and would love to roll over and have sex with Kieran at 6:00 or a 6:30 A.M., whereas Kieran wants that extra hour of sleep but is very interested at 10:00 or even 11:00 at night. As a result, their once frantic sex life has slowed down a lot.

Blasts

Cathy and Paul met at a community college when she was nineteen and he was twenty-one. They married just before graduation, when Cathy was pregnant. They have been together for twenty years. Their daughter is fourteen, and they are still driving her to soccer practice and get-togethers with friends. Their son joined the military when he turned eighteen.

Cathy, now forty, and Paul, forty-two, have active physical lives. She works as a physical therapist in a small clinic and Paul has a successful business as an organic farmer. They are both attractive, fit people whom you would think would be in bed a lot, but they are not. Sex has become an area of contention for them. Days pass, and then weeks with no time for sex, as they see it. They have the usual excuses: work, their daughter, friends, family, and so on.

Cathy misses their old sex life and has read a book that suggested scheduling times to have sex together. She thinks that's what it will take to get as much sex as she would like, but when she brought the idea up, Paul was offended and said, "I am not going to be told when I have to perform. I think the idea of scheduled sex is the least romantic idea I have heard in a long time." Cathy was hurt at his reaction and hasn't brought up a solution again.

The Doctors' Advice

Why are so many people reluctant to schedule sex? We schedule dinner parties, dates with friend, and playdates for kids and don't think of those as inauthentic or forced. We schedule dinner, which is also about appetite, but we don't think we need to wait until we're hungry. We know that a certain time of day is good for eating.

In today's busy, complex world, scheduling makes things happen that might not otherwise occur. And so it is with sex as well. In the case of Johanna and Kieran, the issue isn't so much scheduling as it is finding a schedule. Instead of trying to rebuild a different sexual cycle—because figuring out how to produce a perfect time is just too big a stretch for at least one member of the couple—it might be easier to institute a date night that makes time for romance and for appetite to build and ends soon enough that both parties aren't too tired to have sex. On date night, Johanna can dress seductively, be playful and affectionate, and take the lead if she wants to. The same is true for Kieran and the extra care and anticipation should make up for not having the exact time they both prefer. As a nice gesture, each partner can agree to occasionally have sex during the other person's preferred time of day.

Cathy and Paul are having a power struggle. Cathy has to back off on scheduling and relight the spark between them or it's just going to be a conflict rather than a connection. What she can do is ask if he thinks it's reasonable to have sex twice a week. Paul loves sex so he's going to say, "Sure, sounds good to me." Then she can say, "o.k., make it happen. What's your plan? When?" This puts the onus back on him and also gives him permission and encouragement. It probably will take scheduling, but it's best not to call it that and leave it up to him to make it happen. If it doesn't, then she might say playfully, "All right, sweetheart. I think we've missed four opportunities. What should we do this month? I want you more than once a week." He can say, "Has it really been just once a week?" and if she confirms that is the case, he may be more interested in the original scheduling idea. Or she can put the schedule on her calendar and then, on the days she has reserved, initiate a playful seductive exchange, making it fun and not a performance in his mind.

Chapter 35

Accusations

"Why?" should be an invitation, not an accusation.

A Closer Look

"Why?" means simply "For what reason?" It seems like an innocent word, and it can be. Occasionally we want to know about something in detail that happened in our partners' lives. We want to know what happened, how it happened, when it happened, and the reason it happened. There is a genuine interest in understanding or hearing the story. "Why?" is an invitation to your partner to tell you more.

Unfortunately, in our experience "why" questions are not usually an inquiry for detail but rather an accusation of wrongdoing:

QUESTION: *"Why did you turn that way?"* Answer: *"Because I am stupid."*
QUESTION: *"Why did you forget to pick up the groceries?"* Answer: *"Because I am lazy."*
QUESTION: *"Why are you late?"* Answer: *"Because I am crazy."*

The only seemingly reasonable answer is "Because I am stupid, lazy, or crazy." These "why" questions don't feel like inquiries. They are inquisitions, and you are already judged guilty.

We think these questions are booby traps, even though that may not be your partner's intentions. Usually these questions come to the surface because your partner is put out over something. We suggest that instead of falling or jumping into the trap, you ask a simple question: "Did I create a problem for you? Because I didn't get the groceries?" Or, "Because I am late?" Or, "Because I turned that way?"

Then you can apologize and be empathetic that your partner was inconvenienced or disappointed. You can say, "I am sorry you can't make the dinner you planned. Shall I make pasta?" Or, "I am sorry I am late. I don't like disappointing you." Or, "I turned that way because I thought it was the right way to go and I am sorry you don't agree."

If you are the one asking why something happened or why someone made a decision, you can start to sound like a prosecuting attorney, not a beloved partner. In fact, if the underlying motivation for asking the question in the first place is to catch your partner doing something wrong or disagreeable to you, your partner will know it is a trap and will not like it or you. There are better ways to find out what you really want to know. Think about asking, instead, "What happened?" or saying, "I'm surprised," rather than anything that sets up a dynamic of accusation and defensive reaction.

Eliminate asking or answering "why" questions with your partner. They will only lead to a fight that has no merit, without getting to the real issue or problem.

The Situation
Ripples

Darla was a popular girl growing up. She loved spending time with friends and going out on the town. She had a lot of male friends and an active sex life, but she just didn't want to commit to one man. She worked in men's clothing at a great high-end retail store from the time she was twenty. She loved everything about her job: the clothes, the money, and, of course, the men.

Nathan grew up in South Carolina and was a true southern gentleman. In school he excelled in science, even receiving a scholarship to the state university. He loved studying any kind of science but was particularly obsessed with weather patterns, and he could spend hours looking at the sky through the school's telescope. He would often forget the time and end up staying awake all night.

When Darla saw Nathan at the coffee shop when she went to pick up her morning coffee, she thought he needed a complete wardrobe makeover, so she approached him and asked him where he worked. He answered, "Weather for the state of South Carolina, ma'am."

Darla laughed; no one had ever called her "ma'am." She asked him if he would meet her for a drink after work, and he said, "Yes, ma'am." Darla had met a lot of men, but no one like him. She pursued him and ultimately taught him to be a very good lover.

They married three years ago, when she was forty-five and he was fifty. She is now a personal shopper with her own list of influential men as her customers. Nathan goes to work at the same time every morning and always comes home at 6:00 P.M. to watch the news. Darla's hours fluctuate, so she may go in at noon and come home at 9:00 P.M. or later. Darla often invites Nathan to meet her and her friends for dinner or drinks, but Nathan, with his inquiring mind, questions her about where they are going, with whom, and what for. He asks her so often that she has become defensive and wonders if he thinks she is cheating. For example, when she says she is getting together with two other couples for dinner and would like him to come, he asks "Why?" He always asks her why she wants to get together with those people. Darla feels her choice of friends, even her desire to go out, is being critiqued rather than just enjoyed. Nathan doesn't understand why she's getting so ticked off.

Blasts

Sheri is a lifelong fitness junkie and a personal trainer. Not only does she help others train, but she herself trains every day. Her first husband, Ed, was also a personal trainer. That marriage lasted only a year: She found Ed was physical with his clients in more than a professional way. She packed his bags and literally left them on the porch. That was the end of the marriage.

Alfred was an independent child who loved reading about popular science and tinkering with the electronics his parents always had at home. He was an easygoing, self-sufficient kid. When Alfred graduated from college, he quickly landed a job and was soon promoted, rising to the vice president level in less than ten years. He became head of the company's international technical support division, and he traveled extensively. Alfred had a long-term relationship with a woman in London. She broke off the relationship when he would not make a marriage commitment after six years of being together.

Sheri and Alfred met at the gym, where he watched her work out. His first thought was, "That is the most beautiful woman I have ever seen." After six months of dating he asked her to marry him, much to her surprise and his.

Sheri is now thirty-one, and she and Alfred, who is now forty-three, have been married for two years. She isn't working right now because of a knee injury. She is looking for work but all of her work history is in fitness, so it has been difficult and depressing to not have a job and not be able to exercise as much as usual.

Alfred makes over a hundred thousand dollars a year, and he takes care of their finances. Sheri is never sure what they have to spend; she does not really have any idea of their financial situation. When they were dating, Alfred was generous and bought her lots of presents. He took her to wonderful restaurants, and even took her on a business trip to Paris. She felt like a princess and loved being wined and dined. But he changed after their marriage and now he watches pennies pretty closely. Every time she spends any money, he asks, "Why did you buy that? We don't need to be spending money we don't have." She meekly answers, "Sorry."

He recently saw a bag of oranges and asked, "Why did you buy a whole bag of oranges?" Sheri answered, "Because I like oranges." Alfred countered, "You don't need a whole bag, I don't eat them."

When she bought milk at the convenience store rather than the grocery store, Alfred asked, "Why did you pay more than you needed to for milk?"

Sheri meekly answered, "I don't know. I'm stupid, I guess."

Sheri was desperate to find a job, anything, so she could at least have her own spending money. She was bored, lonely, and depressed.

Sheri indulged in some retail therapy one week while Alfred was away. She went downtown and saw a pair of expensive boots on sale. They were half price, but she hesitated, went and had some coffee, and then went back and bought the boots.

She did some creative pricing and when Alfred asked she said they were much less expensive as they were. Alfred was skeptical because they were clearly expensive boots. He looked in the wastebasket in the bedroom and found the actual receipt for the boots and asked her again, "How much did you say those boots were?" And she lied again, saying they were $99. In fact, they were $450, half the original $900 price.

Alfred was furious. "Why did you go shopping in the first place? You know we are on a budget." She said, "They weren't that much." When she lied again, he pulled out the receipt and said, "Then what is this for?" She started to make an excuse and he interrupted furiously, "So this is who you are! You are not just a liar; you're a thief. Why would you steal my money and then lie to me? Why do you lie? What else do you lie about? Everything? How could you? Especially when you are not contributing to this household any more." Sheri was embarrassed and frightened and stood transfixed with shock.

The Doctors' Advice

These "why" questions are not invitations. They are accusations, and accusations lead to conflict that is damaging to the self-esteem of the partner being interrogated. Only resentment, defiance, or a complete disconnection can result from that type of attack. These questions create an issue that isn't there between Nathan and Darla and, worse yet, it escalates an unexamined issue between Alfred and Sheri. In neither situation is there any understanding of what either partner thinks or feels. It is an emotional dead end.

Nathan doesn't understand that his inquisitiveness feels like a challenge to Darla. She is inviting him to go out with her, and his natural response is that he is interested in where she is going and what she is doing. What we have to find out here is what lies behind this style of reacting to her suggestions. Is he uncomfortable with these friends? Does he look down on them, as she fears he does? Or does he really want to know more about these people and how, if at all, they fit into their lives? What they need is a new format for discussing their friendships or, for that matter, any other area in which they need to explore why they make one choice or another. Nathan's style befits a scientist more than a husband, and it's going to hurt the relationship unnecessarily. He'd do a lot better to express how he's feeling and what he wants. For instance, he may want to know, "Hmmm, what do we have in common with these people?" Or, "Tell me more about your friends. I am uncomfortable with people I don't know." Or, if he does simply want to know more about what Dana is doing, he needs to ask a "what" question, not "why."

Any conversation about the other couples might help Nathan to feel more comfortable or, at least, willing to make new friends. "Why" questions are dangerous because they put one person in the position of defending his or her choice, which polarizes the situation rather than fostering a mutual conversation about how to proceed.

In Alfred and Sheri's case, the "why" question here really is an interrogation. He already knows what she's done, and now he's using it to trap her and punish her, which, we don't need to tell you, is a lousy thing to do to anyone.

He should not be asking her "Why did you do this?" because when the question is asked this way, it makes him sound like a judge, jury, and executioner. He has already found her guilty and is using questions to punish her. Instead, if he really wants to know what happened, he should ask her to sit down and tell him what happened. So, for example, in the best possible scenario it could go like this:

ALFRED: *I am upset that you didn't tell me the truth and that you spent a lot of money while you are not working. You know, that our budget is tight given that we just bought this house.*

SHERI: *I'm sorry I lied—I knew it was too much and I just didn't want you to know. And then when you asked me, I thought I would tell you the truth, but I was so embarrassed that I didn't. I thought I could just take them back.*

ALFRED: *I would appreciate that. I just don't think we need to spend that kind of money on nonessentials right now.*

SHERI: *You know I have been feeling pretty bad about not being able to help financially. I thought I would have no trouble getting another job and that just hasn't been the case. I just wanted to feel better, and I saw the boots and I just let myself do it. And, I have to admit, I did feel better. I was someone with great boots.*

ALFRED: *I understand, and I am sorry I called you those names. I don't really believe what I said. I don't think you are a liar and certainly not a thief. I am truly sorry. And I know it's a hard time for you. But we have to be on the same team about money right now, and I have to be able to trust that you are telling me the truth about things. Even if I don't like what you do, you are an adult and you have the right to make decisions. I don't want you to report to me, but I want you to be responsible and reasonable about our money situation.*

SHERI: *I can do that, but please don't ever yell at me like that again.*

ALFRED: *I won't.*

Bypassing "why" and getting to the question of "Did I cause a problem for you?" will get the accuser to step back and address the real concern. We know you may have questions about "why" your partner does or doesn't do something, but just phrase it in a way that invites your partner to share the story with you. That can add to your sense of adventure or misadventure, and increase the depth of your understanding of each other.

Chapter 36

Sexual Surprises

THE SNAP ··

Your sex life should be full of surprises that never end.
···

A Closer Look

Amazing as the concept is, sex can be boring. But even modest innovations can make a huge difference. Sexual relationships give couples
a unique way of staying intensely connected. Bringing someone you
love to an ecstatic, orgasmic state can sometimes feel like a religious
moment. You transcend rationality together and under the best of
circumstances feel like you have opened yourself up to each other in
a way that deepens your love and trust. Sex can vary from lovemaking to having fun to just releasing tension. But at its most awesome,
there is a feeling that the world has stopped for just this moment of
lust or love or some wonderful combination of both.

Sex is psychologically complex. Certainly, great sex is not just a
matter of knowing how long to rub something. Our desire starts in
the brain, and the brain sends the message to the rest of your body.
If your brain gets negative input—rude treatment, bad smells, or
something else that is objectionable—the whole turning-on process
gets short-circuited.

One thing that can stop the brain from continuing to send the
kind of signals that light up our nerve endings and get the genitals
hard or juicy is the message that the same thing that has happened
every other time is going to happen again. "Oh, he's starting to
rub my breast now. He's doing the usual, going for the right one.

Now he's doing the left one, like he always does. Nice, but I wonder if I put the clothes in the dryer." This is a bit harsh to hear, but men and women who never try a new move, a new pattern, or something a bit edgy—or at least start things up in a different room of their home—can sometimes make even sex boring. In fact, they can make it so boring that many couples stop having regular sex because they've been there, done that in the same exact way so many times that they never really get passionate anymore. We know you are saying to yourself, "Well, what do you expect after ten years?" Or, "Sure, we were like that the first ten years, but it's been twenty-five. Are we supposed to be sex playmates at our age?" This is an understandable reaction, but we are here to tell you that sex can still be exciting, at least occasionally, no matter how long you have been together. This does take a bit of mental energy, but if you can overcome your inertia, you can do great things together. Sometimes your sexual renovation can be as easy as the introduction of a sex toy! Long before *Fifty Shades of Grey* hit the shelves, research showed that both men and women yearn for some variety in their sex lives. New sex toys create new adventures that in turn create an edgier, sexier sex life. To maintain some electricity in a long-term relationship and to keep all the juices flowing, we recommend you create some new moves by expanding your sexual repertoire.

The Situation
Ripples

Lois, thirty-three, is a social worker, and Marcos, thirty-one, is a sales representative for a toolmaker. Their relationship was electrifying the first decade of their marriage. They made love in the living room, in the kitchen, on camping trips, even in the car. It was all fun and exciting and a little naughty. They had both had other lovers in the past, but nothing came close to the excitement and instant arousal they had with each other. They could not seem to get enough of each other.

Now they have what they think is a "good enough" sex life: They make love twice a week and she is generally orgasmic. However, Lois admits that when she read *Fifty Shades of Grey*, she felt envious. It wasn't that she wanted to try S&M, but being tied up sounded sexy and she thought it would be fun to try. Marcos, who's a meat and potatoes kind of guy, didn't feel like reading the book when she suggested it because he thought it was "trash" and not worth his time. Lois thought that if he gave the book a try, it would be sexy for both of them. She's a bit crushed at his reaction and doesn't know how to spice up their sex life without insulting or embarrassing him. She also doesn't want him to think she's weird.

Now that she thinks back about their early lovemaking, it was often and energetic but they really didn't try anything unorthodox; they were pretty conventional. After she read *Fifty Shades of Grey*, she started buying *Cosmopolitan* at the grocery store checkout and discovered a whole range of sexual experiences she didn't even know about.

Blasts

Scarlet calls herself a plain Jane type of girl. She couldn't have cared less about being in the popular crowd growing up. She found her sisters embarrassingly materialistic and immodest and had no desire to imitate them. Scarlet did not want to draw attention to herself or her body. She became a much appreciated bookkeeper for a private bank and started saving for her retirement from her first paycheck on. She lived well below her means and saved enough money for a down payment on a small house by the time she was thirty. Little by little she continued to save and fix up her house, and her friends were delighted and a little envious to see what she had accomplished by saving her money. She didn't date much during this period and she thought she might never marry until she met Milo.

Milo grew up in a happy home where his dad stayed home to cook and his mother earned the salary that kept them afloat. His dad dreamed of writing a cookbook some day, and he passed his love of cooking on to Milo. Milo studied engineering in college and took a job with a large industrial construction company after graduation, but cooking remained his most serious love. He liked being out in the field, and he loved getting back home and entertaining his friends. He had a great group of them who loved to come over on weekends for whatever Milo cooked up.

Scarlet and Milo met when a friend of Milo's who worked for a heating and cooling company went to Scarlet's house to give her a bid on a ductless cooling system. Milo was curious how these systems worked, so he went along with his buddy to Scarlet's home.

Milo was blown away by the little oasis she had created out of what had once been someone's cottage a few blocks from a lake in northern Tennessee. He kept looking at her innovative ideas and how beautifully she had handcrafted her own woodwork. He noted and admired her attention to detail. He asked Scarlet if he could call her and come back to talk more about her house. She eagerly said, "Yes, of course!" The following weekend he invited her to his apartment and made her dinner. It was her turn to be blown away. They seemed to share the same taste in food, décor, and attention to detail. Within a year he proposed and they soon married. Milo is now forty-one and has recently changed careers. He has finally gotten around to courting his first love: cooking. He went back to school at a culinary institute and after graduation was offered a job as a sous-chef. He has thrown himself into his work, for more than one reason. He and Scarlet do not have the sex life he envisioned and sometimes he just stays up late cooking out of sheer frustration. To put it simply: Scarlet is a prude. Milo knew she was different about sex, but he thought that she would unwind, and it would change over time. However, they have been married for twelve years and Milo's hopes for Scarlet being more open about sex have vanished.

When he first fell in love with Scarlet, he was so delighted by her talents and creativity that he didn't mind her uptight approach to sex, and it didn't dissuade him from marrying her. He thought it would get better over time. But she continues to find both nudity and sex somewhat shameful. She needs all the lights to be turned off when they make love and she does not like to undress in front of him. She likes the missionary position and resists changing. He fantasizes about oral sex but the one time he started to move his face down her body, she stopped him cold. He tried to convince her that "fooling around" in the shower would be fun and her response was, "You think it would be fun if we slipped and fell?" He was crestfallen. He believes she really doesn't like sex and is just tolerating him, so recently he has been indulging some of his desires on the Internet. He now frequently waits until she is sleeping and then sneaks over to the computer and explores Internet pornography. He masturbates to orgasm frequently, watching people doing things he would like to do. He also has considered going into sex chat rooms but so far has not done so.

The Doctors' Advice

Lara and Marcos are typical of a lot of couples that have been together for ten years. Both Lara and Marcos say that as long as their sex life is pretty good they can live with it. But "not too bad" really isn't good enough. Couples don't need to settle in to boredom and routine, and they shouldn't be afraid to share their fantasies and desire for some experimentation. Actually, experimentation builds trust and intimacy and if it's forgone, the couple is missing the kind of growth and deeper trust that's essential for a truly intimate lifelong relationship. As we have learned, Lara is not exactly content, and she is not alone. There are a lot of married or cohabiting women and men who have secret sexual fantasies that are not being fulfilled. In fact, *The Normal Bar: The Surprising Secrets of Happy Couples* found that more than three-fourths of both men and women said they would be interested in "kinky sex." Now one person's "kinky sex" might be quite different from another person's! One partner might be wildly titillated merely by wearing a blindfold or by having sex in the kitchen instead of the bedroom. For another, it might mean using toys or having sex on a swing!

Being a meat and potatoes kind of guy does not exempt Marcos from having fantasies that he would enjoy exploring with Lara. He may have felt strange or worried about sharing these fantasies, but his initial discomfort doesn't mean re-approaching sexual fantasy has to be a dead deal. First, Lara needs to handle his refusal to consider the book and find out whether or not that refusal applies to all erotic materials. He be may have rebuffed her specific suggestion rather insensitively, but the idea of pursuing fantasies might not be out of the question.

She can say, "I have some erotic fantasies and I wonder if we can talk about fantasies and maybe read some sexy novels together or watch some sexy movies." Then, she could bring home an erotic movie, starting with major productions like *Body Heat, Basic Instinct, Mississippi Masala, Shakespeare in Love, A Walk on the Moon, Y Tu Mamá También, Mr. and Mrs. Smith, Bull Durham, Out of Sight*, or maybe the original *Thomas Crown Affair* with Steve McQueen. If this is fun, she can suggest they graduate to a sexually explicit film and see which ones turn them on—or not. This is about sharing a bit of adventure with one another, and finding a deeper knowledge of and love for one another. Experiencing such intense arousal together can produce an "out of your mind" experience, and that intensity of pleasure requires so much trust and submission to excitement that going through it together often brings a sense of bonding and connection like no other. This is something no couple should miss.

Scarlet has helped create a situation that she may not be aware of having crafted. Milo has let Scarlet's sexual style dominate their sex life for so long that Scarlet quite naturally thinks the state of their sex life is normal, if not exactly what her husband wants and well within the average experience of most couples. She has said, and she truly believes, that "hotter sex" is a Hollywood creation and has nothing to do with her or other average human beings.

Trouble is brewing because Milo is taking his libido out of the marriage and putting it online. The risk of taking sex almost completely out of your marriage is obvious, but there are concurrent risks that Milo may not be thinking about. For example, Scarlet could wake up one evening and get an abrupt shock with the discovery of her husband's pornographic habit. Or, she might realize he rarely approaches her sexually anymore, suspect an affair, and research his Internet history. Traumatic discoveries are never a good way to awake to a problem or end a marriage. Nonetheless, this kind of scenario happens over and over again, and it is hard to repair.

The real issue is stagnant sex and her lack of joy and sensual connection with her husband. Milo needs to tell her how he's feeling. He's being self-defeating by not honoring his own sexuality and by escaping rather than taking on the real-life situation. He can bring a book home and say that he wants the two of them to look at this book and discuss what it says with a view to changing her feelings about sex and their sexual life together. Some books to begin with might include *The New Naked: The Ultimate Sex Education for Grown-Ups,* or even the *Kama Sutra* or a sensual picture book like Anne Hooper's series of books showing beautiful people making love in interesting ways. If she is not receptive, he needs to let her know that he cannot continue the marriage in its present form. It is time for him to tell the truth about his recent sexual activities online. Win, lose, or draw, she needs to know, and he will feel better about himself by telling her what's really going on in his mind and in the marriage.

He may have to reassure Scarlet that his feelings and need for sex are normal. He should say that he knows pornography is not a good substitute for his wife and that he is happy to go see a counselor if she is willing to accept the fact that their marriage is in trouble and she would like to work with him to save it. She might break down crying, feeling humiliated and shocked. He can be sympathetic and tell her that he loves her but he has been looking at porn because he is so frustrated. It is also possible that she will listen and realize her marriage is in big trouble and that she wants to save it. They could be on the cusp of a totally new understanding of each other and at the beginning of really figuring out how to fix their sexual mismatch.

It may seem that we aren't being sympathetic enough to Scarlet. You may think she is entitled to her aversive reactions to his sexual suggestions. We *are* sympathetic. Obviously, she has some issues in her life that have caused her to shut down sexually and, of course, we would like her to discover what is inhibiting her from being sexually open to her husband. But living with the situation as it is now is not an option. Sex isn't a black box that is contained in a partnership; when it is going badly for one or both partners, as it can and often does, it undermines every other part of the relationship. Treating one partner's sexual frustration and disappointment as just a small problem that can be contained is a delusion. It is a rare marriage that can tolerate, much less thrive in, a situation in which one partner feels undesired or sexual behavior is minimally interesting and infrequent.

Keep adding new sexual experiences and sexual surprises several times a year. We want couples to be open to new sexual adventures together, because it is a way to keep the relationship lively, vital, and intimate and help you and your partner grow.

Chapter 37

DIY: Customize
Your Relationship

THE SNAP

Keep inventing and refining your relationship.

A Closer Look

A traditional nuclear family comprises one man and one woman who are married, with one child or more, living in one home together until the kids leave. This vision, storied in movies and books, is simply not the norm anymore. There's now a 50 percent divorce rate for the general population, a delayed age at first marriage, a large number of people in society staying single at any one time (including one-third of all baby boomers), and new forms of relationships popping up in significant numbers, including gay marriage, long-term dating, and cohabitation that does not end in marriage.

We believe that there are many choices you can make other than getting married and staying married for your entire life. Couples who were once headed to the attorney's office can now head for the counseling or coaching couch to design a lifestyle that works for them. Many couples choose not to live together full time. They are becoming so well known that they have a name (LATs, for "living apart together") in the research literature and, soon, in the census. But even if people look conventional from the outside, there are other subtle but important choices they can make. For example, they don't have to have only mutual friends. They can share some friends, and not others. We know some couples who have released each other from kin duties; they do not attend each other's formal family holidays. They are part of a new breed of couples who are trying to minimize family hassles by not fulfilling unwelcome traditional expectations.

Couples who choose these types of independent lives need to be clear about the new rules and boundaries. You may want to insulate your relationship from many of the influences that create difficulties in traditional marriages, which often contribute to their demise. Many second or third marriages or cohabitations have stumbled when they had to include stepchildren or in-laws; pool money; share housekeeping; or compromise on lifestyle differences friends, or dogs versus cats. However, we do not know of many long-term, loving relationships that allow partners to have sex outside their relationship. Some couples do negotiate a "don't ask, don't tell" policy that seems to work for them.

Others, particularly people who believe in polyamory (having committed relationships with more than one person) openly negotiate non-monogamy guidelines. The vast majority of couples practice monogamy because it is a sacred part of the marital commitment to them and/or because they could not emotionally handle the idea, much less the reality, of the person they love making love with someone else. But even monogamy isn't a given anymore. People make their own marriage contracts.

We are not advocating throwing everything sacred about marriage up in the air. But we do believe we are in an era of new freedoms and innovations that may make relationships more satisfying to partners. Although your parent's marriage might be what you want, it isn't necessary to pick it as the model. Open your mind to new ideas of what brings out the best in you and your partner and use that as the foundation for building a customized relationship for the two of you.

The Situation
Ripples

Delilah was raised in a small, conservative town in Idaho. Her parents were deeply religious and they attended church at least three times a week. She married a young man from her church when she was twenty, and they had a baby girl immediately. Everything changed when the baby was born. Her husband was angry that the baby was a girl, and his reaction to their daughter horrified Delilah. He would not hold the baby, and he wanted Delilah to try for another pregnancy immediately. Delilah eventually packed up her daughter, took half the money from their savings account, and ran away.

Her parents helped her file for an annulment. They loved her and their granddaughter, and no one would be allowed to threaten either of them again. Delilah was greatly relieved, but now she was confused. She could not imagine being in a relationship again, but she also could not see a role for herself in the world unless she was someone's wife.

Delilah stayed single until her daughter was eighteen, and then she met JP, who was eleven years older. He was a good-looking guy with a confident, good-natured personality. JP was a self-made man who had put himself through school. He liked people and had a gift for sales, and he found a niche for himself in marketing. He looked like a great package when Delilah met him and he was, but not without some baggage.

JP met and married his first wife as soon as he got his first job, and had two children in quick succession. That marriage lasted seven years, until it ended when he had an affair. To this day, he doesn't quite know why he couldn't resist his lover. He had thought he loved his wife, but when he met Cheryl, an attractive coworker who was in the same sales force, he was sure that marrying his wife was a mistake and this woman was his true love.

Hurt and furious, his wife took the kids and filed for divorce. His head spinning from the quick succession of events, he immediately married Cheryl. That marriage was a disaster. His ex-wife hated the new wife and Cheryl didn't know how to relate to his two boys, who promptly took a major dislike to her. This caused numerous battles in his new home, and JP found himself fighting with his new wife about his kids almost daily. Their marriage lasted less than a year, but not before she became pregnant with his child. JP found himself supporting three young children.

When Delilah, now thirty-eight, met JP, forty-nine, he had become an advertising executive. He had an appointment at her skin care clinic and they were immediately attracted to each other. He asked her out to coffee and many coffees led to dinner. Over time, they discovered each other's complicated family system and it drew them together—they felt like they wanted to be each other's one loyal and true partner. They married and thought they could be just one big happy family, but the kids were not supportive of their relationship. Putting the whole group together just isn't working. Nonetheless, JP keeps trying to put "special family days" together, but the older children often don't show up and his youngest son is openly hostile to Delilah and her daughter. The marriage is now three years old and the family situation is not getting any better.

Delilah is very close to her daughter, who is now newly married and has just had a baby. Understandably, Delilah wants to spend a lot of time with her grandchild. But JP would like her to spend weekends and vacations with him and his boys, because he still believes they can have the close family ties that JP is looking for. But their get-togethers are awkward, at best, and Delilah would really just like him to go do his thing with his sons and leave her to have some private time with her daughter, son-in-law, and grandson. The two of them are having trouble dividing up their time in a way that pleases both of them.

Blasts

Candace knew as soon as she started reading fashion magazines at age nine that she wanted to be a designer. She was industrious and determined when she attended The Cooper Union School of Design, and her professors noticed that she was a standout, exceptionally original talent. She was offered a position immediately upon graduation with a well-known, over-the-top-expensive handbag company whose products started at about a thousand dollars. Handbags had long been her passion and she could not have been happier at the company. She stayed there eight years and worked night and day. Her work was applauded, and she was snapped up by another equally prestigious handbag firm and promoted to head of the company's North American office. She recently launched her own line of handbags.

The man she would fall in love with came from a quite different background but shared Candace's intelligence, diligence, and passion for work. Xavier's dad was an eye doctor and his mother had been a model in her native Stockholm. His parents met when she was in Chicago on a fashion shoot and developed an eye infection. They had no reservations about their interracial relationship and married within two years. Two years later Xavier came along, and a year after that, his sister, Jada. Both kids were exceptionally good-looking and smart. However, being an interracial family at that time occasioned some issues for both parents and children and those times helped make the family very close and protective of each other.

Xavier followed in his father's footsteps and became a pediatric ophthalmologist. He works at the university so he can take care of patients and also do research. He met Candace at a friend's party, and they fell into an easy friendship that quickly morphed into a love affair. They have been together for three years now and have been commuting between Candace's townhouse and Xavier's condo. It is a thirty- to forty-minute commute and Xavier thinks it's a waste of time and money. But more than anything, he misses Candace when they are not in the same place. He has asked Candace to marry him, and when she accepted, he took it for granted that they would live together after they got engaged.

However, Candace likes things the way they are and doesn't see why they have to change something that works so well. She loves Xavier and enjoys their time together. They share a love of golf, tennis, and boating and, best of all, they are great friends and lovers. They both say that one of the best parts of their relationship is how often they make each other laugh.

Now in their mid-thirties, they both wanted a partner who did not want to start a family at an early age, or maybe at all. Candace says she just never had the urge to have a child, and time slipped by. Xavier loves kids but felt he didn't have the time to help children at the hospital, do research for the hearing impaired, and take care of his own family.

But Xavier had never considered not living with his wife. When he told his family that he and Candace were going to be married they were thrilled but when he told them they might not live together, they were up in arms and thought it was disrespectful to marriage and to their reputations. His parents wonder if she really does love him or if she has something else going on. Some of his aunts and cousins are personally insulted and have wondered out loud if there is something racial about this, if perhaps Candace isn't really at ease with being a full member of the family. Xavier doesn't know what to do; he understands where Candace is coming from and he trusts her love. But he would prefer to live together and he doesn't want his family to feel insulted. In an effort to persuade Candace, he has said, "My sister thinks this is ridiculous, and my mother is hurt, and I wonder why you don't want to please them because you know how important they are to me. And, of course, I really want to see you every day."

Candace is touched by Xavier's situation. She loves him and his family and wants to please them, but she put it this way: "Xavier, you know who I am. You know the hours I work and the time I need to think and be creative. I need some alone time. Yes, I could manage living with you. I adore our time together. I want to be with you a lot. But this is a time to grow my business. We don't have kids. If we decide to, then I would reconsider. But, we can do this differently and have a wonderful marriage. Do we have to be like other people instead of going on with something that has worked so well for us?"

It's a tough situation but if they don't come to a solution soon, this might polarize family relations, and that would be hard on such a close and loving family.

The Doctors' Advice

JP is putting old wine into new bottles. It just doesn't work. It's almost impossible to change partners and keep every older tradition intact. We think that the more players involved, the less energy and space there is for the primary pair. JP and Delilah have a pretty crowded schedule that doesn't leave a lot of room for new traditions. This doesn't mean family ties get broken, but they do get changed. JP needs to put his relationship with Delilah front and center, and she will have to take some time from being a doting grandmother to invest in JP. We want them to be a couple first and make some fair decisions about how to divide their time while not shortchanging their marriage.

It might help to make a calendar. Each person can choose one tradition with their respective families that is inviolable, and they will attend that event together. Other than that, they can get together with their own kids on their own. We would like them to block out at least one overnight outing a month for the two of them that involves no one else. They also need two weeks' vacation for just the two of them. There are special occasions, such as weddings, births, and funerals, that they would probably want to attend as a couple.

There is no reason for them to blend these families unless it's convenient and fun. Each of them has obligations and they need to refit them, not abandon them, around their work and new relationship. This also applies to friends. They do not have to make all of their old friends "couple friends." What may have worked previously might not fit them. We want this marriage between JP and Delilah to be fun and fulfilling for them, and that can only work if they carve out the time and energy to make that happen. One of the best gifts they can give their kids is showing them how a good marriage works.

Candace has worked hard to have her own business and build a good life for herself. She is with people every day; she oversees her team of designers, meets the wholesale customers, and travels to the factories in China almost monthly. She has a life that supports her and gives her the time and energy to be with Xavier.

Candace has no doubts that she loves, respects, and admires Xavier, but she wants to be fresh, fun, and awake when they are together. And she has never felt so loved, understood, and accepted as she does by Xavier. Sleep is a problem when they are together all the time: She has jet lag from her various trips, and he has late-night calls, emergencies that make his at-home time unpredictable.

She likes to be alone in her house sometimes. She likes her neighborhood exactly as it is. Xavier likes the simplicity of a downtown condo and has no desire to live in her neighborhood. Candace really worries that if they were together more, it would be less romantic and they would have more conflicts because she really does need time to herself. She doesn't see why anything has to change simply because they are getting married.

We agree with Candace under the "if it isn't broken, don't fix it" rule. He has to decide if he really needs to be married in the traditional way, or if they can have a great relationship under this new conceptualization of how to conduct a lifetime relationship. He has to be honest with himself and see if he is unhappy in this arrangement, or if it is family pressure that is making him unhappy about commuting back and forth to each other's place.

It seems to us that they are both truly in love, and what they really need is a plan they both like and that they think will meet their needs for togetherness and independence. For example, they could agree to have three or four nights around the weekend together and two or three weeknights apart. They can figure out which days they are least likely to need each other's participation at a dinner or mutual appointment, and which times away are best for work or individual endeavors. Candace can ask Xavier, "Just how much time do you need to feel loved and taken care of? When do you feel lonely and how can I help make that less likely to happen?" And each of them can lay out what they need and how much separation they need, and let each other know if either one of them violates those needs. In other words, they can plan a personal strategy so the marriage gets nourished and they can know when they are not getting enough of each other, and have a strategy for getting back to what they need.

They have the power to create their marriage and customize their lifestyle. It only has to work for them—not for everyone—but for them. However, the fact that Xavier's family feels something is wrong with this picture is becoming a negative influence. That may be hard, but Xavier has to stop getting advice from his family and stop complaining and giving them the wrong picture about Candace. He needs to tell them that he and Candace are happy and that she adds a lot to his life. He has to tell them he and Candace need their support for however they put their marriage together. Your friends and family may be well meaning, but their constant discourse about your life can screw things up. In this case, Xavier's feelings or worries about their living arrangements should be expressed to Candace, not friends and family.

Chapter 38

Confessions

THE SNAP

Don't confess to make yourself feel better.

A Closer Look

Most people need a filter, not a faucet. Being open doesn't have to mean making a true confession. Confessions may seem to offer a way out of feeling guilty and ashamed because of something you have done but wished you hadn't. Confessions don't release you from your emotions, however; most of the time they make you feel worse as you watch the agony and distress you are causing your partner. Once you start telling your secret, there is no taking it back or un-telling.

If your confession is about sex and it is in the past, there is nothing you can do to change what happened. We believe the burden belongs to you, and not your partner. By confessing your wrongdoing, the emotional burden is shifted to your partner, but you will still have guilt and shame. The burden your partner will now carry if you confess is broken trust, and once trust is badly broken it is difficult to repair. Your partner might be plagued by flashbacks, a seemingly endless series of questions, betrayal, self-doubt, humiliation, fear, hurt, and anger—to name a few of the emotions that could haunt him or her for years.

The Situation
Ripples

Giselle was nicknamed "gazelle" by her friends after the fast antelopes in Africa, because of her swift turnover of boyfriends. And

239

there were a lot of boyfriends/lovers. None of her friends could keep count, but they confidentially guessed that she had more than 100 lovers. When anyone asked her how many lovers she had, she quipped, "Not enough."

She went on to explain, "I have a high libido and I enjoy sex with a variety of men. It's no big deal when guys do it. Why should it be a big deal when women have lots of lovers?" She did formulate her own ethical standards and boundaries: always using condoms; a don't ask, don't tell names policy; and never dating a friend's beau, even if they weren't together anymore. Her women friends are important to her and she holds that boundary firmly.

After she graduated from college and got a job in a public relations firm, she was much less sexually active and more discreet. She didn't have a lot of extra time and mostly she used weekends to catch up and recuperate. She dated only occasionally, but she did get serious with a guy she met from another public relations firm when they were thrown together on a project. She moved in with him when she was twenty-six and that lasted a year. She was faithful the entire time, but he wasn't. She forgave him, but the relationship was different after that. They eventually separated as friends.

Miles grew up in a rural community in eastern Oregon with two brothers and two sisters. His parents ran a cattle ranch. He worked on the ranch as a boy but didn't like rural life and eventually left for college in Miami. During his second year of college he met a young woman from Japan who was studying law and technology. She was the first woman he dated since leaving Oregon, and he was completely enthralled by her beauty, her culture, and her intelligence. At the beginning of their senior year he asked her to marry him, and she accepted. They became engaged and then moved in together. This was the happiest time in his life. But things changed when Miles wanted to set a wedding date. His fiancée confessed that her parents had not known about Miles or the engagement and when she told them, they demanded she come back to Tokyo immediately. She explained to Miles that she loved him but her parents would not allow a marriage between them and she must leave. Miles helped her pack and took her to the airport, and that was the last time he ever saw her. He tried calling and emailing her but received no response. Over the course of the next year his heart healed. He made new friends, joined a chess club, and took up fly-fishing.

A group of the guys from work invited Miles to go with them to New York for a long weekend, and that is where he met Giselle. She was working in Washington, D.C., and came to New York for a friend's wedding. She was having a glass of wine in the hotel lounge. He sat on the stool next to her and they started chatting. They agreed to meet for breakfast the next morning and ended up spending the rest of the day together.

They have been dating for two years now, and Miles has recently asked Giselle to marry him. He has told her he can move to D.C., where he already has a job lined up if he wants it. Giselle is in love with Miles and can see spending the rest of her life with him. She feels he would be a solid partner and a good father. Giselle feels economically secure and ready to go on to the next stage of her life, but she has some inner turmoil. She feels guilty that Miles doesn't know about her wild child past. She is worried that he will meet someone from that period who will spill the beans. She has been trying to get the courage to tell him about her past, but she is not sure how much to tell. She's worried that Miles might be disgusted with her if he knew the range of her sexual and romantic experiences. There were some public scandals, like the time she inadvertently got the dean of students fired when they were discovered having sex on his desk. And she had a lover who didn't tell her he was married and the whole sorority she had joined was witness to the angry wife coming in and threatening her with a lawsuit. There was the awful incident of the girl who publicly accused her of giving her fiancé herpes. She hadn't done it, but the rumor floated around for a very uncomfortable couple of months. Any one of those stories, or more, might jump out of her past.

Blasts

Naomi grew up on the wrong side of the tracks and started working when she was twelve, cleaning homes and babysitting. Her mother, a single parent, worked two jobs, and between Naomi and her mother they were able to pay the rent and keep the younger two kids fed and clothed. Life didn't seem that tough at the time. Everyone she knew was poor and everyone worked two jobs to get by.

After graduation, she moved to Lexington, Kentucky, and got a job as a representative for a cosmetics company. She was quick to pick up aesthetic details and was good at demonstrating her product lines. She now made enough money to get her own condo and help support her mother. She dated but had not been serious about anyone until she met Ayden at work. He is a sales rep for a commercial lighting supply company in Greenville, South Carolina.

Naomi is now thirty-one and Ayden thirty-six, and they have been married for three years. Naomi is on a leave of absence from her job. Naomi and Ayden had a child thirteen months ago who had some health problems, so she is staying home longer with her son than she'd originally planned. She used to travel, but now she is homebound. Ayden still travels almost every week, and often for days at a time, especially when there is some important convention to attend. At one of the conventions he met Isabella, a beautiful woman and a well-respected salesperson whom he needed to talk to, so he asked her if she had time for a drink. There was instant chemistry and magnetism. After a few drinks they decided to have dinner, and they ended up in her room all night.

Ayden felt guilty but he couldn't get her off his mind and they spent the three days of the meetings together. When he got home, he told himself that was the end of it, but he found himself calling her. When she suggested he meet her in Chicago, he agreed. Short meetings went on like this for the next six months, with Ayden's guilt growing deeper by the day. When he looked at his young son, he realized how much he was putting at risk, and he finally got the courage he needed to end it with Isabella. But he couldn't stop thinking about her and didn't know what to do. He finally went to a relationship coach for advice.

The Doctors' Advice

A confession can simply shift the burden from the partner who created the problem. We know it can be tempting to want to get a mistake or misdeed off your chest, but we find that relief is usually short-lived when your partner becomes saddled with worries.

Giselle worried that Miles might not understand her own history because she knew he had had only a few sexual partners in his life before he met her. She was worried that some of her girlfriends from that time, or someone who had spread nasty rumors about her before, would somehow surface and make Miles feel bad, maybe even tricked. Of course, we feel that these days people expect their partners to have sexual experience, but it's never clear how much is too much for someone's personal morality. We think it is possible that if Miles knew the full extent of Giselle's adventurous spirit, he might have felt bad about it, not necessarily to the point of leaving, but not thrilled. Still, even with the possibility that some malevolent "buddies" from the past might take it upon themselves to inform Miles, we believe that the best choice is to leave the past in the past. We see nothing good coming from Giselle spilling unnecessary confessions. She enjoyed that time of her life—but that was then and it really has very little to do with now, except that it may have given her more than enough sexual adventure and made it easier for her to settle down and not feel deprived. Miles really loves and respects her, and they can agree that if there is gossip about either of their pasts they will disregard anything anyone says. Chances are that it will never come up and we just can't see that she owes him any information that doesn't bear on their present relationship.

If we think you shouldn't talk about your past because it's disruptive, you can imagine how we feel about Ayden confessing his affair. What could this do to his marriage? Now, we recognize this is a controversial issue among coaches and therapists. Many therapists feel a relationship cannot heal if the affair is not admitted and dealt with in therapy. There might be circumstances in which this is completely true and justified. But the question here is, is confessing *always* the best thing to do? We think not.

The person who broke the marital contract should, if possible, have to deal with the consequences and not hurt the other partner. It would be good for Ayden to talk to a coach or therapist about what happened so he can set better boundaries and can stay away from behavior that is unworthy of a husband and might jeopardize his marriage and his relationship with his baby son. Naomi and Ayden have a good marriage and love each other. We don't believe that telling Naomi about the affair would be good for their relationship. We believe in focusing on the good in your partner, your relationship, and yourself, and protecting the relationship, even from serious mistakes like an affair. We recognize this is a controversial call—but we stand by it.

Ayden has to stop kidding himself, though. Dr. Lana tells her clients, "After 8 it's a date." Business should be concluded earlier or the situation can lead to a compromising outcome. Another piece of advice: Drinking creates vulnerability and offers an excuse for destructive behavior. Drinking or getting high puts everyone concerned in dangerous territory. If the whole purpose of drinking or drugging is to remove inhibitions, and if you are committed to your partner and you don't want to complicate business relationships, then alcohol should be avoided or kept to a minimum as an accompaniment to good food. A single glass of wine or one cocktail is the safe limit. Two drinks is dangerous; three drinks is relationship suicide.

Chapter 39

Celebrate Every Occasion

THE SNAP

Celebrate every occasion until the next one comes along. Even better: Invent a few of your own.

A Closer Look

We believe celebrations are important because they draw attention to something or someone meaningful in your life. Celebrations also highlight shared memories of the good times in your life together. Couples need to remember what they've shared and experienced over the years. Celebrating your anniversaries and birthdays is good, but it's not enough. If possible, celebrate events like the day you first met, your engagement, your best vacation ever, a positive occurrence at work, and the end of a big project. Look for and relive all the good experiences you have shared.

It is easy to let one day drift into the next and have a year or longer of nothing special happening, and that makes any relationship dull. A celebration a month seems like the right tempo to us. Creating shared experiences to celebrate doesn't have to be elaborate or costly; in fact, the best ones are often free. You can take a picnic to the place that is special to you, write a letter full of praise celebrating your life together, or go for a walk hand in hand and talk about your favorite vacation together. You can also make special experiences into rituals: Have breakfast in bed on Sunday mornings (prepared the night before), go to the outdoor market on Saturday mornings, or watch a romantic movie every Wednesday night. Have coffee or tea at the same spot each week. For those of you

245

with young children who say, "We can't do that," we say, "You can and you'd better." The very best thing you can do for your children is to have a good marriage, and these celebrations and rituals vastly improve your chances of having a marriage go the distance. Make it happen: Exchange time with a neighbor, hire a student for an hour, or trade babysitting with someone else who has kids. You can do it. It is important to continually celebrate your life, your love, and your gratitude toward each other.

The Situation
Ripples

Penelope likes "stuff." When she was a child, her mother took her to the store as a reward for being good. Penelope could buy one item, but what she and her mother enjoyed together was that she was thrilled by everything she saw. As they went up and down each aisle at the department store, Penelope would gasp with joy at all the beautiful toys, clothes, housewares, and sporting goods. Everything was exciting to her.

Francisco's background was quite a contrast. He was born in Portugal. Both his French mother and Portuguese father were teachers who wanted him to see the world. So, when he turned eighteen, he came to Washington, D.C., to attend college. His first job was with a large construction firm, and since he was fluent in English, Spanish, Portuguese, and French, he was soon promoted to the international division of the company. They needed someone who was an energy field auditor, so they put him into a training program that he enjoyed a lot. Francisco was an ambitious man and a quick study.

Francisco met Penelope in the Los Angeles airport, where she seemed completely lost. Never one to ignore a pretty lady, he asked if he could help, and she answered, "I don't even know what terminal I am in or what terminal I am supposed to be in." He smiled, looked at her ticket, and walked her to the right check-in. When she was ready to leave, she turned around and gave him a lingering hug and a kiss on the cheek and said, "You are my Prince Charming, rescuing a damsel in distress." Later he didn't remember what she said, but he could not forget her perfume.

She was walking through security when he asked her for her phone number, but she could not hear him, so he persuaded a passenger in line to take his business card to her and ask her to call him. The Good Samaritan passenger did just as he asked, and a week later, when Penelope returned from her trip, she called.

Penelope, now thirty-two, and Francisco, thirty-nine, are madly in love and agree on most things—where to live, what to do, places to go, friends. They are highly compatible, except that, according to Penelope, Francisco just doesn't "get it" when it comes to celebrations. He travels worldwide and he usually wants to link their anniversary celebration to a trip he happens to be taking for work. His business trips require interaction with other people in the company or with clients. Francisco usually takes an extra day or two, but it's always connected to his work.

Penelope doesn't like some of the places they go and Francisco probably wouldn't pick them himself, but he argues that these trips are expensive and that this is a way to "kill two birds with one stone." It's not that Penelope doesn't enjoy some of his friends and colleagues. She does. But she does not feel special on these trips and has openly disagreed with his opinion about combining their anniversary with work. So far, nothing has changed.

Blasts

Mira's mother was Turkish and her father a blond, blue-eyed American, and her looks have always been an alluring mix of the two cultures. When she was a child, Mira's mother had knickknacks all over the house from "the old country," and Mira hated the clutter. She resolved that her own house would look quite different. Mira eventually turned a love of mathematics into a successful tutoring business.

Ken, the man she was to marry, was an only child of well-off parents, but he lived within walking distance from his cousins. He was a good student, not great, but he had other talents: He was very good with people and had tons of friends. He has pleasant memories of his family, except for the time his mother left for a few months; he was never quite sure as a child what happened. At the time he was scared because he was quite close to his mother, but his dad assured him she would be back. She did come back, and even though he asked about where she had been, where she went or why was not discussed. As he later learned as an adult, she had run off with an old boyfriend who had become an extremely wealthy man. They had traveled Europe for two months, but she would not leave her family and she came back. The incident left its mark, however. He was always afraid his mother would disappear again, and even though she never did, he couldn't quite shake the fear that some morning he would wake up and she would be gone. Even much later, while he was in medical school, he found that he was relieved whenever his mother answered the phone.

Mira and Ken met in their late thirties, when Mira's dad had a mild heart attack and she took him to the hospital. Ken met with them before her dad went home to discuss his aftercare. Mira thought he was attractive in a geeky sort of way but was surprised and initially alarmed when Ken called her at home. He quickly apologized for startling her, and asked her if she was free for dinner the next weekend. She agreed, and they dated steadily for several years before moving in together.

Ken likes to buy Mira presents, and he often takes his spare time to look for things she might like. Mira acknowledges his kindness, but she really doesn't reciprocate. She has said numerous times, "I don't really need anything," and she often forgets his birthday and their anniversary, or she remembers it at the last minute and they hunt around for a restaurant that has a table. Since their anniversary is during the Christmas season, they often end up at a place that doesn't please either one of them. Ken is feeling bad about all this.

He wants to celebrate things in a bigger way and he feels stifled by Mira's disinterest. Sometimes he thinks she doesn't love him that much and that he is just convenient for her. He knows that some of his insecurity comes from his childhood trauma caused by his mother's sudden disappearance, but it is not something he feels he can control. He feels that if Mira loved him enough she wouldn't forget the celebrations that are so important to him.

The Doctors' Advice

There's a shortage of joy in most relationships—and joy is absolutely essential for a relationship to thrive. Couples need to create or find reasons to commemorate and celebrate to keep their relationship thriving. When Dr. Lana turned fifty, her son wrote in a birthday card, "Lana celebrates every occasion until the next one comes along." We believe celebrating the simple moments in life reminds us of our good fortune and brings joy to our lives and the lives of others. (Take a look back at Chapter 17 to get ideas of meaningful ways to celebrate and praise your relationship in your partner's love language.)

Francisco has figured out the practical answer to their anniversary celebration by combining business with pleasure, but practicality is not romantic and it's not really a celebration. To get out of this stalemate, Penelope might compose a list of fun things to do and another list of all the times they might want to celebrate, such as birthdays, the day they met, Cinco de Mayo, the summer solstice, the day he got his citizenship, and so on. Then they could research ways to celebrate an occasion. For example, Squidoo.com has many ideas on how to make a day or event special. Not all of them require money; For example, they could have a picnic, or read a Dave Barry book (or some other humor book) together, or make a special dinner at home together, or have friends over for a dessert party. If Francisco finds an idea he likes (and one that is not too expensive), he will probably sign up for a few of these ideas.

Penelope may not get the exact anniversary celebration she wants, but she can add new celebrations to their life that will make it feel more intimate and joyful.

Mira is a no-nonsense kind of lady, and she has no idea how hurt Ken is about her lack of attention to and appreciation of his attempts to celebrate her—and them. We think both giving and getting various kinds of gifts or experiences is an affirmation of the relationship, and that Ken has a right to feel uneasy about her lack of participation. The gift doesn't even have to cost anything, but if it shows that you know your partner and you have taken time to think of what makes him or her happy, then it adds to the love and bond between you. We want to stress that joy comes from both giving and receiving: It's important to note that part of the joy of giving is seeing the other person's appreciation of the gift. If there is no real gratitude, it undermines gift giving. And if the gift is inappropriate, it undermines intimacy.

We recognize that giving or receiving a gift is fraught with danger and can create anxiety that make a lot of people want to avoid gifts altogether. But, celebrations are important and people need to feel gifted (or have their gift accepted), even if that gift is a nice day together at the zoo or a lavish dinner. Ken wants more emotion and gratitude from Mira and he wants her to show joy about him and the relationship. Mira has to see the world on his terms as well as her own.

As Ken and Mira start to have more fun celebrating occasions together, Ken can tell her how important these special times are to him, and that it brings him joy to see her laughing and smiling. As dates that are important to him start to come up, he needs to be honest about the value these celebrations have to him and he has to tell Mira exactly what he would like her to do for him: "Please make a reservation a week in advance for dinner at Juno's on my birthday. It is important to me." If he wants to make sure he puts it in the right framework and doesn't sound whiny or too hurt, he can script his message ahead of time (see Chapter 12). For those of you who think telling someone exactly what you want them to do takes away the romance, we don't agree. Mira simply doesn't think that way, but she does love him and wants to please him. We want them to succeed at celebrating and creating new memories.

The less you celebrate, the more your relationship may start to look just like a business partnership. This is especially true if your partner's love language ranks giving gifts or spending quality time together at the top of their list! The loss of these acts becomes more than a minor irritation; it starts to make your partner feel unimportant and unloved. We think this is a serious issue because these kinds of celebrations and special rituals help define you as a couple. If your lives become merely functional, without special moments, the relationship becomes less intimate. You need stories to tell, moments to remember, and celebrations to look forward to. Life together should be joyful, and we want you to continually celebrate all you have and create new occasions to celebrate in your future.

Chapter 40

Dessert

Dessert first, please.

A Closer Look

You know the drill. Come home. Do all the chores. Check the email or pay bills. Make dinner. Call your mother. A thousand other things, and then you get into bed and go to sleep. You meant to chat and talk about your day together. You meant to make love, but you were just too tired. You meant to plan a trip to the Bahamas, but there was just too much work to do and you decided it was better to put the money into a newer car. The subject varies, but the theme is the same: We do the practical thing and forget about romance, or we just use residual time rather than prime time.

We squeeze in joy rather than putting it before other life needs. We think of it as optional, when it really isn't. And let's face it: Sometimes we really would much rather have dessert than an appetizer or even our entrée, but we wait until after the meal is done and by then we are too full or we have spent too much on the other part of the meal. And so we don't get dessert and it really was the part we wanted the most.

We believe that sometimes dessert has to come first, that something sweet can often be more important for having a joyful life than something "practical." Or to put it more concretely, sometimes you should just skip dinner and make love. Better to have sex together and a peanut butter sandwich later than to make a great dinner and be too full to want to make love. To our mind, we get our priorities wrong and, ultimately, that hurts the relationship.

The Situation
Ripples

Paige usually became the leader of whatever group she joined. She was pretty, charismatic, and savvy. She intuitively knew what to do to make people feel good. She's just one of those people everyone seemed to enjoy being with. She was never rude or dismissive of anyone; she liked most people.

Dmitri's parents were first-generation Greek. His father was a doctor and his mother a high school teacher. A good education was very important to his parents and they insisted that Dmitri and his brothers attend the best schools, study hard, and be active in sports and leaders in their community. They were religious and devoted to their extended family and to each other. Dmitri now has a high-paying job in Silicon Valley, where he works ceaselessly, specializing in search engine optimization. He barely considers his job to be work because he loved it so much. When he met Paige he told her he could hardly believe he was getting paid for working, since his job just seemed like fun to him.

Paige and Dmitri met at work on a project when she was brought in to be part of the team. Paige is a social media strategist, and Dmitri was impressed with her insights and her perspective. He was especially intrigued by the way she approached problems; her way of thinking was so different from his! At first he wasn't sure about her advice, but he did as she suggested and his product was the best launch of the year for the entire company.

He invited her to dinner, supposedly to thank her for her help, but it did not take long for them to become lovers. They became inseparable and got married within a year and a half after that first dinner. Both of them had big families and large numbers of friends, so they ended up having a huge wedding. It was a glorious setting, and no expense seemed to be spared. They looked handsome together and made all their guests feel comfortable. At that moment, they were the perfect couple.

Paige left the software company and went to work for a financial securities firm. And Dmitri had two big promotions in two years. They both continue to love their work, which sometimes seems like it is twenty-four hours a day, seven days a week. Both of them thrive on challenge and even though their hours doing their work seem to have increased exponentially, it has not dampened their enthusiasm for their careers. There is, however a "fly in the ointment": Although they have been happily married for two years, they are starting to have problems because they are not in the same sleep cycles.

Therapists call this the "dove and the owl" syndrome. Paige is up early in the morning and out the door at the crack of dawn, doing her run and then going to the office. Dmitri gets up a bit later, lingers over his coffee, looks at the news on the Internet, and then gets to work. He doesn't know how to go to bed early, so he is often working at his desk long after Paige has gone to sleep.

They overlap on hastily thrown-together dinners occasionally. Sometimes they go for a run together, and they have friends that they see on weekends. The problem is that there doesn't seem to be any time when they are not either tired, sleeping, distracted, or with people for conversations about life, love, their future, or other important topics.

Paige misses the togetherness she used to feel with Dmitri and is wondering what is wrong because he doesn't seem that interested in sex anymore. Dmitri is thinking she cares more about being with her friends than with him, and she gets up early to avoid him. They have brought these worries up to each other, but somehow their dialogue never resolves these feelings. Neither of them feels reassured, and no changes have been made.

Blasts

Renate and Jason have been together for twenty-five years. They met when his aunt and her uncle got married. They had so much fun at the wedding that they started dating immediately, but it took them a few years of dating and another couple of years of living together before they married. They also took some time before they had children. They wanted time to be a young couple together first, and they both were glad they had made that decision. Of course, now they are middle-aged and still have children at home, and this complicates their life. Still, they feel those years of being young and child-free were worth it.

Renate, now fifty-one, is part-owner of a luxury consignment-clothing boutique and Jason, fifty-four, owns a motorcycle dealership. She opens her store at 10:00 A.M. and closes at 8:00 P.M., and Jason opens the bike shop at 6:30 A.M. and closes at 7:00 P.M. They have a rolling dinnertime because their two teenage kids, ages fourteen and sixteen, come home and then leave again for various activities. By the time they are alone, it is usually about 9:30 or 10:00 P.M. After straightening up the house, checking email, and returning personal phone calls, it is usually at least 11:00 P.M.

When they get in bed, they often just fall asleep, but every now and then Jason reaches for Renate to indicate he'd like to make love, and her response is less than satisfying to him. She usually says yes with her body language but, more often than not, she adds, "But could we make it quick? I am really tired." Jason wants a whole lot more enthusiasm than that, but he's tired too, so he either makes it quick or says, "later" and falls asleep. Neither one of them feels that their sex life is in good shape, and they've talked about it, but their routine hasn't changed. A recent conversation sounded like this:

> JASON: *You know, I don't like it when you kind of blow me off. I mean, you could show a little more interest."*
> RENATE: *Well, if you'd come to bed when I'm awake you might get a different attitude.*

JASON: *It doesn't matter what time I come to bed. You are always tired and sometimes you pretend to be asleep. And that really pisses me off. Do you think I am really so out of it that I think you are really asleep?*

RENATE: *No, I don't think you're "out of it," but I think you are kind of lazy. I mean you reach for me and it feels mechanical, and that's a turnoff. Frankly, if that's the offer, I'd rather sleep.*

JASON: *Here we go again. Good night.*

The Doctors' Advice

In fact, most couples would have a better sex life if they stopped making it the last thing they do in the day. If you are more energetic and awake, sex will be more energetic and innovative. Sex after 11:00 P.M. is rarely quality sex. So, why not have sex when you are fully awake and excitable? Have the dessert of your relationship first. Keep the best part of your relationship in the foreground. Have fun together, make love, be silly, find new adventures together, and keep the spark between you glowing.

Dmitri and Paige have a common couple problem: They are busy being busy and the relationship is getting their leftover time and energy. They are not giving their primary relationship prime time. It's easy to be sucked into this vortex and become entangled with work, friends, sports, extended family, church, and dozens of other things and not have time for each other. This is a national disease, but it is not recognized as such. Like many of their friends, they take pride in being the busiest because busy seems to have the highest status in our society these days.

But busy is not compatible with intimacy. Intimacy takes time, prime-time scheduled and unscheduled time. It needs one-on-one time; it just can't happen the right way if the only time you talk about important subjects is when other friends or family are present. It has to be just two partners, having time to talk when they are at their best and most focused on each other.

Dmitri and Paige are still young, but their relationship could slip away if they don't build the right foundation now. The foundation has to begin with prioritizing quality time to communicate. Quality time can't be wedged into sporadically salvaged time. We know that they love their jobs and that their success depends on giving their jobs enough time, but they don't need to sacrifice their relationship because of their work. Actually, couples need only half an hour or so a day to have a meaningful conversation, but it has to be a really focused and intimate period and not just a news brief of what happened that day.

One thing they can do is this: Half an hour before Paige is ready to go to bed, they can go to the couch to snuggle and talk for a while. Paige and Dmitri do not have children yet, which does make getting this quality time for communication easier, and if they establish good habits now, it will help them immeasurably later.

Renate and Jason are ruining their sex life by relegating intimate time to leftover time. It's causing a lot of stress on their relationship. Late at night is rarely prime time. You need energy for great sex and you need time to make sex interesting, varied, and intimate. Renate is right: Jason's overtures are rather lazy. This isn't so awful if it happens occasionally, but if that's all there is, it's going to diminish her interest in making love. Jason is in the unenviable situation of being rebuffed or getting a lukewarm response, but he's not taking responsibility for setting up what he gets. Renate is treating him rudely, so his anger is understandable, but he has not taken that as a sign to take a different approach and help solve the problem.

We think sex is a highly important way of being intimate. It creates a connection that nothing else does. It's not an "add-on"; it's not what you squeeze into small spaces of your life. It really needs to be at the center of a relationship—the sweetest, most delicious thing you do with and for each other. It deserves prime time. Renate and Jason have to back up and re-establish sex as an important part of their lives that requires a different time slot. They need to take the time from some other part of their life, and they haven't done that yet . . . but it will take a reorganization of prime time.

They should go over their schedule and see what prime-time slots they are willing to give up and take back for themselves. For example, they have a two-hour time slot for the kids to drift in and get food, but they can make it a one-hour window and take back some time by assigning their kids to either help clean up the kitchen or help put the house in order. If their kids don't come in during that time period, they can have cold cuts available for them to just grab and go. The point here is that there are probably other times that would be much better for the relationship—if the kids have sports on Saturday morning, that might be the time to linger longer in bed. Right now, though, they have to stop having these accusatory confrontations and look at the problem as a mutual fiasco, as opposed to either person's "fault."

Here's one way this couple can revise their conversation: Think of something sweet every morning when they are washing their faces or brushing their teeth, something they can say to one another that shows love and affection and maybe, occasionally, desire.

Putting that kind of romance and admiration back into your relationship is much more likely to create sizzle later in the day, more than just a random arm over your partner's body. Finally, just moving up their mutual bedtime an hour or so would solve the problem of fighting fatigue and reinvigorate their sex life.

The number one priority of your daily life as a couple is to enjoy each other for some period of time every day. This time to connect and savor the good each of you brings to the other has to be exercised, maintained, and upgraded regularly. Intimacy is just like software: If you want to keep your Internet and smart phone effective, you have to stay current, and you have to keep learning and changing.

We do not want you to put off the best part of your relationship until your work is done. Your relationship as a couple is primary and should have prime time, not whatever time and energy you have left after everything else is done. We want you to have the yummy stuff first, so you don't miss out.

Your primary relationship is one of the biggest investments you will ever make and it will be one of your riskiest if you don't give it lots of Tender, Loving, Care. Making an intimate connection with your partner daily is one of the best ways to protect your investment. Use your partner's love language, give it your best time and energy, and find joy in each other every day. All of this takes minutes, not hours. It is a sweet kiss hello or goodbye, an "I love you" text, cuddling before sleep, a love note, or a new sex toy. If you want to keep the fire going, you have to fan the flames and feed the fire with new fuel.

References and
Further Reading

Amato, Paul, Booth, Alan, Johnson, David R., Rogers, Stacy J. "Alone Together: How Marriage in America is Changing." *Journal of Marriage and Family*, February 2008.

Chapman, Gary D. *The 5 Love Languages: The Secret to Love That Lasts.* Chicago: Northfield Press, 2010.

Cheek, J.M., Briggs, S.R. "Shyness as a Personality Trait." Perspectives from Social Psychology. London: Cambridge University Press, 1990.

Craft, Mandala. *The Joy of Living: Unlocking the Secret and science of Happiness.* New York: Crown Publishing, 2007.

DeSteno, David, Condon, Paul, Desbordes, Gaëlle, and Miller, Willa. "Meditation Increases Compassionate Responses to Suffering." *Psychological Science*, August 21, 2013.

Dickson, Jane. *Debrett's Manners for Men: What Women Really Want.* Woodbridge: Antique Collectors Club, 2008.

Gordon, Cameron L., Arnette, Robin A.M., Smith, Rachel E. "Have You Thanked Your Spouse Today? Felt and Expressed Gratitude Among Married Couples." *Personality and Individual Differences*, February 2011.

Gottman, John; Silver, Nan, Michael. *The Seven Principles for Making Marriage Work.* New York: Three Rivers Press, 1999.

Gottman, John. "Research FAQ's." Retrieved from www.gottman.com/research/research-faqs .

Hanes, Tracii. "Natural Ways to Increase Serotonin & Endorphins." August 12, 2013. Retrieved from www.livestrong.com/ article/89032-natural-increase-serotonin-endorphins/

Hendrix, Harville. *Getting the Love You Want: A Guide for Couples.* New York: Henry Holt & Company, LLC, 2007.

Hertenstein, Matthew; Weiss, Sandra. *The Handbook of Touch: Neuroscience, Behavioral and Health Perspectives.* New York: Springer, 2011.

Hiller, Tobey, and Ziegler, Phillip. *Recreating Partnership: A Solution-Oriented, Collaborative Approach to Couples Therapy.* New York: W. W. Norton & Company, Inc., 2001.

Huq, Zaki. *Emotional Language: The Art and Science of Communication for Human Development.* New York: Emotional Language Consulting, Hay Group, 2011.

Klinenberg, Eric. *Going Solo: The Extraordinary Rise and Surprising Appeal of Living Alone. Happily Ever After—Separately.* New York: Penguin, 2013.

Lyubomirsky, Sonja, *The Myths of Happiness: What Should Make You Happy, but Doesn't, What Shouldn't Make You Happy, but Does.* New York: Penguin Press, 2014.

Mayo Clinic Staff "Stress relief from laughter? It's no joke." July 23, 2013. Retrieved from http://www.mayoclinic.org/healthy-living/ stress-management/in-depth/stress-relief/art-20044456

NationMaster. "Countries Compared by Lifestyle > Leisure > Leisure Time > Leisure time across demographic groups > Total. International Statistics at NationMaster.com", OECD Social Indicators, 2009. Aggregates compiled by NationMaster. Accessed November 15, 2014. http://www.nationmaster.com/country-info/stats/Lifestyle/Leisure/ Leisure-Time/Leisure-time-across-demographic-groups/Total.

Northrup, Christine; Schwartz, Pepper; Witte, James. *The Normal Bar The Surprising Secrets of Happy Couples and What they reveal about Creating a New Normal in your Relationship.* New York: Harmony, 2013.

Parker-Pope, Tara. "When Sex Leaves the Marriage." 3 June 2009. http://well.blogs.nytimes.com/2009/06/03/when-sex-leaves-the-marriage/

Raison, Charles. "Balance," *TedX. Atlanta.* 13 Sept 2011. http://tedxatlanta.com/videos/09132011-balance/charles-raison/

Restak, Richard. *The New Brain: How the Modern Age is rewiring your Brain.* New York: Rodale Books, 2003.

Schwartz, Pepper. *Prime: Adventures and Advice on Sex, Love and the Sensual Years.* New York: William Morrow, 2008.

Seligman, Martin. *Positive Psychology to Realize Your Potential for Lasting Fulfillment.* New York: Free Press, 2002.

Seligman, Martin. *Learned Optimism: How to Change Your Mind and Your Life.* New York: Vintage, 2006.

Shapiro, Dana. *You Can Be Right (or You Can Be Married): Looking for Love in the Age of Divorce.* New York: Scribner, 2012.

Stoessel, Lise ,Tracy. *Living Happily Ever After—Separately.* Brandylane Publishers: Virginia, 2011.

Stoppler, Melissa. "Endorphins: Natural Pain and Stress Fighters." Retrieved from: www.medicinenet.com/script/main/art.asp?articlekey=55001.

Wallis, Claudia "The New Science of Happiness." *Time,* January 2005. Retrieved from http://content.time.com/time/magazine/article/0,9171,1015832-1,00.html

Acknowledgements

E very book is a team effort. First, we want to thank our agent Helen Zimmermann, who helped create this wonderful partnership with Seal Press. Our editor Stephanie Knapp helped shape both the style and content of the book. Among the people who have helped us at Seal, none were more critical for this book's existence than Laura Mazer, who "got" our message, and acquired the book for Perseus. Thanks also to Krista Lyons, publisher, Beth Partin, our excellent copy editor, and production coordinator, Tabitha Lahr. We appreciate our publicist, Anna Gallaher, and vice president of production Jane Musser, who oversaw both the production and design.

Of course, we are grateful to our partners and families, who unselfishly gave us the space to create, even though they missed us when we were writing. Being loved and supported makes all things possible. Finally, we both feel thankful for each other. We have shared a joyful and fascinating friendship and collaboration. In fact, so much so that it is hard to see the book completed. Our friendship however goes on, with many intriguing conversations and consultations, ahead.

About the Authors

Pepper Schwartz is Professor of Sociology at the University of Washington where she teaches classes on human sexuality and intimate relationships. She is the author or co-author of 22 books including the *New York Times* best seller, T*he Normal Bar: The Surprising Secrets of Happy Couples*. She is Past President of the Society for the Scientific Study of Sexuality, the Love, Sex and Relationship Ambassador for AARP, and has won awards for translating academic work into a more readable format for the public. An expert on matchmaking and dating, she created the matching algorithm for PerfectMatch.com, wrote *Dating After 50 for Dummies* and is on a team of four relationship experts for *Married at First Sight,* the hit show on arranged marriage on the FYI channel. She has often appeared on *Oprah, The Today Show, CBS Morning News, Good Morning America* and other major television shows. Pepper blogs frequently for CNN.com, hisandhersvacations,com, (a romantic travel site) and ARRP.org. She lives on a horse ranch near Seattle, Washington, and has two adult children, Ryder and Cooper, who both do relationship and other kinds of counseling. Her life partner is Fred Kaseburg.

About the Authors

photo © Ingrid Pape-Sheldon

Lana Staheli, Ph.D. is a coach on relationships and life strategies, has been in private practice for over 40 years. Dr. Lana is the relationship expert for KIXI 880AM in Seattle. She has written several relationship and self-development books, including *Triangles: Understanding, Preventing, and Surviving Affairs; Affair-Proof Your Marriage; and Bounce: Be Transformed: Change Your mind, Change Your Life, Change The World.*

Dr. Lana has been featured in the *Seattle Times, Washington Times, Gannett News,* and other syndicated newspapers from Anchorage, Alaska, to Miami, Florida. She is a contributor to *Parent's Magazine, YM, Woman's World, First For Women, Reader's Digest, and Cosmopolitan* (International and U.S.) and others. She has been quoted for online articles for the *Washington Post, MSNBC,* and *ABCNews.com.* Lana has been a guest on Fox *After Breakfast, The Maury Povich Show, Good Morning Texas, Town Meeting, KOMO News, AM Northwest,* and *Northwest Afternoon,* plus others. She has participated in hundreds of radio programs and has spoken to audiences around the United States, Europe, and China.

Dr. Lana is a founding member of the board of directors for the Center for Women and Democracy at the University of Washington and the Founding Chair of the Global Networking Program. She is a member prestigious International Women's Forum and current president of the Washington State Women's Forum. Lana is also a former member of the Board of Harvard University's Kennedy School of Government.

Dr. Lana, along with her husband of nearly 40 years, Lynn Staheli, M.D., has traveled to over 60 different countries offering medical advice. They created a non-profit Global-HELP.org that has now had 10 million downloads of information for health care workers to use in their own environments throughout the world

Dr. Lana answers questions on her website www.askdrlana. com; and is a requested speaker for national and international groups. You can find her on facebook.com/AskDoctorLana.

Selected Titles from Seal Press

The New I Do: Reshaping Marriage for Skeptics, Realists, and Rebels, by Susan Pease Gadoua and Vicki Larson. $17.00, 978-1-58005-545-1. A new perspective on the modern shape of marriage, this guide offers couples a road-map for creating alternative marital partnerships.

Otherhood: Modern Women Finding A New Kind of Happiness, by Melanie Notkin. $17.00, 978-1-58005-571-0. Melanie Notkin shares the funny, sexy, and sometimes heartbreaking stories of today's well-educated, successful women who find themselves childless in spite of their desire to be mothers.

Better than Perfect: 7 Strategies to Crush Your Inner Critic and Create a Life You Love, by Elizabeth Lombardo. $16.00, 978-1-58005-549-9. A proven, powerful method for shaking the chains of perfectionism and finding balance in life.

Got Teens?: The Doctor Moms' Guide to Sexuality, Social Media and Other Adolescent Realities, by Logan Levkoff, PhD and Jennifer Wider, MD. $16.00, 978-1-58005-506-2. Adolescent health and sexuality experts provide parents of middle schoolers a way to decode their teen's health questions and behavior.

The Goodbye Year: Wisdom and Culinary Therapy to Survive Your Child's Senior Year of High School (and Reclaim the You *of You)*, by Toni Piccinini. $16.00, 978-1-58005-486-7. Part self-help, part therapy, and completely honest, this sensitive companion is for mothers facing the life-changing transition that occurs when children graduate from high school.

Under This Beautiful Dome: A Senator, A Journalist, and the Politics of Gay Love in America, by Terry Mutchler. $24.00, 978-1-58005-508-6. The true story of a journalist's secret five-year relationship with a member of the Illinois Senate reveals the devastation caused when gay and lesbian couples are denied acceptance and equal rights.

Find Seal Press Online

www.sealpress.com

www.facebook.com/sealpress

Twitter: @SealPress